CAMBRIDGE LIBRARY COLLECTION

Books of enduring scholarly value

Polar Exploration

This series includes accounts, by eye-witnesses and contemporaries, of early expeditions to the Arctic and the Antarctic. Huge resources were invested in such endeavours, particularly the search for the North-West Passage, which, if successful, promised enormous strategic and commercial rewards. Cartographers and scientists travelled with many of the expeditions, and their work made important contributions to earth sciences, climatology, botany and zoology. They also brought back anthropological information about the indigenous peoples of the Arctic region and the southern fringes of the American continent. The series further includes dramatic and poignant accounts of the harsh realities of working in extreme conditions and utter isolation in bygone centuries.

The Life, Diaries and Correspondence of Jane Lady Franklin 1792–1875

Jane Franklin (1792–1875) became well known in the middle of the nineteenth century for her tireless campaign to discover the fate of the lost Arctic expedition led by her husband, Sir John Franklin (1786–1847). The editor of this volume, Willingham Franklin Rawnsley (1845–1927), was Sir John's great-nephew, with access to the family papers. The four sections of this work, first published in 1923, address Jane's life before her marriage in 1828; the period when her husband was posted to the Mediterranean; life in Tasmania, where Sir John served as governor; and Lady Franklin's quest to learn the fate of her husband's expedition in search of the North-West Passage. Given appropriate context, the extracts illuminate her interest in European travel, her activities in Tasmania – especially in education and the treatment of female convicts – and her movements over the globe after searches discovered evidence of her husband's demise.

T0370637

Cambridge University Press has long been a pioneer in the reissuing of out-of-print titles from its own backlist, producing digital reprints of books that are still sought after by scholars and students but could not be reprinted economically using traditional technology. The Cambridge Library Collection extends this activity to a wider range of books which are still of importance to researchers and professionals, either for the source material they contain, or as landmarks in the history of their academic discipline.

Drawing from the world-renowned collections in the Cambridge University Library and other partner libraries, and guided by the advice of experts in each subject area, Cambridge University Press is using state-of-the-art scanning machines in its own Printing House to capture the content of each book selected for inclusion. The files are processed to give a consistently clear, crisp image, and the books finished to the high quality standard for which the Press is recognised around the world. The latest print-on-demand technology ensures that the books will remain available indefinitely, and that orders for single or multiple copies can quickly be supplied.

The Cambridge Library Collection brings back to life books of enduring scholarly value (including out-of-copyright works originally issued by other publishers) across a wide range of disciplines in the humanities and social sciences and in science and technology.

The Life, Diaries and Correspondence of Jane Lady Franklin 1792–1875

EDITED BY W.F. RAWNSLEY

CAMBRIDGE
UNIVERSITY PRESS

CAMBRIDGE
UNIVERSITY PRESS

University Printing House, Cambridge, CB2 8BS, United Kingdom

Published in the United States of America by Cambridge University Press, New York

Cambridge University Press is part of the University of Cambridge.
It furthers the University's mission by disseminating knowledge in the pursuit of
education, learning and research at the highest international levels of excellence.

www.cambridge.org
Information on this title: www.cambridge.org/9781108075084

© in this compilation Cambridge University Press 2014

This edition first published 1923
This digitally printed version 2014

ISBN 978-1-108-07508-4 Paperback

The Life, Diaries and Correspondence of Jane Lady Franklin 1792-1875

JANE LADY FRANKLIN
By Miss Romily

The Life, Diaries and Correspondence of Jane Lady Franklin

1792-1875

EDITED BY

WILLINGHAM FRANKLIN RAWNSLEY

LONDON, W.C.1
ERSKINE MACDONALD, Ltd.

PRINTED BY
THE STANHOPE PRESS, LTD.
80 STROOD HIGH STREET
ROCHESTER

Preface

THIS book should have been published long ago, when Lady Franklin's name was in everybody's mouth in all lands. But as it describes the earliest beginnings of colonization in Australia, New Zealand and Tasmania, and gives a lively account of the travels in all parts of the globe where Lady Franklin and her niece, Miss S. Cracroft, were often the first European ladies who had been seen ; and as it also gives an intimate sight into the character of her heroic husband, there is still much in the diaries and letters of great interest to all English-speaking people throughout the world.

I must record my thanks to Miss J. Lefroy and Mrs. Austin Leigh, who, taking up Miss Cracroft's work of decyphering, copying and arranging the large mass of correspondence, have made my work possible ; also to Dr. Guillemard, who has gone carefully through the MS. when typed, making wise suggestions and corrections ; and most of all.to the kind help and sympathy of my wife.

In part IV. I have quoted from the *Life of Franklin*, by Sir A. Markham and that by Mr. H. D. Thraill, who had been allowed the use of many of the letters now placed in my hands by the owners. I have also to thank Mr. Philip Lyttelton Gell for his personal contribution of reminiscences of his grandmother

W.F.R.

Lady Franklin's Life may be divided thus:

Part I
Before Marriage
1792-1828

Part II
" The Rainbow " in the Mediterranean
1830-1833

Part III
Tasmania
1837-1844

Part IV
Sir John's Last Arctic Expedition and After
1845-1875

Supplement to Part IV
American Letters
1849-1859

Contents

PART I.

BEFORE MARRIAGE, 1792-1828

PART II

" THE RAINBOW " IN THE MEDITTERRANEAN, 1830-1833

PART III

TASMANIA, 1837-1844

CONTENTS

PART IV

SIR JOHN'S LAST ARCTIC EXPEDITION AND AFTER
1845-1875

List of Illustrations

The
Life, Diaries and Correspondence of Jane Lady Franklin

PART I

CHAPTER I

PARENTAGE—FAMILY ASSOCIATIONS

L ADY FRANKLIN'S father, John Griffin, of 21
Bedford Place, London, a liveryman, and later a
governor, of the Goldsmiths' Company, was of a
Huguenot family, from the Pays de Caux. Born in
1757, he married in 1786 and died in 1852, at the
great age of 95. He was a silk weaver of Spitalfields,
and a man of education and wealth, and fond of travel.
His wife was also of a Huguenot family, her grandfather, Jean Guillemard, having been brought over
as a child from Normandy to London.* He had four
sons—John, Peter, Isaac and James—the eldest of
whom, John Guillemard, had a son, John, and a
daughter, Jane. This John was the uncle so often
alluded to in Lady Franklin's letters, and Jane, born
in 1765, was her mother. She married John Griffin
in April, 1786, and died in 1795, leaving four little
children—John, who died in 1804, Frances, Jane and

* Dr. Guillemard has still the armoire in which the child was smuggled
on board ship.

LIFE OF LADY FRANKLIN

Mary. The children, who were only eight, seven, four and two years old, were brought up by Miss Peltreau, whose charming portrait by Downman we are able to reproduce, and who acted as both governess and mother to them until they were grown up. She lived at 21 Bedford Place with them, which was a big house well adapted for the large dinners and receptions and the little dances which the girls and their father delighted in ; we know that the house had thirty-seven windows on which £25 10s. 6d. was paid as window tax.

The Guillemard family were also " silk men," as they were then termed, and very well off. Mrs. Griffin's brother, besides having a house in Gower Street and a farm near Bath, gave £40,000 for Clavering Hall, near Saffron Walden, in Essex ; and throughout the eighteenth and nineteenth centuries we find them among the ranks of literary men and ecclesiastics who had mostly received their education at the University of Oxford.

The three daughters of John and Jane Griffin, with whom we have to do in these pages, married in the inverse order of their birth. Mary the youngest was married at the age of twenty-one to Mr. Simpkinson, Q.C., afterwards Sir Francis Simpkinson, in 1814 ; Jane when 37 married, as his second wife, the great Arctic explorer, Sir John Franklin, in 1828 ; Frances at 43 became the wife of Mr. Ashhurst Majendie, in 1831.

As frequent references are made in these pages

LADY SIMPKINSON

to various members of them, it will, I think, be interesting to hear something of each of the three families into which the sisters married.

THE SIMPKINSONS

This family was also connected with the Goldsmiths' Company. Many of them, having taken Holy Orders, devoted themselves to the work of public school education.

The father of Mary's husband was a Rev. John Simpkinson, Rector of Cliffe, Kent, who had married Renée, daughter and co-heir of Abraham *de Wesselow*. This name had originally been *Wesselofski*, and Abraham had been Ambassador of Peter the Great to the Court of Vienna, but after the death of his friend the Czarevitch Alexis, in 1718, he fled and settled in Geneva, and, having changed his name, died there in his hundreth year in 1782. It was in Geneva that their daughter, Renée, was born.

John and Renée Simpkinson had one son—John Augustus Francis, who went to Christ Church, Oxford, was called to the Bar, and was knighted in 1845. He died in 1851. He, too, had been born at Geneva, and he it was who in 1814 married Mary Griffin. Their family consisted of two sons and three daughters. The eldest son, *John Nassau Simpkinson*, educated at Rugby and Cambridge, was from 1845 to 1855 a master at Harrow, where he married the sister of Dr. Vaughan, the headmaster, later Master of the Temple, and had a large family. The youngest daughter died in 1921.

John's brother, *Francis Guillemard Simpkinson*, was in the navy. He sailed with Franklin in his earlier commands, and with Admiral Belcher in his voyage round the world in the *Blossom*, and was one of " Humboldt's lieutenants," of whom two were appointed by each nation to take synchronous pendulum observations, etc., in various parts of the world. He was sent to Van Dieman's Land. He was also a water-colour artist of very considerable merit, and a friend of Prout and Turner. Latterly he lived at Cannes, and, when fifty years of age, assumed, in 1869, the name of De Wesselow.

Their three sisters were *Louisa*, who married James Dixon, F.R.C.S., the well-known ophthalmic surgeon ; *Emma* ; and *Marianne Jane*. The latter married an Italian, the Marchese Annibale Paulucci dei Calboli-Piazza, of the Guardia Nobile of H.H. the Pope; he died in 1865, in the same year as his wife, leaving three sons, of whom Raneiro (to call him by the first of his seven names) was Italian Minister to Portugal and later Ambassador to Japan. He had a son, Fulcieri, who greatly distinguished himself in the late war. He had a public funeral and a street called after him in Rome, and received on his deathbed a special gold medal for valour from the hands of the King. Raniero was appointed in 1922 Italian Ambassador at Madrid.

THE FRANKLINS

Towards the end of the seventeenth century Francis Franklin had a farm at Sibsey, near Boston, in Lincolnshire. Of his thirteen children, John, born 1710, married Mary Hall, one of the eleven children of Thomas Hall, yeoman, and his wife Elizabeth, the heiress of Thomas Willingham. Both of these families lived in the adjoining parish of Stickney. This John Franklin had ten children, of whom the eldest son, born 1739, was christened Willingham. When John died his widow moved to Spilsby and set up a business there. At Spilsby Willingham had a large family of five sons and seven daughters. Henry, the eldest, died in infancy. Thomas Adams was the foremost man of the neighbourhood in raising a troop to fight Buonaparte. Sir Willingham, Captain of Westminster School, Scholar of Corpus and fellow of Oriel, Oxford, was a distinguished scholar, and died Judge of the Supreme Court of Madras. James, a major in the Indian Cavalry, has the distinction of having been in charge of the first survey of India. Sir John, the youngest, made himself a name famous for all time by his Arctic explorations, and was the discoverer of the " N.W. Passage." Of the daughters, we have in Sir John and Lady Franklin's letters frequent allusion to Isabella Cracroft, whose daughter, " Sophy," lived with Lady Franklin and travelled with her during the eight and twenty years of her widowhood. Of the other sisters, Mary lived and died unmarried at Spilsby, and Hannah Booth, Sarah Sellwood (mother of the first Lady Tennyson), and Henrietta Wright all settled in the Spilsby neighbourhood. Anne Peacock lived in London. They made a numerous clan in what was called " Spilsbyshire," and the Arctic Seas exhibit on many a cape, inlet and bay the names of various members of the family or their places of abode in Lincolnshire.

THE MAJENDIES

The de Majendie family lived in the fourteenth and two following centuries at Bezing, in the old French province of Béarn, in the Lower Pyrenees ; one, André de Majendie, being persecuted and banished at the instance of the intolerant Roman Catholic party, went to Amsterdam in 1667, and from his grandchildren are descended the French branch, which still remains at or near Bezing, and also the English branch, which settled in Exeter in 1700. They had fled to Holland on the Revocation of the Edict of Nantes, in 1685, and passing on to England, like many other Huguenot families, have remained here ever since. Dr. J. J. Majendie, the son of the first émigré to Exeter, had for his mother the daughter of a Devonshire clergyman. He became chaplain to the French Chapel of the Savoy and then preceptor to Queen Charlotte, and subsequently Canon of Windsor, and died in 1783. His son, Henry William, succeeded him as tutor to the Queen's younger son, William, and voyaged with him on the *Royal George*. He became successively Canon of Windsor and St. Paul's and Bishop of Chester and Bangor, and died in 1830, the year that his pupil ascended the throne. His brother, Lewis, married the daughter of Sir Henry Hoghton, whose wife, Elizabeth, was the only daughter of William Ashurst, of Hedingham Castle,

MISS PELTRAU (PELLETRAU)
From a Drawing by Downman in the possession of Dr. Guillemard, of Trumpington

A SCHOOL-GIRL LETTER.

Essex. And it was their son, Ashurst, who became the husband of Jane's eldest sister, Frances, and inherited also the lordship of Hedingham Castle, to which his nephew, Lewis Ashurst, succeeded, who had married Lady Margaret Lindsay, daughter of the Earl of Crawford and Balcarres. There are several notes extant from Queen Charlotte which show the pleasant terms on which the " preceptor " lived with the Royal family.

John Griffin's three daughters were all not only extremely well educated and unusually travelled but all very pretty girls. Many letters testify to this.

Miss Peltrau—whose name, as it seems, really was Pelletreau—did well for them ; she ruled the house and Miss Van Emden acted as governess and when Frances went to school she brought at times a schoolfellow to stay with them, whom Miss Peltrau seems to have welcomed with open arms. We have a regular school-girl letter dated January 29th, 1806, written by a Miss Wrey, of Tawstock Court, a house which the Wreys have owned for six centuries, to Frances, then aged eighteen years old. The letter is half chat and half politics. In it she says, " Do send me some intelligence of Miss Van* and Miss Peltrau, also the general opinion on the loss of Mr. Pitt " (who had just died) ; " I confess I am one of those who think we shall do quite well without him, particularly if my friend Lord Sidmouth or Lord Castlereagh be chosen to supply his place.

* Miss Van Emden, their school mistress.

CHAPTER II

1815

An Exciting Easter in Rome

The following pages are taken from Jane's voluminous Diaries of Travel.

In 1815. Amongst other things, happily no longer existing, she saw the galley slaves at Toulon, five or six hundred in number ; those guilty of murder chained to their benches and never leaving the ship, others working in chained gangs in the streets.

One volume of small quarto size has 177 pages with thirty-five lines to the page. It is called " Journal of a Tour in France, Italy and Switzerland, containing Nismes, Aix, Marseilles, Toulon, Hyere, Nice, Genoa, Lerici, Massa, etc." Volume three of this year continues the tour of the father and his three daughters through Tuscany to Pisa, Leghorn and Florence, where they spent four months and then went on to Perugia and Rome, their first sight of Florence on this journey being on February 25th and of St. Peter's, June 29th. This volume is a larger quarto forty-five lines to a page of about 550 words. To Florence no less than ninety-five pages are given.

An undated copy of one journal gives the account of their first introduction to Rome. This must have been in 1815, and tells how, after overcoming many difficulties with the hotels and livery stables, "we got away from Bolseno, now a poor village built on the ruins of Volsinium, the ancient capital of the Volsci. We had to pay for six horses, the hotel-keeper refusing to move with less, and passed through a wild country, beautiful with oak and broom by Montifiascone, famous for its wine. In the church of St. Floriano is shewn the tomb of a German prelate, who died there in his travels from drinking immoderately of it." Having at last arrived at Viterbo, by moonlight, the Journal goes on, " We delivered our passports at the gate to be taken and signed by the governor. We had heard that the Albergo Reale was probably filled with the suite of the King of Spain, who was here on his way to the baths of Lucca, which induced us to go to the Angelo, a secondary inn, where we found very bad accommodation and a very extravagant bill*—bad butter and milk—the latter tasted like liquid goat's cheese.

" On our arrival here a number of reports were spreading relating to the appearance of the King of Spain here. It appeared he and his suite, among them a queen and her son, had all precipitately fled from Rome, not to go to the baths of Lucca, but to get out of the way of Murat, who was said to be advancing towards Rome, through which he had demanded a passage for his troops of the Pope. The latter was said to be going off to Civita Vecchia, whence many fugitives were running and ministers were coming

---

* This recalls Sheridan's remarks on the inns, "The Sun refused us candles to go to bed by and the Angel treated us like the devil."

out. We found the next morning we could not get horses to get off early; we must wait till the Duchess's horses could return. The King of Spain, though it was said that he had put fifty horses in requisition at each post, was not going to move from Viterbo to-day, but other people were coming in—the old King of Sardinia, the Sardinian and Russian ambassadors, etc. We seemed to be running into the midst of tumult and danger, but it was not till we had set off about one o'clock and found ourselves now actually approaching Rome that we began to feel adequate fear of the danger. I do not speak correctly, for though we all felt that some revolution was taking place and that we were advancing to meet it, it was only F——who seemed cast down with dismay. She now bitterly lamented the folly which was leading us thus heedlessly on, and would willingly have turned back to Viterbo, or gone (if there were any road) to Civita Vecchia. Mr. Guillemard, my uncle, while he only pitied or smiled at her fears, did not remove them. He said he had no doubt in his own mind that some tumult was taking place; that our situation reminded him of his when he entered Paris at the commencement of the Revolution.

" We were told that the King of Spain had left Rome the preceding day; they had begun to distribute about the streets the news of Buonaparte's capture, which had just arrived by the Florence courier. Coming at this juncture, without time to be confirmed by other accounts, and seemingly at the moment when it might be forged for political purposes, they said nobody seemed to believe it. My uncle, who when we first began our journey together was always talking of the impossibility and the madness there might be in trying to get to Rome, now seemed to have his whole heart fixed on it. Thirty years he had been going to Rome. 'Oh, Rome, Rome, Rome!' and was he now to come back within sight ? A distant view would not suffice him. He must touch Rome before he should be satisfied."

Before reaching Ronciglione they met a diligence from Rome, which told them that all was quiet at Rome, but that reports said that Murat was coming and the Pope going to fly away, but a Neapolitan gentleman arrived now who said he did not believe that Murat had any hostile intentions against Rome but was going to make war against the King of Sicily, but people were frightened because his troops were going to take possession of Ancona and must pass through the Pope's territory. These representations allayed Fanny's fears and they set off early in the morning.

" We were escorted during the whole of this stage by about half a dozen of the Pope's cavalry guard, who were returning to Rome after having escorted the King to Viterbo ; the King of Spain protected by escort of the Pope in his own dominion ! They were mounted on pretty good, long-tailed, dark chestnut horses, but were in themselves rather deplorable looking soldiers. Their uniform was a dingy green, faced with red and gold lace, with red tufts and gold loopings (no feathers) in their cocked hats.

They asked if they should escort us, and though Deguine politely thanked them and refused, they continued by the side of the carriage, and at length asked for ' pour boire.' We were not suprised to find such degrading conduct from such deplorable looking soldiers. They had a pistol pouch on their saddles and immense long swords dangling from their sides. They had all dirty trousers, some with boots beneath, and some with dirty white stockings hanging in folds over their dirty shoes. They had no gloves." These Jane contrasted with the papal Swiss guards on duty at St. Peter's, who, she says, " looked well dressed in steel armour, steel helmets and steel waistcoats ; all large, fine-looking fighting men."

It is of these Swiss guards that Jane tells the wel-known tale, how a French soldier thus reproached a Swiss for being a mercenary. " Vous ne vous battez que pour de l'argent, tandis que nous ne nous battons que pour de l'honneur." " Bien," replied the Swiss, " tout le monde se bat pour ce que lui manque."

After they had reached the Eternal City the journal becomes more interesting.

" *Monday, 20th of March.*—We walked to the Piazza Colonna, where we got a hackney coach, delivered at different houses our letters of recommen-dation (nobody at home), and then having an hour and a half before dinner, hour of $\frac{1}{2}3$, set off as if running a race to see as much as could be possibly crowded into so small a space. I was of my uncle's opinion, that it was best to get a general idea of objects before examining detail, but this was not even a general

idea. However, there was one reconciling consolation. If Murat came and we were obliged to scamper
off to Civita Vecchia we might perhaps be able to
recollect that we had glanced at all these things ;
so in the space of an hour and a half we saw the Pantheon, the Capitol, the Forum, its buildings, etc.
After dinner it was approaching evening and we set
off to walk for an hour, and found the Corso filled with
carriages which drove up and down, making the sweep
of the Piazza del Popolo, where they often stand still
while people sit quiet in them looking at what passes.
We lingered in the Piazza ; the moonlight streamed
upon the Egyptian column, and as we returned it
mingled with the light from the smart lighted cafés,
the lamps, and Madonna lanthorns, and the torches
of the green stalls which are suffered to encroach
into the streets. Almost all the carriages moving
on the Corso were calashes, a good many gentlemen
but no lady walking. As English we felt ourselves
privileged, and were countenanced by seeing others.
The palm stalls, which were filled with fritters the
day before, were now full of fish, lobster, small fish,
dried, etc.

"*Tuesday*, 21*st*.—F—— and I went before breakfast
to Vasi's paint shop, in the Rue Baliano, where we
found prints coarser and worse and dearer than Menal-
doli's, where we had been the day before in the Piazza
di Spagna, a disagreeable, stupid, ugly conceited
man ; he told me when I asked for books he had not
got them, that, having his itinerary I had everything ;
it contained the substance of all the rest. At Menal-

doli's I bought a book of beautiful prints illustrative of Grecian and Roman instruments, furniture, etc., for only one scudo ten pali, or about five shillings. During the morning we went up Trinity stairs to Monte di Pincio, where my father and uncle went into the French Academy to deliver a letter Mr.—— had procured for us from M—— to M. Le Thiere, director of the Academy, while F—— and I walked upon the Terrace. We could not show ourselves after the foolish complimentary letter which the Genoese gentleman, without having seen us, had written to his friend. We afterwards lingered a little in the forum, but (having lost our guide and having no cicerone) without much purpose. We went to. the Coliseum, where we found my uncle. After looking at it for ten minutes we returned home to dinner. In the Corso, round a library where the papers are read, was a great number of people ; we supposed there was news, and on enquiry found that a manifesto of the Congress against Buonaparte had just arrived by the courier from Florence. We saw this afterwards. It was the declaration of the eight United Powers who signed the Treaty of Paris, stating that "as Napoleon Buonaparte had by invading France violated all the treaties of good faith, it was impossible ever more either to make peace or treaty with him ; he was put out of the protection of the laws and delivered over to public vengeance. At the same time they declared that in order to secure the peace of the legitimate sovereign of France and the French nation, and to make this "impotente et dilettuoso delirio " return to the nothing from whence he came, they would assist with their forces and by every means in their power the French nation or any other power he might attack. It was signed at Vienna on the 13th March (so had been only eight days coming here) by the eight allied Powers, Austria, France, Great Britain, Portugal, Prussia, Russia, Spain and Sweden. This decree had been printed under authority of Lord B—— at Florence, on the 18th. It proved the total falsehood of the news we had heard at Vienna of Buonaparte's having been taken near Grenoble and carried prisoner to Toulon. Nobody on the road nor here at Rome had heard of this news of ours, and doubted it when we told them."

At Easter they went to the Sixtine Chapel, the Marquis d'Origo, to whom they had an introduction from Prince Aldobrandini, having brought them a permit in order to hear the Miserere. It began at four and it was not over till six.

"There was an immense crowd of people and a great number of English ; more than half the ladies were English, many dressed in black, as were all the Italians. I saw not the slightest appearance of devotion amongst them or amongst any.

"The English were laughing and talking; the politics of our situation in Rome were discussed, and weariness expressed at the length of the music. ' How long will it last ? ' said a lady behind me. ' Till all the candles are out.' They had none of them begun to die away and I did not know what this meant—a man was perpetually balancing himself on the precipice of the screen to trim the high wax lights which stood there in candelabra; the toddling extinguishers excited a general smile. When all the candles were out, however (before this the contending mixture of night and day had spread a fine light over the chapel), and the Miserere began, a general and solemn silence took place. Some responsive voices were heard amongst the congregation. It was good and beautiful. We sat on benches before two square box galleries of crimson and gold standing on each side of the aisle, which are meant for sovereigns and princesses, and within an iron or bronze grating with a door in the middle and a row of eight lighted candelabra on the balustrade. Sitting at the end, I saw all the people beneath me; this ante-chapel we were in as well as the space enclosed between the walls and partition on the inner side were crowded. I saw Prince Esterhazy's brilliant star and fierce eyes shining amongst the bystanders beneath us. We had hit also upon the Princess in going into the Pantheon in the morning. I saw all the cardinals pass by, their long violet trains held up by bearers, powdered hair stiffly sticking out in curls at the bottom. They all seated themselves under the wall on the opposite side to the partitioned crowd—a row of priests sat before them. The Pope's throne was empty. I looked for him for a long time, but he was gone, in consequence of Murat's requesting a passage for his troops through Rome to join those he had at Ancona, pretending the passage by Abruzzo was not practicable for his artillery. A proclamation published from the papal palace stated that as there was reason to believe the Government of Naples had designs against his temporal kingdom and his sacred person, he had judged it necessary to leave his people of Rome for a short time, and retire to a neighbouring city of his dominions, not mentioned. He appointed a provincial government during his absence, the president of which was the Cardinal della Somaglia, Vicario di Roma. The cardinals did not long stay behind. There was a smaller number of them this evening than when my uncle was at the Pope's chapel the day before, and the next morning only four, it is said, remained. We went to the Doria Palace the next morning, where the two Cardinals, brothers of Prince Doria,* had gone off. The Portuguese minister, too, had gone off. Buonaparte, instead of being taken near Grenoble on the 10th, was now said to have entered Lyons on that day. A great many people were going off amongst the English.

"The next day, *Thursday, 23rd,* we heard nothing new to frighten us, and there were no horses to be had if we had wished to go away. F—— and I, in the fear of being called away, we knew not how soon, set off with my father early before breakfast to see St. Peter's. There was some singing in a side chapel, which sounded beautifully in the distance, a great many confessionals were occupied with the priest sitting in the centre, and people kneeling on each side. They had wands

---

* This is reckoned the finest and largest palace in the world. It is not a little curious that the Prince Doria of to-day has just married the devoted English woman who saved his life by her assiduous and skilful nursing ever since the war. July, 1921.—ED.

or rods in their hands. I saw an officer in scarlet come forward before one of the confessionals, fall on his knees before the priest, receive a stroke of the wand on his hand, and rise and walk away.

"We unfortunately missed to-day seeing the washing of the feet of the apostles, who are pilgrims, priests and deacons, which ought to have been done by the Pope and which one of the cardinals did for him. The benediction from the balcony of the church also, and the illumination of the cupola of St. Peter's did not take place. The latter would not have taken place if the Pope had been there, as he had determined to put an end to it, judging rightly that it was less an object of adoration than the cause of making St. Peter's a profane promenade. In the evening we went to see the Pauline chapel in the Vatican ; a number of carriages and people returning made us believe something was over which we had lost. We found, however, the chapel brilliantly illuminated with lights and multitudes of poor dirty people all on their knees. There was nothing going forward, the most perfect silence and quiet reigned. There would have been something grand in this if the people had answered to it, but they were all clownish faces, smiling and staring with admiring wonder at the sight, remaining on their knees mechanically and kept there seemingly by the pleasure of looking at the lights.

"In returning to dinner we found a basket full of things coming out of our room and a young English-man following them. He apologised, said he had left them here when he went to Naples and came to

THE CARDINAL'S BLESSING

recover them—had come from Naples to Civita
Vecchia with the Prince of Wales—had had great
civility from Buonaparte and Murat ; the former had
told him that he had done with the commotions of
public life and was settled quietly for life in his retire-
ment of Elba. Murat had given his word of honour
as a king that whatever might happen in Italy he
would protect the English. The Queen of Naples
had fainted when she heard her brother had exposed
himself by leaving Naples.

"*Friday, 24th.*—At three we went again into the
Museum for a little while and then to hear the Miserere
in the Cappella di Corso in St. Peter's. A great part
of the service was in a monotonous Gregorian Chant—
the conclusion was fine music of Cimarosa's, candles
going out, and noise of clapping of hands as at the
Sixtine. While this was going on I saw in another
part of the church (for we did not remain in the chapel
all the time) a cardinal attended by priests and fine
scarlet-liveried servants and trainbearer, seat himself
in a confessional and give his blessing or his absolution
to the people at the end of a long rod with which he
touches their heads as they kneel before him. The
priests of some higher order received it first, standing
and then seated themselves below the Cardinal-
Bishop ; then inferior priests, servants, and the multitude who put themselves on their knees in groups.
It was curious to see the Cardinal's good-natured
carefulness, for fear the long trembling rod should
at last tap too hard on their heads or come into their
eyes.

"Before we went away, the balcony above St. Veronica's statue was being lighted, I suppose they were going to display the sacred relics, the lance of our Saviour and the divine handkerchief.

"This is Good Friday, but there were no shops that I observed shut up during any part of the day, but still more than usual abundance of vegetables in the streets. Our landlord, I believe, had a scruple of conscience in dressing meat for dinner for us; he asked us if we did not make maigre, and Deguine said it was the only day throughout the year in which he himself did. Good Catholics, he said, to-day would refrain not from meat only, which nobody could think of touching, but from eggs, milk, butter, (I saw however, little men and women in butter at the shops); nobody would eat anything till twelve o'clock, and even nurses would not give suck to their infants till towards that hour. My father did not choose to go without his meat."

After visiting the Villa Media, where Buonaparte had established the Royal Academy of France, founded by Louis XIV. in 1666, they are taken by Mons. Le Thiere to Canova's workshops, and Jane writes a good account of all his fine sculptures, which has a prominent interest sufficient to entitle it to be inserted here.

"Mr. Le Thiere came this morning, as he had appointed to take us to Canova's workshops, full of relievos, bits of statues, etc.; they occupy almost the whole of one side of a dirty narrow street which leads out of the Corso. The Chevalier had been

A SCULPTOR'S WORKSHOPS

apprised of our visit and was ready to receive us. He is a little man between fifty and sixty ; he was of an intelligent and benevolent expression of countenance, with light eyes and dark hair, a long face, not nearly so handsome, however, as his bust, which has a great deal of the *beau ideal* in it ; he speaks French indifferently, but speaks very little, appears exceedingly modest and what he said was mostly in Italian to Mr. Le Thiere, who repeated it. We rather hurried through the rooms, Mr. Le Thiere fearing, I believe, to detain him from another party. There are nine little workshops opening into one another. We saw, besides the plaisters* of the fine things we had already seen at Florence and the Vatican, a beautiful Paris, naked, with his Phrygian bonnet in his right hand, which holds the apple turned behind and resting on his hip at the back, as if hiding it from the fair candidate. The Empress Marie Louisa represented as Concord, seated upright on a fine sculpted chair, with her feet on a cushion as footstool, a tiara on her head. Mr. Le. Thiere seemed in a passion, he had made it so ugly. She has the most simple and insignificant and even ugly face, with a smirking pleased expression. It is said very much to resemble her ; it is a very fine statue, notwithstanding her ugliness and stiffness. It was made by Buonaparte's order, as well as another of his mother, Madame Letitia, represented sitting in an easy reclining attitude with her tiara on her head—the plaister is here in the same room, the original is in Paris.

* Jane always spells this word with an "i" and the London City Company of Plaisterers still do the same.

29

" An enormous plaister of Buonaparte, represented like the Roman Emperors, naked, with his robe clasped by an eagle medallion, and his right hand stretched out holding a little Victory, at which he is looking. It is a very strongly marked, fine head, uncovered, resembling him, but full of the *beau ideal*. One would imagine from this statue, setting aside its colossal size, that Buonaparte was a very tall man. I understood that this statue had been paid for since Buonaparte was in Elba ; on our second visit the man said the marble was in Paris and one in bronze in Milan.

" Colossal statues of Ajax, not finished, and of Hector naked with helmet on. A group or part of a group of ' Beneficence,' belonging to the monument of the Princess Marie Christina of Austria, aunt of the Emperor, which is in the Church of the Augustines at Vienna—the part we saw was in plaister and represented Beneficence, a fine female figure looking down, and gravely leading an old, bent, infirm man, whose arm she has under hers and draws him forward. A little girl with her petticoats tied in a knot about her naked waist, and her hair done up in a little knot at the top of her head, forms part of this group; she is accompanying the old man.

" A figure originally meant for Madame Lucien Buonaparte, and since converted into a muse with a lyre ; another of Elisa, Buonaparte's sister, also converted into a muse, sitting on a chair. A group of Hercules dashing Lichas by the foot, a plaister which

A FAMOUS SCULPTOR

I scarcely saw. The group of Theseus killing the centaur, very fine. We saw the group divided, it being not yet finished or joined : the centaur and the hand grasping his throat was one part, the other was Theseus, a figure with a little drapery and helmeted without his grasping arm ; one leg of the centaur is also with this part ; these are colossal and very fine. I was particularly struck with the action of the hinder part of the centaur, which identified the beast with the man and shewed how much the animal was affected by the gripe of the latter, the left knee of Theseus pushed into the stomach of the centaur man.

" A lovely little Hebe scarcely emerged from childhood tripping lightly on, almost in the air, her shoulders and bosom naked, and her light gauze petticoat falling in full folds and a sash that binds her waist and is tied in a large smart flying knot behind ; her right hand is elevated above her head, which makes her shoulder-blades advance a little and her elbow go behind ; she has a very long face, hair bound with a band ; she seems intended to hold a vase, which, however, is not in her hand, though it is in the print. In her left she has a golden cup. This figure has been purchased for three thousand sequins by Lord Cawdor ; it is small, not at all bigger than life. , I think he has made three, but this is the best and last.

" A group of the three Graces, entwined and caressing, quite naked, the centre is rather the tallest, and reclines her head on one side a little affectedly ; their hair is sedulously dressed.

" The Duke of Bedford has ordered Canova to make a similar group for him, with some alteration in their coiffure—they are not at all larger than the natural size. This group he was about when we went the second time. A very fine standing figure of Peace, with beautiful limbs and drapery, with a gilt branch of olive in her right hand, of which the elbow is rather behind her, resting on an elevated column on which is a gilt illustrative inscription slightly inclined; she has wings raised behind ; a serpent is trying to climb up the column, which she treads under her right foot. This statue is beyond the natural size, very beautiful, and is going to the Emperor of Russia. A sitting, graceful figure drawing, representing the daughter of the Prince Esterhazy; '1805,' is in gold letters at the back of her book ; she is looking intently at her model, upright and head a little erected from her tablet, which she holds in her left hand, while her right is in the act of holding the pencil, a small grey mark in the marble is in her forehead—the marble is full of spots.

" A most lovely dancing nymph, her head bewitchingly on one side, her right hand with raised finger, and her left elbowed on her hip with a garland swung upon her wrist, her cymbals hanging on a stump beside her. This is bought by some individual in Fiori, in Italy, the Pope's territories, who desired Mr. Canova to make him a statue without fixing any price.

" Besides these we saw a good many fine busts which we had not time to look at. I recollect one of

Cimarosa and some reliefs ; one good one of Socrates defending Alcibiades, also the plaister group of Icarus and Dædalus; a fine thing, which was the first Canova executed. Mr. Le Thiere said it was true to nature, but had not the *bcau ideal*. The old man, with his intent, adopting look as he regarded the youth, appeared to me excellent, as well as the pleased proud smirking look of the boy, who has the wings tied on his shoulder. We saw also a great colossal figure in marble of the King of Sicily, helmeted like a warrior, and draped like a Roman emperor, his right arm extended, his left elbowed on hip and covered by drapery.

" Mr. Canova is now employed on a most enormous statue of Religion, fully clothed and helmeted, not beautiful, which is to be placed in St. Peter's. It is twenty-four feet high—I should have thought it double. Canova said if it could have been made twice as large it would not be too large for the building. He intends it, I believe, to stand isolated on the pavement before one of the tribunes. It is a full petticoated stiff figure, looking straight forward.

" Mr. Le Thiere said of Canova that the ladies ought to build an altar to him, for great as he was in everything, he was superlative in his females ; this was speaking of Hebe, etc., for nothing can be in greater contrast than his light natural-sized figures and his colossal religious ones. He is a little reproached for giving too much uniformity to all his features. He has a style of beauty of his own, a defect, however, which scarcely any artist, however great, is exempt from."

The journal tells of daily drives and sight-seeing a week after Easter. An uncle brought them the news that Buonaparte had entered Paris on the 20th, and the King had left it on the preceding day. Four days later they hear that King Joachim has entered Florence and the Grand Duke was fled to Pisa. Hearing that three Swiss and three English were going to Naples, they settled to accompany them. Mons. Le Thiere brought them passports from the Neapolitan consul, in case they should fall in with the armies— and on Sunday, the 9th, they left Rome and eventually returned to London.

CHAPTER III

1815

Napoleon at Elba

It was in one of the picture galleries in Florence, in March, 1815, whilst people were in a state of anxiety in consequence of the escape of Buonaparte from Elba, that Frances and Jane Griffin were introduced to Lord Ebrington, who had been in Elba three months before and had talked more than once with that wonderful man. The conversations which then took place were published in pamphlet form a few years later, and called a " Memorandum of Two Conversations between the Emperor Napoleon and Viscount Ebrington, at Porto Ferrajo, on the 6th and 8th of December, 1814." The copy before me is the second edition, dated 1823. This reappeared in nearly identical form in *Macmillan's Magazine* for December, 1894, entitled, " A Conversation with Napoleon at Elba." Frances wrote out her notes of Lord Ebrington's conversation with her and Jane, which though begun in the public gallery was probably carried on in their own rooms or in those of their mutual friend, Mr. Banks. She tells how the Emperor was riding with a guard of fifteen or sixteen horse, and seeing Lord Ebrington, he sent to ask who he was, and hearing he was an Englishman, asked whether he was an officer or a merchant or what. Hearing he was just a traveller, he said, " Oh ? vous êtes donc un ' gentleman.' " He told one of the guard to bring a horse, saying, " No doubt you can ride ; he is a quiet animal." " Oh ! we understand horses very well in England." They rode and talked and met on horseback more than once, and the Emperor gave him a private audience from 8 to 11.30 p.m., and told him to ask any questions he pleased about his past life. " Don't apologise, I told you to speak freely ; I shall be angry at nothing you say."

Questioned about the murder of the Duc d'Enghien, he said he had had proofs that he was implicated in a plot for his assassination, and that he was formally and properly tried, and that it was Talleyrand who dissuaded him from seeing him at the last, saying " N'allez pas vous compromettre avec un Bourbon."

He expressed great contempt for Talleyrand, who he said had but one talent and that was silence. He spoke, Lord Ebrington says, lightly of the talents of his marshals, but had words of praise for Massena, Soult, and Davoust, and thought Murat a pleasant companion, but in military matters a fool, and lazy— a " magnifico lazzaroni." He dwelt with some humour on his admission and that of his army in Egypt to Mahometanism. He was excused circumcision and allowed to drink wine on condition of doing a good action after each draught, and we know from Falstaff that to drink is in itself a good deed. He said that during the fortnight at Tilsit the Emperors Alexander and Francis and the King of Prussia dined together.

Alexander he called a " veritable Grec." You could not trust him. Francis was honest, but without much capacity; and as for the King, they all rose early from the table to get away from him—he bored them to death—but the Queen was quite charming.

Louis XVIII. Napoleon spoke of as a very benevolent, good kind of man, but not fit to be king of France. Napoleon had a great plan for creating a new aristocracy, partly of young members of the old nobility and partly by merit from the ranks, but it needed time to do this. Princes and dukes he could set up, but he owned that he could not make " de vrai nobles," and King Louis would find it impossible to set up on a firm footing men who had for twenty years been " enterrés dans les greniers de Londres."

Of course Lord Ebrington could not tell these eager listeners all that the Emperor had said, nor could Fanny jot down all that she heard, but as hers differs in some details from the printed account, it will be best to transcribe a few pages just as she wrote it. She tells us that—" During the conversation Napoleon fixed his eyes on the Englishman within a few inches of his face. The latter at first retreated, but finding that Napoleon advanced upon him and not choosing to be nailed against the wall, he kept his ground. Napoleon often tapped him on the shoulder. Lord Ebrington thought him very handsome; not a dignified nor severe, but a pensive countenance ; with eyes on the ground when not speaking, but then very animated ; he often laughed and shewed his teeth very much, which are very fine. He did not seem very fat. ' Don't they say in Paris that I am too fat to move ?' He coughed a little. ' I hear from Paris that I spit blood and that I can't live six months.' (mimicking the manner of a consumptive person).

"His marriage with Austria, he said, was the most fatal occurrence that had happened to him ; he was very averse from it, but the Austrian Court was never quiet until it had inveigled him into it. An alliance with Russia would have been more proper for him, but the Princess was only thirteen. ' Rather too young,' he said.

" 'On the occasion of my marriage a very fatal presage occurred—the fire at which the Princess Schwartzenberg was burnt. It affected the French very much.'

" ' But you did not mind it ?'

" ' Pardon me, I did. I have never been fortunate since. Do you not know the same thing happened on the marriage of Louis XVI. with Marie Antoinette ?'

" 'It is said that your son is a child of great talents.'

" ' Je ne le connais pas, je ne l'ai jamais vu j'ai toujours été à la guerre.'

"He said he was much attached to Josephine, but it was necessary that France should have an heir. The Emperor Alexander, he said, was a brave man and ' un bon homme,' but a very bad general. Blucher a brave man, but not a good general, and he behaved like a coward when made a prisoner after the battle of Jena.

"He spoke of Belgium. 'When I was made Emperor I took an oath to preserve France as I found her; Belgium was then annexed to her.* The Rhine and Italy I conquered, and I had a right to play for them and to lose them, but not for Belgium; therefore I would not agree to the conditions of the Allies before they entered France. They required its cession. I would not have yielded it for the crown of France, and would not resume the crown on that condition. After the battle of Leipsic the Allies were not sincere in their offers of treating; they wished only to ensnare me.'

" He spoke of the Bourbons. He had no antipathy to them; he might have poisoned them all in England, but he would not do it. But they were not calculated to be popular with a people like the French. Madame d'Angoulême he had heard was plain and awkward. ' Il fallait pour l'ange de la paix du moins une femme spirituelle ou jolie.' ' The King of England is a very good man, but he hates me.' ' Certainly,' said Lord Ebrington, ' he has never spoken well of you but once, when you had changed your wife. "He has done a good thing," he said. " Oh, that I could change Charlotte." ' ' I never wished to conquer England or to be at war with her. I like the English.'

" ' It does not appear,' replied Lord Ebrington, ' else how came you to make all our poor travellers prisoners. What harm had they done you?'

" ' And how came you to make my poor merchants

---

* Bruges was taken by the French in 1794 and Belgium incorporated with the French Empire. In 1815 it became part of the Kingdom of the United Netherlands. In 1830 of the Belgian Monarchy.—(*Chamber's Encyclopædia*).

prisoners before the declaration of war ? I cared
as much for my merchants as you for your
travellers.'

" ' He said that he understood English, though he
did not speak it, and had all the English papers. Lord
Wellington was equal to any of his generals, if not
superior. ' I believe it is now pretty well acknowledged that I am the best general in Europe, yet I
make ten mistakes a day. *Ten,*' he repeated, holding
up his fingers. Marmont's treachery to him was his
final destruction. When he arrived at Paris and
found it shut against him he turned to Marmont, whose
intentions he had heard of, and said, 'I hear, Maréchal,
you are to turn against me.' He denied it firmly
and the same night he set off. He believed he should
have succeeded but for this.

" Moreau, a brave man, he had great regard for,
but he was spoilt by his marriage. He loved his brother
Lucien very much ; he was the cleverest of all his
brothers, but they quarrelled about his marriage . . . .
He denied poisoning the wounded at Jaffa. ' But
there were a few, ten or twelve, wounded men whom
I was obliged to leave there. The physicians had a
consultation as to what was to be done with them,
for they could not be moved, and the Turks are very
cruel to prisoners, scooping out their eyes and torturing
them in various ways. I said I would give no opinion,
but if it were myself I should prefer taking a little
opium to such a death. I asked how long they might
live. They would hardly survive twenty-four hours
was the answer. I said I would wait twenty-four

hours. When the time was expired there were still two or three alive.'

" Lord Ebrington asked how he came to remain six weeks at Moscow, which proved his ruin. ' I consulted the thermometer records for the last thirty years, during all which period the frost had only twice set in within three weeks of the time it did that year. I don't object to being sent to England, but I won't go to St. Helena alive. The English newspapers say but one thing which is true of me, that I am writing my history. I am doing so.'

" He spoke of Mr. Douglas, Lord Glenbervie's son, as the most talented Englishman he had seen ; only twenty-five, but with a head of forty.

" He did not despair. ' All is not finished yet. You will acknowledge that I have a better chance now than I had when I was a lieutenant in the army. You will see that Louis will not be on the throne in a year or two at most.'

" The Emperor of Russia had at Tilsit suggested an elective monarchy, but he had said at once that it was impossible ; a candidate could only be found once in an age, a Caesar or an Alexander.

" Lord Ebrington said, ' You will have the satisfaction of being placed in a great triumvirate after your death, together with those two.'

" 'Not now,' said Napoleon ; ' I should if I had had the good fortune to be killed at the battle of Moskwa, but now my glory is tarnished.'

" 'Everyone was surprised you should have survived your glory.'

" ' I know it. My enemies thought I was a bankrupt, but my affairs are not yet irretrievable. They put pistols in my way on purpose, but they were mistaken I was not such a fool as to use them.'

" ' How do you live now ? Very temperately, I suppose ?'

" ' No, I never lived so well. I go to bed at eight or nine, rise at twelve and read or write till four in the morning, then sleep till seven or eight.'

" ' I thought I should find you very stern and severe.'

" ' Yes ; the world does not know me. I am thought very violent, but I am not at all so naturally ; I have been obliged to feign it to awe people. My portraits have never expressed my real character. They all represent the Emperor, not Napoleon.' "

Fanny Griffin thought that the young viscount had been dazzled by being admitted to familiar conversation with the great man, and believed all he said too easily; but when she takes notes of what Mr. Banks, a man of mature judgment, told her of his conversation with Napoleon, she ends with, " Mr. Banks believes Louis Buonaparte to be a kind good-hearted man without any selfish views or ambition," an opinion on which she makes no comment.

" Among other things Napoleon said to Mr. Banks that the Duke of Wellington was a most extraordinary man, very superior to Marlborough. ' It is true,' he said, ' that he had the best troops in the world ; I always allow one-third more in proportion against the English than against any other nation.'

" Mr. Banks was also well acquainted with Lucien

Bonaparte at Rome, and said he was the only man
there who had a lamp burning before the Madonna
night and day in his hall.   He complained bitterly
of Napoleon for persecuting him on account of his
marriage with a woman of very decent family whom
he loved. ' Lucien,' Mr. Banks said, ' received the
English very well at Rome ; perhaps with a view of
securing a retreat in case of a change in his affairs.'

So far we have quoted from the notes made by
Fanny when with her sister Jane and her father at
Florence, or a few days later at Viterbo, from which
place the latter writes and speaks of the " meeting,
on March, 1815, with Mr. Banks, who introduced
Lord Ebrington to them, who talked to them, describing
very fully his visit to Elba in December of the previous
year."

In Lord Ebrington's published account the Emperor
asked how people would receive him if he came to
England, " Serais-je lapidé ? "   The answer was that
war having ceased, the feeling against him was subsiding
and he would be perfectly safe.   But he said he thought
he would still always run some risk at the hands of
the London mob.   Of the French he seemed to have
no fears.   Some, he said, had called him a traitor
and a coward, but it is only the truth that hurts one ;
and the French knew very well that he was neither
the one or the other.

He had kept those who served him well paid, and
when Lord Ebrington asked whence he got the means
for doing this, he said, from the "domaines extraordi-
naires," a fund of two hundred million francs, which

he explained were " des contributions de mes ennemis,
l'Autriche pour deux paix m'a payé par articles
secrets 300,000,000 francs, et la Prusse aussi enorme-
ment," but when asked if he had got much from
Russia, he said, " Non, je n'ai exigé d'elle que de
fermer ses ports contre l'Angleterre." He referred
again to the French love of receiving, but dislike of
spending, money, when, after upholding the necessity
of an established religion, he combated Lord Ebrington's observation that there was a great indifference
generally throughout the country about public worship,
by saying "Eh! non; le Francais aime bien son curé,
sa messe, pourvu toujours qu'il n'aye pas à le payer."
He often had petitions from villages for a parish
priest, to which he always assented "à condition qu'ils
le payeraient "; this they as constantly declined,
but he allowed no priest in his armies ; " car je n'aime
point le soldat devot." But it would appear from the
letter following, written but a week or two after these
conversations in Elba, that Napoleon, though he did
not like to trust himself in England, was too optimistic
in his faith in the reception the French would give
him on his re-appearance from Elba.

The letter was written to a Miss Cramer by Fanny
Griffin, from Marseilles, in January, 1815, as they
were going out to Italy, and speaks of the feeling in
the South of France towards Napoleon just before
he abdicated and was sent to Elba.

" En arrivant à Avignon nous avons trouvé la difference
la plus marquée dans les sentiments du peuple de celui de Lyon,
et ce sentiment nous ne l'avons plus trouvé changé depuis. Dans

PROVENCE HOSTILE TO NAPOLEON

toute la Provence le gouvernement passé est détesté. J'ai pris chez vous l'habitude de dire l'Empereur; je m'en suis vite defait en trouvant que ce nom choquait toutes les oreilles ; le peuple, toujours violent, surtout dans ce pays, ne prononce ce nom qu'en y mélant des injures ; et le nom ridicule de Nicolas qu'on a peutetre inventé par esprit de parti est celui par lequel on le designe le plus souvent. Il n'y a rien de plus vrai que les dangers qu'il a couru en traversant cette province, et les craintes qu'il a éprouvés. En plusieurs endroits on s'est assemblé pour le menacer, et enfin à Argon, petit village ou nous avons passé, voyant son effigie pendant, il a cédé à ses craintes et s'est déguisé en courier jusqu'a Aix. A Freyjus nous avons couchés dans l'auberge ou il avait passé deux jours avant de s'embarquer. . . . on ne nous donna pas des details bien interessantes, il s'enfermait toujours à écrire dans se chambre, et il était inquiet de sa sureté, comme de raison, car c'aurait été une mort misérable que d'étre assassiné par des paysans. Il parait mauvais qu'il n'eut pas une garde suffisante pour le mettre à l'abri de l'insulte. A Marseille l'esprit est encore plus violent, la raison en est claire, leur commerce était detruite et la guerre les faisait mourir de faim . . ."

The above description, written in January, 1815, must refer to the feelings of the people of Marseilles and Provence towards Napoleon before he was compelled to abdicate in April, 1814. The " Hundred Days " did not begin until the middle of March, 1815. As to his life in Elba, he said it was a death in life.

CHAPTER IV

1816—1821

THE FIRST MEETING

In 1816 they started again for Switzerland and took up their residence in Geneva. Two little duodecimo volumes of seventy-two pages with two hundred and fifty words to a page give a very intimate account of their life; each book full of gossip and chat covering one month. In this year these determined travellers made their fourth visit to Florence and their third to Rome.

The following account of the painting of Jane's portrait by Miss Romily is taken from the Geneva journal :—

"We (Fanny and I) went by appointment to Miss Romilly at one o'clock to have our portraits taken.

"I sat first and longest, but not without interruption, she being afraid of nothing so much as worrying me and producing fatigue. It seems to be her object to seize as much as possible the character and natural expression of the face by making it talk and laugh and to move and be at ease. She talks and laughs incessantly herself; hears what you have to say and catches your real expression, while you forget yourself in speaking. She asked me questions, made Fanny read to me, made me pay attention to what she read, requested her sister, Mrs. Dance, to play on her harp, and as much as possible diverted my attention from the painful feeling of embarrassment which one necessarily

feels in such a situation. Miss Romilly seems a young woman of
the most amiable temper and quick sensibility. I could not
help liking her very much when I saw how her beautiful complexion
caught as it were the reflexion of the stupid blushes which once
or twice I felt heating my cheeks. Mrs. Dance came in repeatedly.
She assists her sister in the subordinate parts of the picture, such
as the ground, and is in this respect of great service to Miss
Romilly, who would not otherwise be able to get through the
quantity of work she is called upon to do. Mr. and Mrs. Huber
were admitted for a moment ; they came in to see Lady Elizabeth Conyngham's portrait, which Miss Romilly said she had put
en pension since the day before, because so many people came to
see it, that she was perpetually subject to interruptions. Mr.
Massot also came in as, I believe, he is in the habit of doing, and
was requested by her to sit down and look at what she had done.
He examined me for some time with great exactness, and having
pointed out something to alter, pronounced it admirable.
' C'était une resemblance à faire rire,' he said. He was not a
minute in looking at Fanny's, but directly pronounced it correct.

"I was drawn with my hair flat, à l'anglaise, perfectly simple,
in a plain muslin frock with a low neck and my pelisse thrown
back on my shoulders ; she arrested me in an attitude I accident-
ally fell into and said she should choose that, submitting it before
she completed it to Mr. Massot's approbation. She carefully
hid the portraits from us, never suffering them to be looked at
till finished. We left after two or three hours' interrupted sitting
and promised to go again and be finished on the following day."

It was on this their third journey to Rome that
Jane and her father witnessed the washing of the feet
by the Pope. There was a terrific crowd struggling
to get into the upstairs room at the Vatican, and the
huge Swiss guards keeping the crowd back, but Jane
says, "we weakened the resistance of the sturdy
steel-clad arm that was pushing us back, by a bit of

money, and we slipped in." The spectacle was curious, but so obscured by the cluster of attendant cardinals they could see little and soon came away.

The 1817 journal has this notice at the beginning : " This book is meant for my own reading only, though I would not absolutely deny my sisters from looking into it should it fall into their hands when they can no longer ask my permission. I may here say the same of all my private journal books."

After twelve pages of notes on a course of lectures on architectural and other remains in Britain from the earliest times, the rest of the volume describes the sights of London—the Abbey, Tower, Mint, Custom House, etc., and the neighbourhood round London. The sisters always wished to get their knowledge at first hand. She is properly pleased with the new bridge at Waterloo, " under which the Duke of Wellington passed with the Prince Regent in the royal barge with a salute of 202 guns, on June 17th, 1817." She notes in the Abbey that the north transept is crowded with monuments and wooden cases like sentry boxes, containing waxen figures in full drapery : " One of these is Lord Nelson, dressed in the very same clothes, the coat excepted, which he wore when he received his death wound." This curiosity is now placed in an upper chamber with similar effigies of the Stuart kings, etc., to which admission is only given to few. These waxen figures were used at the funerals of the celebrated people they represent. The effigy of Nelson whilst in this transept stood close to the monument of Miss Nightingale, by Roubilliac.

SUNDAY MEMORANDA,

APRIL 10.... 2nd Sunday after Easter

APRIL 17.... 3rd Sunday after Easter

APRIL 24.... 4th Sunday after Easter

MAY .... Rogation Sunday

MAY .... Sunday after Ascension

MAY 15.... Whit Sunday

MAY 29.... Trinity Sunday

FACSIMILE OF LADY FRANKLIN'S 1865 DIARY

DINNERS AND DANCES

The sisters at this time saw a good deal of the Rogets, an interesting and clever family of Huguenot origin, Dr. Roget being the compiler of the famous Thesaurus. They give parties and dances and go to exhibitions of pictures and statuary at Somerset House. Jane goes to see the first imported Wapiti deer kept in the royal mews, and indeed she goes everywhere where there is anything important to be seen, from wild animals to " painted glass," and is perpetually educating herself in the most painstaking manner. Her father being a member of the Goldsmith's Guild, she goes by water to a City company banquet at Richmond and sees the Thames steam packets for the first time, which she speaks of as " passing by in full motion, the wheels at the sides cutting the water and moving as if by a volition of their own, and the tall black tube with its volume of smoke issuing from it like a mast on fire."

Jane describes one of their own parties as " a dinner and evening party united " with eighteen to dinner and seventy afterwards and dancing, and in the following week a " more homely and quiet dinner party " of ten ; amongst these was a Mr. Pratt, of Tottenham, just returned from the Continent.

The journal proceeds as follows :—

" Mr. Pratt is returned from Italy a hero of romance, a knight of chivalry, and his adventures are too curious not to be recorded. He related them to us by degrees, and not without some questioning on our part, during a long morning visit which he paid us a day or two previous to his coming to dinner. Mr. Pratt left England in July with a younger brother ; he was about

D   49

LIFE OF LADY FRANKLIN

six weeks in Switzerland and went into Italy before the autumn.
On his return to Rome in December, after leaving Naples he went
to a party at Torlonia's—where he met a young Italian lady,
called Madame Pio (this is her maiden name—I do not know her
present one), the wife of a French general who in Buonaparte's
time had been commandant of the city. This lady, addressing
Mr. Pratt as an Englishman, without having any previous acquaintance with him, told him that notwithstanding she and her husband were strongly attached to each other, her family, which
was one of the most considerable in Rome, and more particularly
her mother, who was a relation of Cardinal Gonsalvi's, had determined in consequence of the change in political affairs which had
taken place, to separate them and to marry her to another. For
this purpose they had procured the sanction of the Government
and the promise of a divorce, and in order the better to effect
their purpose, had enticed them both to Rome, where they were
each kept in a species of confinement. She had no resource, she
said, but to throw herself on the generosity of an Englishman to
deliver her from the cruel machinations forming against her.
She entreated Mr. Pratt to effect her escape. He was an Englishman, she said, and that was the reason she appealed to him.
She could not trust to an Italian or a Frenchman : they would
give her fair promises, but till those promises were actually
fulfilled she would never feel secure of their good faith; but the
English were a generous, a highminded, a noble people, a nation
of *preux chevaliers*, despising the thought of danger, and never
betraying the cause entrusted to them. Few young Englishmen
could have resisted such an appeal, and Mr. Pratt, though apparently one of the most sober and least romantic of young Englishmen, did not hesitate a moment. He adopted the lady's cause,
effected her escape from her mother's home and carried her off.
The alarm had been given, and troops and police were stationed
on the roads to apprehend them in their flight. They were joined
at Ponte Molle, within a few miles of Rome, by the husband and
brother of the lady. They made their way undiscovered through
files of armed troops, travelling by night, sometimes on foot and

sometimes on horseback. At one place they could get nothing but a *white* horse, a bad colour for travellers furtively escaping in the dark. They sheltered themselves from a tempest in a cavern in the rocks and quenched their thirst with rainwater collected in one of the large bells which hang about the neck of the cattle. Through all hardships, difficulties and dangers, however, they arrived safely at Florence, but here they were arrested by the police. Mr. Pratt had taken the precaution of having his brother's name in his own passport turned into a woman's, so that the lady passed, I suppose, for his wife. He had also a separate passport for her in case it should prove necessary. The lady, however, fortunately could speak English extremely well, and persisted, when questioned, to speak nothing else, and after considerable difficulties, and though it is supposed that the lady was strongly suspected not to be the person she pretended to be, they succeeded in getting off.

"They avoided the papal territories of Bologna and crossed with much danger and difficulty the Pistoja mountains and came into the King of Sardinia's dominions. They now flattered themselves they were almost in safety, but dangers of another kind awaited them. They were travelling in a coach drawn by two horses with a cabriolet for the driver in front, and were descending the steep Montagne de Chavannes above Montmellion in Savoy. The husband and brother were descending on foot, the lady and Mr. Pratt were alone in the carriage. It was frosty weather ; they were on the edge of a precipice, and one of the horses slipped, dragging the other and the carriage along with it. Mr. Pratt saw what was going to happen ; he saw the first wheel turn over the edge of the precipice and, clasping the hand of his companion, they both resigned themselves to instant and certain destruction. The carriage dashed down a height of about fifty feet, when it pitched upon its head upon a rock where the multitude of light packages and bandboxes (purchases that had been made at Milan) broke the fall. It bounded again, however, three or four several times, though with diminished violence, and the last time it balanced itself long enough on the edge of a precipice to enable

Mr. Pratt to rush out, dragging his companion along with him, and to seize the horses' heads so as to drag them from the edge of the descent. The ground, however, on which Mr. Pratt and his companion were standing was too precipitously steep to be maintained, and they had scarcely set foot upon it, when, losing their ground, they both fairly, and hand in hand, rolled down the precipice upon a thick bed of snow. They received scarcely any injury, and when they came up to the top again they found the spectators, amongst whom were the husband and brother, all standing with open arms to embrace them, like persons miraculously rescued from the jaws of death. The country people who were witnesses of this extraordinary escape cried out ' a miracle,' and declared they would erect a cross upon the spot to commemorate the event. The driver, who in the first stage of the accident had been thrown out of the cabriolet, had his head much lacerated, but was not dangerously wounded, and the horses, though materially injured, were not killed. After having so wonderfully escaped this imminent danger, it might be presumed they would not have much to fear from any other which could await them during the remainder of their journey, and they accordingly arrived safely at Toulouse, the lady's destined place of refuge, where Mr. Pratt resigned his trust into the hands of her husband and made his way to Paris. Here he was met by his poor brother, who, deprived of his passport and ignorant of the reasons of his brother's capricious departure from Rome, had been merely informed by him that he was gone and had been left to shift for himself. Mr. Pratt was the bearer of some letters from the lady and her husband to their friends at Paris, and amongst others to Mr. Le Thiere, a relation of the General's—he there heard our names mentioned, and when Mr. Pratt told us of this circumstance, he asked if we knew Mr. Le Thiere well. ' Oh, yes, very well,' I said. ' Intimately ? ' inquired Mr. Pratt. ' Intimately,' I replied, believing that on this account we were going to have more interesting details communicated to us. ' Then, if that is the case,' said Mr. Pratt, ' I cannot tell you some things which I should otherwise perhaps have communicated.'

LITERARY REUNIONS

How provoked I was ! for Mr. Pratt had already dropped some hints which excited my curiosity. This heroine it seems is not above twenty years of age, handsome but not pretty, with a fine expression of countenance—she is highly accomplished, plays on the lute, and speaks with fluency almost all the languages of Europe. She has been in England and was at the battle of Waterloo, where her husband was made prisoner ; her life has, in short, been a series of the most extraordinary vicissitudes and adventures. Her husband is about forty, and she was only twelve years old when she married him. She had a son seven years of age, who was at Rome with her at her mother's. Mr. Pratt offered to her at Toulouse to go back to Rome and steal the boy, but this she would not allow."

In January, 1818, the journal, which is of octavo size, but so fine and small is the writing that there are often forty-two lines to the page, yet all easily legible, tells us that the Griffins " organized a book society, which differs from any other that I am acquainted with by the circumstances of its meeting every month at the house of the respective members in succession for the sake of forming a literary conversazione and and arranging its internal affairs."

At the February meeting several new members were proposed to make up the number of twelve. The Griffins proposed Mr. d'Israeli* and told him that they had done so. The ballot came on at the March meeting.

"A balloting box, borrowed by Dr. Roget from the Medical Society, was now brought forward, in order that the members proposed at the last meeting might be duly elected. Mr.

* Probably Isaac, father of the Statesman. The Disraelis were very friendly with the many Huguenot families who lived in Hackney.

d'Israeli was first balloted for. The box went round, and when the draw was opened a black ball was found. It excited a momentary surprise, but was, of course, attributed to accident, and the box therefore went round again, but what could exceed our consternation and astonishment when a second black ball was discovered! Mr. George Gregory blushed as he reluctantly took it out. Everybody looked surprised, and not surprised only, but alarmed. How much more reason, then, had *we* to be so, who had proposed Mr. d'Israeli, who had prevailed with him almost against his inclination to become a member of our society, and on whom must necessarily devolve the task of communicating to him his rejection! ' I am sure,' exclaimed Mrs. Debary, ' it is not *me*, for I *know* Mr. d'Israeli, therefore it is not likely to be *me*,' I stopped her by saying that if all those who had not put in the black ball were to tell us so, the person who had done it must be discovered, and that this would destroy the nature of the ballot. It was thought impossible that this second black ball could be the effect of accident; notwithstanding, Mr. George Gregory said he would give Mr. d'Israeli a third trial after having first proceeded to another candidate. They were preparing then to ballot for Mr. De Warris, when a thought suddenly struck me. ' Is not the putting the ball into the *right* hand drawer approving ?' I said. ' No,' said Dr. Roget ; ' just the contrary.' ' Oh, then it's me, it's *me* !' I exclaimed, and ashamed enough I was to make this confession, for ' *aye* ' and ' *no* ' were written in large characters on the box, and blindly disregarding these signs, I had followed my own senseless fancy, never once suspecting that as in driving along the road so in putting your hand into a balloting box:

' If you go to the left, you'll be sure to be right,
If you go to the right, you'll be wrong.'

" My stupidity seemed to be strongly felt by all the party, for there was very little joking about it ; they all seemed to think I must find it an unpleasant topic, and dwelt very little upon it, and I too was mortified and somewhat borne down by the sense of the exposure I had made of my stupidity."

VISIT TO HOLLAND

Throughout her many domestic journals we find Jane to be very shy of the advances of young men, but she is pleased to have the company of elderly gentlemen, whom she describes as " mild, inoffensive and obliging," and her sister Mary admitted that the idea of a wedding always made her uncomfortable. Jane, until she was quite middle-aged, was tormented by an annoying form of nervousness which made her change colour for no adequate reason. She often alludes to this in her private journals.

In August they go for nine weeks to Holland, and on returning go for a month's visit to Brighton, where Jane writes up her Holland, Netherland, and Paris journals, an octavo volume of two hundred and forty-four very closely written pages. In one she even gets twenty lines of legible writing into the space of two inches.

Brighton was a very different place then from what it is now. But in 1817 Jane did not find it much altered from what it was when she visited it in 1805. Her " Journal at Brighton " begins thus. " It is twelve years ago since we were last at Brighton— it was in the summer of 1805, the year after my poor brother's death, I was then thirteen."

The next MS. is called a " Domestic Journal," and extends from December, 1817, to September, 1818. They were all gathered for Christmas week at Ascot " as usual," at the house of Mr. Simpkinson, who had married Mary Griffin.

On Easter Monday, March 23rd, 1818, Dr. Roget interested them in an expedition which was fitting out at Deptford for the North Pole. Mr. Dollond,* the well-known telescope and marine instrument maker, gave them a letter of introduction to Captain Ross of the *Isabella*. And here, as this is the first mention of her future husband, Jane shall tell her own tale.

" She (the *Isabella*) was the largest of the four, but was only about 370 tons and with a crew of fifty.   The *Alexander*, a smaller vessel, was commanded by Lieutenant Parry, and both of these are destined to explore the North West Passage to the Pacific.   The two others, the *Dorothea*, Captain Buchan, and the *Trent*, Lieutenant Franklin, are going directly to the Pole.   All these vessels have been made unusually strong, and the sleeping places of the men, instead of hammocks, are berths with sliding shutters, in order that the men may sleep the warmer.   The decks of the *Alexander* are so low that it is not possible to stand upright on them.   I saw on the deck of the *Isabella* a great number of deal chests containing coloured beads, and some harpoons for killing the whales, and saws for cutting the ice . . . . . . On board the hulk from which we descended into these vessels was the sealskin canoe belonging to the Esquimaux who is to accompany the expedition on board the *Isabella* as interpreter."

He had been performing some feats in the water with this in the earlier part of the day, before Lord Melville and other " people of consequence." Jane says, " We were conducted over the *Alexander* by a young officer, whose name I scrupled to ask, which I am sorry for, as I should like to have fixed my attention upon his fate in the future reports of the expedi-

---

* The Dollonds were Huguenot refugees of good family and considerable scientific distinction, Fellows of the Roget Society and inventors.   John, founder of the optician's business near St. Paul's, was born in 1706 and was the son of a Spitalfields " silk-man."

tion." This was a regretable shyness on her part, for it might possibly have been Lieutenant Franklin of the *Trent*, her future husband, who was then rendering her his first service. This Arctic Expedition was Franklin's first voyage to the far North, when he commanded the brig *Trent*, 280 tons. She sailed April 23rd, 1818, and reached latitude 80°. 34', but being beset by ice and both vessels damaged, they had to return, reaching England October 22nd, 1818. The voyage, though ineffectual, was notable as being the first Arctic voyage of the century.

Jane adds a note at the end of this volume, that Easter day, 1818, falling on March 22nd, as noted above, was on the earliest date possible, and had not happened to fall thus since 1761, nor would it do so again until 2285.

The months of August and September found the family again abroad. In October they re-visited Brighton. The last sixteen pages of volume three of these domestic and very private journals are a marvel of minute penmanship, but for the most part entirely devoid of interest for the general reader. All the same, from 1819 to 1821 their life in London fills volumes. They were indefatigable and somewhat omnivorous sightseers. After describing a sort of astronomical lecture in the East London Theatre, in Goodman's Fields, called by the fearful name of Walker's " Eidouraneon," or vision of the heavens, Jane says, " We have been also to see the ourang-outang at Exeter Change ; the copy of Leonardo da Vinci's picture in Pall Mall, and the new and beautiful panorama of

Athens," ending with " I saw the Duke of Gloucester there ; he came in with his umbrella in his hand, accompanied by another gentleman," a bathos which is hardly exceeded by the Wordsworth parody in " Rejected Addresses."

> " I saw them go, one horse was blind,
> The tails of both hung down behind,
> Their shoes were on their feet."

In January, 1820, King George III. died, but Jane saw no great signs of grief in London, nor was the accession of the Prince Regent likely to be an occasion of any great jubilation.

The next two volumes of the journal describe with painstaking minuteness, a tour in Scotland lasting from the end of July to mid-November, 1821. They travelled comfortably and kept careful accounts, which show an expenditure of £250. The journey between London and Leith was performed by sailing-packet at the rate of thirty miles a day and in very indifferent weather.

They returned in the same manner, and, being becalmed off Cromer, they landed. They could only get a gig, but, undaunted, by turns driving and walking, reached Walsingham, where they took coach by *The Times*, which brought them to Aldgate in fourteen hours, the distance being 115 miles and the fare for each twenty shillings. The driver, who changed horses every seven miles, told them that, with now and then an interval of rest, he did the journey every day of the year.

CHAPTER V

1821-1828

JANE'S ENGAGEMENT AND VISIT TO RUSSIA

It is rather a curious coincidence that Sir John Franklin's two wives should have been friends before either of them was married.

From a large quarto of 194 pages, closely and minutely covered, and called "Home Journal, 1825 and 1826," we hear a good deal about the early friendship between the Griffins and Franklins at the time when Captain Franklin was starting on his second (land) expedition with Dr. Richardson to the North West. In 1825, we read how Jane and Fanny left, on February 5th, the little presents which they had been preparing for him to take on his expedition, Jane's present being a silver pencil case, with his crest on the seal at the head, and a pair of fur gloves, which he had himself named as the most useful present he could receive.

On the 14th we are told that Captain Franklin took his last leave of his poor wife, who had never been well since the birth of her daughter, but who was most courageously anxious that her condition should not be any impediment to his departure. He embarked at Liverpool on the 16th and she died on the 22nd.

A month before this Jane speaks of a dinner party

at their house at which the three most interesting
individuals were Captain Franklin, Sir George Staunton
the Envoy to China, and Mr. Sharp, known on account
of his talent for conversation as "Conversation
Sharp," and we find her calling on Mrs. Franklin,
when ill, and being admitted with her sister Fanny
when no other callers were.

The Spring of 1825 saw our travellers in Normandy,
and Jane gives an interesting account of the Abbey
of Fontevraux, the burial place of our early English
kings. The Autumn found them again in Scotland
and the northern counties of England.

Besides a full journal of their tours, Jane wrote in
1823-4, on a large quarto of 262 pages and with
750 words to the page, what she calls a "Home
Journal." This she finished on her thirty-third birthday. The time and care she must have devoted to
these journals is almost incredible.

In the Spring of 1826, Jane and her father went to
Guernsey, next year to Denmark, and the next to
Russia. And after returning from Guernsey they
went for August to France and thence to Spain,
returning to Bayonne in November and not reaching
England till December 18th.

The following is an extract from a letter to Mr.
Griffin from their friend Mr. Isaac Disraeli, over whose
admission to their book club Jane had made her
embarrassing blunder.

" My dear Sir,
" . . . . Let me congratulate you on your happy return from
the perilous adventure of Spain ; and that your escort proved

AN IMPENDING ENGAGEMENT

faithful, and held no secret communication with the Posadas
and the Guerillas, and, finally, that you have escaped from the
Inquisition, for heresy there is still a matter of delicate discussion,
and an *Auto da Fé* might serve as a proclamation of war against
England !

"*A Griffin Carbonadoed* might have been painted on one of the
holy flags held by a *San Benito* ! Think what you have escaped
from, and don't be too fond of Catholic emanicipation.. . . .
                              " Believe me, dear Sir,
                                    " Most truly yours,
                                          " I. D'ISRAELI.
" J. Griffin, Esq."

Whilst Franklin was still in the Arctic regions the
Griffins were planning a visit to Holland. This was
carried out in August, 1827, and they were back about
the time that he landed in England.

The little volume which gives a minute account of
all they saw and did devotes forty pages to the town
of Doberan, though they only spent four days there.

Franklin, who never lost any time in setting about
any enterprise which he was taking up, was soon
renewing his acquaintance with his late wife's friends,
and though he did not formally request Mr. Griffin's
permission to address his daughter Jane until July,
1828, they had clearly made up their own minds
some time before that. Hence, in a journal of 1827,
we read, under date October 29th, amongst other
cards, "Captain Franklin's, two,"and next day"Captain
Franklin called apologising for lateness, said he had
called the day of his arrival in England (a month ago)
and just before he went down to Lincolnshire. He
said his travels were nothing to ours. He had called

LIFE OF LADY FRANKLIN

a cape, he told father, by his name. His child was in town with his sister, Mrs. Booth. He hoped we would come and see the child and also his Arctic drawings at his house."

" *Wednesday, 31st.*—Went to see the drawings. Saw the original sketch-book of Lieutenant Back, some coloured, some pencil. Daughter pretty and very fair, but rather sickly. Mrs. Booth, a plain but very intelligent and learned woman, showed me on an oiled-paper map Point Griffin. Felt very nervous."

The relatives were evidently aware of Jane's admiration for Franklin, for she enters in her journal, " Mr. S. (her brother-in-law) asked if I had succeeded in meeting Captain F. in the Arctic circle, that being the report, and whether some cape or bay was not christened by our name." A week later we find—

" *Thursday, November 8th.*—Came up to town with Mary. Captain F. had called in evening and written note begging acceptance of reindeer tongues and three pair of shoes made by native Indian women, for Mr. Griffin, Miss Jane, and Mrs. Simpkinson, in token of his grateful remembrance of kindness."
" *Saturday, 10th.*—Party to Capt. F. He sat on my right."

In 1828 the Griffins were again in Holland on their way to Russia. Over several years there are many mentions of a Spanish political exile called Antonio Alcalá Galliano, who maintained himself and a clever young son in London, by giving lessons in Spanish. The Griffins were always kind to him and often had him to dine with them. Jane speaks of buying a snuff box in Holland as a present to him. She renewed her acquaintance with him many years later in Spain,

62

just before his death. He was then not only recalled from exile but a member of the Government.

The father's consent had by this time been obtained, and her friends constantly congratulated her on her engagement, which Jane takes very quietly. They embark at Travemunde, near Lübeck, and we learn in the St. Petersburg Notes of 1828 that Captain Franklin is likely to join the party. Accordingly we find that when Mr. Griffin's party arrived at St. Petersburg, on Sunday, September 14th, 1828, they at once called on him and carried him back to tea and dinner with them, after which they lionized the place together. Captain Franklin's fame as a great Arctic explorer had preceded him, and all, from the Empress Mother downwards (who invited him to dine with her), were ready to do anything they could for him. His introductions naturally were to the Admiralty, but the Admiral was able to open all locked doors and passed him on for special attention to the General, who was in charge of the Grand Duke Michael's palace. The General was in full uniform, his breast covered with orders, and with other high officials in attendance. "Captain F.," Jane says, "seemed to have nothing to say ; and told me that he was vexed he had not on his uniform. I said he had better apologise, and at his request I did it for him. This seemed to please the General, who begged Captain F. to think nothing of it. But I saw him whispering to the attendants and looking at me. I think he was enquiring through them who I was, for though before he paid little attention to me, he now came up and entered into conversation and henceforward paid me great attention, and on going away said he hoped I should remember Petersburg with pleasure." To this Jane, with prompt courtesy, replied, " Not with pleasure only, but also with gratitude."

They next went to the Mint, and though when she wanted to buy a coin, brand new from the Mint, she was told they could not be sold, she noticed that one was taken and wrapped in paper and presented to Captain Franklin with a complimentary little speech about the great value of his recent Arctic voyages, a subject on which they asked him many questions.

Captain Franklin was particularly bent on going to the Academy of Sciences, but Jane liked better the Imperial Library, where she saw letters of Henry VII., Queen Elizabeth and Mary Queen of Scots, also the latter's prayer book and an illuminated parchment with her writing at the foot of one page. " *Ce livre est a moi, Marie Reine.*"

Jane was evidently proud of the high estimation in which the scientific men, as well as the naval men, held the Arctic explorer. On the 23rd September, upon their leaving Russia, the Admiral, who had acted as their guide on many occasions, presented Franklin with a quarto book he had written, and a set of his charts, with this inscription in the book, " From Adm. K. to Capt. F. as a small token of his respect for that celebrated navigator and explorer, to whom science is so much indebted."

On another occasion Jane says that at a meeting and banquet of scientific men one sat by her, and

This bust, a cast of which is at Greenwich and another in the Tasmanian Museum, was modelled
in London by Sig. A. Lucche'si from a small wax bust, the property of the editor, made, probably
for his first wife, by the French sculptor David, in Paris. Sir John's last surviving nephew, the
Rev. Canon Wright, who was quite remarkably like his uncle in face, sat to Lucche'si for the final
touches. Canon Wright died in 1920. Age 89.

smiling very good-humouredly, " asked if I meant to go out with Captain F. on his next expedition, thus telling everybody his just acquired knowledge of our engagement."

As they passed through Hamburg, Captain Franklin met the Professor of Astronomy at Copenhagen, whom he declared he would have walked a hundred miles to see.

Early in October, 1828, they were in Amsterdam, and here Jane, who delighted in going for a ramble with Franklin before breakfast, " early one morning climbed to the cupola of the palace, where thirty-four bells, great and small, hang, the chimes and the hours being struck by clappers on the outside of the bells." On October 12th they visited Leyden, and came home from Rotterdam to Gravesend a month before their marriage, after an extremely pleasant sort of pre-wedding honeymoon.

PART II

CHAPTER VI

1830

MARRIAGE, TRAVELS AND APPOINTMENT IN TASMANIA

ON November 5th, 1828, Jane Griffin was married to Captain John Franklin. In 1829 he was knighted and received the D.C.L. degree at Oxford.

Lady Franklin was always eager for her husband to be actively employed; and in 1830 when his chance came she wrote to him, " I look with remorse on our career of vanity, trifling and idleness." This was only since their wedding in November, 1828, and included the honeymoon ; but she grudged every month of inaction, having never any sort of value for domesticity. But really after his ten years' arduous work as an Arctic explorer, Franklin had been enjoying a well-deserved repose, till on May 23rd, 1830, he was appointed to command the twenty-six gun frigate *Rainbow*, then fitting out for service in the Mediterranean. He returned in December, 1833, with the warmest testimonials to his judgment and ability from the Commander-in-Chief, Admiral Sir H. Hotham, and from the British Consul at Patras, where he was mainly occupied as senior naval officer in Greece in preserving order and protecting the inhabitants, for which he was made in 1831 by King Otho a knight of

the Redeemer of Greece (K.R.G.) and on his return
to England a Knight Commander of the Guelphic
Order of Hanover (K.C.H.)

Lady Franklin had not been very well, and it was
settled that she should not go out to Malta, where the
Rainbow would probably be, but wait a few months.
Sir John and his wife now begin a constant correspondence, each writing in small characters on thin paper
and often at great length.   This came more naturally
to Lady Franklin, who, however, rallies Sir John on
the length of his descriptions and his patience in writing
the same things to various members of his large family
circle.

His first letter after leaving England is dated
H.M.S. *Rainbow*, Gibraltar, 16th December, 1830,
but we have a still earlier one from his wife written
eight days before.

Lady Franklin to Sir John Franklin.

" Bedford Place, London.

" 8th December, 1830.

" Though I have written to you so lately, I am unwilling to
let the first mail go off without profiting by it.   I received your
letter yesterday, and of course have reason to consider that you
are now again at sea, and I trust you will have a more prosperous
voyage than heretofore. . . . .

" I think, my love, if you agree with me that as we are not
likely again to take an empty house on lease in London (town)
the utility of preserving more furniture than we now want for
present use and for storage is very chimerical.

. . . " It is possible on your return from your present service
that you may have two or three years to wait before you succeed
in getting another ship, but why not strive during that interval
to resume your chieftainship in your own peculiar department ;

A WIFE'S GOOD COUNSEL

and if you did so, and came back as usual with an increase of credit and fame, surely a ship when you liked to ask for it would be the least and a natural reward for your services.

"I am speaking with a view to a continued state of peace, but if war were to break out, then you might hope to complete your service almost without interruption.

"You cannot think me wanting in feeling towards you in saying this; for I am not singular in my feelings, am I? Has not Parry (and surely not without the full concurrence of his wife) declared to you his intention as soon as he returns from Australia to resume again his baffled enterprise, unless, he added, *you* should have returned first from the ship he prophesied for you, and should be beforehand with him? Does not the gentle and loving Mrs. Richardson, though her husband is even now in full and active employ, long that he should return to the sphere which has made him what he is, and has he not himself, even with duties to occupy him which might well exonerate him from any sluggishness of feeling, solicited such employment.

"I should not have said all this now when you are so happily recommencing your career of active life, had not your perspective aspirations after quiet induced me to dwell upon it, and the almost unmingled satisfaction I feel at our having been forced out of our career of vanity, and trifling, and idleness, a career which I look back upon with feelings very akin to shame and remorse, forced them from me. We might have employed our time better, but I am obliged to confess I see no hope that we should have done so. . . . . .

"When all the latent energies of your nature are elicited, not I only, but all the world (most proudly do I say even literally that *all the world*) knows what you can do, and England has acknowledged with shouts which almost drowned the declaration, that :—

"'In the proud memorials of her fame,
"'Stands, linked with deathless glory, Franklin's name.'"*

* The concluding lines of the prize poem at Oxford in 1829, by Thos. Legh Claughton, first Bishop of St. Albans.

Officers and ladies not being allowed on the *Rainbow*, Lady Franklin spent the winter of 1831-2 with Sir John at Corfu, but left in March for Alexandria in the American corvette *Concord* (twenty-four guns), Captain Perry. After visiting Cairo they re-embarked from Alexandria for Jaffa, went to Jerusalem and Jericho, then to Cyprus and Rhodes and so to Constantinople.

Sir John writes to his wife from Patras, February 22nd, 1833, with news of an attack made by robbers on Mr. Wordsworth and Mr. Robertson, as they returned from Thebes to Athens. Next day two other travellers arrive who confirm the news, adding that Mr. Wordsworth and Mr. Robertson were travelling with Mr. Milnes (the future Lord Houghton) and that the first two were badly wounded. They gave the robbers all they had, which was but little, but the rascals supposed them to have more, and stabbed them several times. Mr. Wordsworth, being the biggest of the party, was supposed to be the purse-bearer, and his daughter, Miss Elizabeth Wordsworth, tells me that they shouted, " That fellow has the money," and went for him again. He was reported to Sir John as lying at Athens in a high state of fever and that considerable alarm was felt for his recovery, as there was no surgeon at Athens.

However, in March the travellers arrived at Patras and rather than wait for the next steamer, had hired a boat, and though detained for a day or two by a furious gale, had got to Corfu, whence a steamer would take them homewards.

AN EARTHQUAKE AT CORFU

In 1831-1832 Sir John and his wife managed to spend the winter together at Corfu. In March, 1832, she is at sea *en route* for Malta and Alexandria, and writes to her sister :

" I spent a week at Potamo with the Leeves, learnt my Greek alphabet there, attended a Greek school, witnessed a Greek marriage and wandered on the steep romantic hills behind the village, which are covered with olive woods, interspersed with small orange gardens and tufted on every knoll with cypress trees. The weather was beautiful, and yet I never felt well all the time I was at Potamo.

*   *   *

" Potamo is not generally considered healthy, and I was warned not to go there, but the Leeves do not agree in this statement, and ought perhaps to know best ; there might also have been something peculiar in the atmosphere, though imperceptible to the eye, previous to a smart shock of earthquake which occurred the morning after my return to town.

" Certain it is I think that the earthquake agreed with me. I was the better afterwards, which does not prevent my dreading ever to feel another. This feeling is universal. Like me, most novices think they should like to feel a slight shock once, but having done so they never wish for another.

" This of 29*th February* was rather severer than usual. It was 7 o'clock in the morning when I, as well as the majority of sleepers, I believe, at Corfu, was awaked by the shaking of my bed to and fro in a very strong yet slow and equable manner. ' Surely,' thought I, ' this must be an earthquake' ! but I was surprised to hear no noises, screams or exclamations, except some bumping sounds overhead so much weaker than those always produced there, from one cause or another, that I could not attribute my oscillations to that circumstance. Presently all the church bells were set a ringing, and so immediately and simultaneously that one would have thought the earthquake

71

had set the clappers going, instead of the bell ringers appointed to this warning office having been able so quickly to rush to their posts. The shock was not repeated as is often the case. They are not uncommon at Corfu, but for a series of years they have not done any serious mischief. This is not the case, however, at Santa Maura, where they are very frequent and often make the houses fall down. Some days previously to the earthquake the front wall of our house was cracked and the window of the anteroom to the drawing-room fell altogether in, and was smashed, but this was owing to the firing on the esplanade upon the Queen's birthday. The winter at Corfu is said to have been fine beyond all example, and I am told, even by those who are in general its best advocates, that I cannot judge fairly, but must judge too favourably by this specimen. I am not, however, disposed to draw my conclusions too favourably, but to the general loveliness of the weather to the *eye* I cannot but give ample testimony.

"I am with Owen (her maid) the sole passenger on board this little steamer and of course I have every comfort it commands. It is only half the size and power of the *Messenger*, but is reckoned a safer sea boat. It has *very* short masts, lateen sails and scarcely any bowsprit and is the oddest looking thing imaginable; its commander Lieutenant Harvey is the best natured person in the world ; the General, to do me honor, not only gave me his own boat to come on board but accompanied and conducted me to my cabin, bringing cakes, milk and butter for me when he returned to the shore ; but Lady Valsamachi and the ' Count ' and Col. Campbell stayed with me to the last.

" I have left Messeri behind, not without regret, finding that Dr. Kirkland has hired an Egyptian servant at Malta.

*   *   *   *   *

" Messeri is a most valuable servant, clever and intelligent in everything.

*   *   *   *   *

" Owen is not what I wish as to usefulness when left alone. As I am now in the lazaretto she serves as an humble companion as well as a waiting woman. In the wide vaulted halls of the lazaretto she and I are the only inmates. A capitano overlooks what is going on, shrinking from our approach, another acts as servant of all work, and a third called a spenditore (who is not an inmate) goes to market.

"On Sunday if the wind is fair for Alexandria I am to step on board the American corvette the *Concord* (Captain Perry), but he will not receive me unless he can be sure of making weigh, otherwise he would put himself into quarantine. My quarantine here is nine days, so that I shall save three by stepping into the ship.

*   *   *   *   *

"I add to my list of places where you should address a letter to me, Charles Lander, Esq., British Consul, Dardanelles.

*   *   *   *   *

"Ever your most affectionate,
"J. F."

Lady Franklin to Sir John Franklin.

"Malta.
"Lazaretto Harbour and Lazzaretto.
"8th March, 1832.

"After the passage in the African Mail Steamer from Corfu.
"My dearest Love,
"We arrived here after a pleasant passage of forty-seven (or forty-eight) hours, being with O. the only passengers, and had the ladies' cabin to ourselves."

*   *   *   *   *

1833

By Christmas Sir John was back at Portsmouth and Lady Franklin was preparing at Alexandria for her voyage up the Nile. She did not get back to England until near the end of 1834.

In 1833 Sir John and his wife were both moving about in East Mediterranean waters, but without meeting, and each of them took every opportunity that offered of visiting places of classic interest in Greece

73

and the Islands, and also on the Eastern shores of the Mediterranean from Jaffa to Constantinople. All the time, however, there was a constant interchange of letters between them, and a regular correspondence between Lady Franklin and her sister. Their letters were generally very long.

The following is an extract from one of them :

Lady Franklin to her sister, Mrs. Simpkinson.

" *Messenger*, off Corfu,
"27th October, 1831.

" My dear Mary,

*   *   *   *   *

" We spent forty-eight hours at Malta, sleeping on board in order to save the trouble and expense of going to the Lazaretto, and accepting the hospitality of our steamboat companions who had established themselves in its desolate and spacious halls, for our meals. With the exception of the mosquitoes which abound there, our friends seem quite satisfied with their abode in the Lazaretto. The rooms are of enormous size, with arched and exceedingly lofty ceilings, bare of all furniture, except what is hired expressly by the inmates, and so empty that you may walk through one after another and do not meet a living soul. You feel yourself to be master of the deserted palace, because no one dares to approach you, and there was something to me rather captivating in the place from this sense of freedom and sovereignty which it creates. It reminded me of one of those castles in fairyland, where the enchanted lady lurks in some secret and unsuspected corner while the adventurous knight, who has entered unbidden within the walls, wanders on from chamber to chamber, lost in its magnitude and wondering at its desolation. Certainly if all Lazarettos were like the magnificent one at Malta, spacious and cool within and looking without upon the sunshine, and the water and the batteries there would be no great hardship in being forced to a week or fortnight's repose in them ; at the same time,

LETTER FROM DR. ARNOLD

that we, only because we came last from Gibraltar, which is in perfect health, or from England where the cholera exists, I believe, only in imagination, should be subjected to such imprisonment, is very vexatious."

1835-6

In 1835 they were in England together and correspondence for a time ceased. The year 1836 begins with the following letter from Dr. Arnold of Rugby.

"Fox How, Ambleside,
"January 8th, 1836.

" My dear Sir,

" I find by a letter which Mrs. Arnold has this morning received from Miss Hatch that Lady Franklin and yourself are now in London. I trust that you will not impute my long delay in answering your kind letter to the least indifference on my part or insensibility to its value ; but I knew not where to answer it, and have been waiting ever since for some information as to your movements, that I might know where a letter would find you. I felt truly obliged and gratified by your kind remembrance of us ; and I can assure you that both my wife and myself felt Lady Franklin's and your congratulations very sensibly, and thank you very much for them. Will you also express my best thanks to Lady Franklin for the walking stick of Athenian olive which she sent me by Simpkinson. She could scarcely have given me anything which I should more value, for I am in the habit of making walking sticks a memorial of particular spots for which I feel an interest, and, therefore, even independently of its value as her gift, a stick of Athenian olive is to me a very delightful companion in my walks, and reminds me that there are other places in the world besides the hedge rows and meadows of Warwickshire. We are here indeed in a country very different from Warwickshire and are greatly enjoying the change. The weather has been generally so delightful as quite to confirm my impressions of the superiority of Westmorland as a winter residence.

LIFE OF LADY FRANKLIN

"Mrs. Arnold unites with me in very kind remembrances to Lady Franklin and yourself, and believe me to be,

"My dear Sir, very truly yours,

"T. ARNOLD."

The offer of a post as colonial Lt. Governor of Antigua, in the Southern Group of the West Indies was made to Sir John. But his friends advised him against accepting so unimportant a position.

Little time was lost by Lord Glenelg in finding a more important colonial governorship, namely, that of Tasmania, or Van Dieman's Land as it was then called.

Sir John writes on April 3rd, 1836, to Lady Franklin at 17 Marine Parade, Dover.

"My letter of yesterday would have prepared you for my acceptance of the Governorship of Van Dieman's Land, which I had the pleasure of conveying personally to Lord Glenelg at his own home. His Lordship was evidently pleased that I had done so, and he expressed a hope that you would like this climate and the adventure of going to such a distance and into another hemisphere, as he had understood you had been an extensive traveller. All our friends, and even your father, say I could not do otherwise than accept it, and I find there is a great deal of patronage in the Governor's gift when vacancies occur. . . . . . .

"I propose going down to Chatham to-morrow afternoon to sleep at Richardson's and to stay Sunday with him, and shall endeavour to prevail on him and Mary and baby to accompany me to Dover on Monday. If so, we shall contrive to be with you by dinner on Monday. . . . .

"Your father and Fanny are gone to see Glover's (Arctic) pictures.

"The Government House is a good one and has a park of thirteen acres around it. Mr. Sellwood went down yesterday, his daughter Louisa being about to marry Alfred Tennyson's brother, Charles."

Part III

CHAPTER VII

Life in Tasmania in 1837

SIR JOHN had made a complete round of his Lincolnshire relations in the summer, and during the last half of 1836 they seem to have been too busy with preparing for the voyage to Tasmania to give much time to letter writing, and as the family were all in reach of one another in London, there was no need for it. They left England on board the ship *Fairlie*, taking with them Sir John's daughter, now a girl of thirteen, and his niece, Sophy Cracroft, the constant and devoted companion of Lady Franklin for the rest of her life.

The new Governor landed at Hobart Town in January, 1837, and Lady Franklin hastens to send news of this to her father.

Lady Franklin to Mr. Griffin.

> " On board the *Fairlie*,
> " Hobart Town,
> " 6th January, 1837.

" We are happily arrived at our destination after a brisk but rather stormy passage from the Cape of five weeks and two days.

·   ·   ·   ·   ·   ·

" It is now eight in the morning, and at eleven the members of the Executive Council with the Commandant of the Troops,

who has been acting as Lieutenant Governor since the absence of
Colonel Arthur, come on board, and then Sir John makes his
public landing, while we ladies walk quietly through the garden
to the Government House. The weather is almost as cold as the
name of the month, though here it is the middle of summer, but
the season is remarkably inclement. The harvest should have
been at Christmas, but it is not yet ripe for the sickle nor likely
to be, and a few days ago there was a hurricane resembling those
in the West Indies, which blew down houses and overset boats
and was altogether such a thing as was never remembered before.
In consequence of this and of the large exportations of cattle
which have taken place to the new colonies in New Holland,
provisions of all sorts are extremely dear.

.   .   .   .   .   .

" With these exceptions, the island seems to be in a most
flourishing condition—everybody growing rich, the convicts
behaving well, etc. In a fortnight's time we are told we may
expect a visit from the Governor and Bishop of New South Wales,
which perhaps we could have dispensed with at this moment,
but we must do our best to receive them.

.   .   .   .   .   .

" The place looks beautiful, though the weather is so gloomy,
and everybody seems in high spirits."

We now pass over two years—Lady Franklin had
already, in company with Mr. Gunn, a botanist, and
Mr. Gould, the celebrated ornithologist, explored the
Southern and Western coast of Tasmania. She now
in 1839 pays a visit to Melbourne, and to her surprise
is called upon to receive and reply to an address from
the residents.

The following address presented to Lady Franklin
by the leading members of Melbourne is written on a
sheet of foolscap, one half of the third side and most of

the fourth being covered by a double column of autograph signatures, sixty-five in number.   A copy of this is appended.   The original is worthy of being carefully preserved.

To Lady Franklin.

" 6th April, 1839.

" The undersigned Civil Officers, Magistrates, Clergy, Land Owners, Merchants, Stock Proprietors, and other inhabitants, residing in Melbourne,

" Hasten to express their gratification on your Ladyship's safe arrival, and at the same time to allude to the pleasing circumstance of Melbourne having been selected for the honor of first welcoming your Ladyship to the shores of New Holland.   They cannot allow the occasion of your Ladyship's arrival to pass without referring to the amicable feeling entertained by them for their sister colony of Van Dieman's Land, with which their intercourse is greater than with the colony of New South Wales.

" They are well acquainted with your Ladyship's character for kindness, benevolence and charity, and they beg to express their admiration of the private and public virtues of your distinguished consort, the intrepid and fearless explorer of the Northern Polar Regions, whose name has become, by his fame, the property of the English Nation.

" They express their hope that the appearance of Melbourne, the creation of only eighteen months, together with their beautiful and fertile district, may impress your Ladyship with a favourable opinion of their enterprise and industry, and of the superior advantages of this colony for the promotion of colonization.

" They cannot conclude without expressing their sincere and heartfelt regret that the rapidity of your Ladyship's movements should deprive them, not only thus early, of your presence, but also of the gratification they had looked forward to, in being allowed the honor to give on the occasion of your Ladyship's arrival, a public entertainment.

" With their best wishes for your Ladyship's health, and with a conviction that your journey through the interior of New South Wales will be everywhere considered an honor by the inhabitants,

" They remain, with respect,
" Your Ladyship's most obedient servants,"

Here follow sixty-five autograph signatures :

Whendale
James Simpson
D. C. McArthur
John Dunbar
James Smith
W. F. A. Rucker.
H. W. Carrington.
Skene Craig.
Henry Ward Mason.
William Easey.
Charles Williams.
J. Y. Johnston.
William Hignett.
George Lilley.
Thos. Penny.
Andrew Scott.
James Montgomerie.
J. C. Grylls, Clerk.
J. B. Alexander.
Geo. Sinclair Brodie.
James Forbes, A.M.
Robert Campbell.
Thomas Strode.
William Meek.
P. W. Webb.
John O. Denny.
W. D. G. Wood.
T. Pittman.

Robt. J. Webb.
Fredk. Wigan.
T. H. Bolger.
John Carey.
Charles Howard.
John Mansell Scott.
John H. Smith.
John Brock.
G. Smith.
P. Cussen, M.D.
P. Nodin.
Richard Henry Browne.
William Forlonge.
John J. Peesy.
John Pascoe Fawkner.
Charles Gray George.
John Mc.Nall.
John Wood.
R. Massie.
Robt. Ewing.
Donald Gordon McArthur.
W. H. Bacchus.
Daniel MacKenzie.
Thomas Thorneloe.
John Green.
John Cobb.
B. Baxter.
W. Harper.

LIGHTNING GROWTH OF MELBOURNE

Barry Surgeon.
William Waterfield.
S. Benjamin.
John Sutherland.
Wm. Wedge Darke.

J. R. Murphy.
C. H. le Souif.
J. M. Buckley.
Robert Russell.

Lady Franklin's reply.

" Gentlemen,
" The unexpected and undeserved honor you have been pleased to confer upon me in presenting me with an address has taken me so much by surprise that I feel considerable difficulty in expressing my sense of the honor thus conveyed.

" I cannot but rejoice in the circumstances which have led me on my first visit to Australia to land at Melbourne, since it has suggested to its inhabitants to remind me with such cordiality of the amicable feeling which exists between two countries so naturally and nearly related, and so capable of aiding each other's welfare.

" The erection of this substantial, well-built and populous town in a spot where eighteen months ago were to be seen only the few rude huts of the first settlers, is a remarkable instance of what industry, enterprize and wealth can effect in circumstances favorable to their development ; and must be a subject of congratulation also to those elder and almost parent colonies which see their own energies thus reflected in you.

" I regret that it is not in my power to make a longer stay amongst you and to visit any part of your beautiful environs.

" Your kind and flattering allusion to my husband is very gratifying to me. I beg to thank you for it, and to assure you that it will always give him as well as myself the highest gratification to hear of the continued and increasing prosperity of Melbourne.

" JANE FRANKLIN.

" Fawkner's Hotel,
" Melbourne.
" April 6th, 1839."

LIFE OF LADY FRANKLIN

Sir H. Elliott, G.C.B., in his book, *Diplomatic Recollections*, published 1890, says " When I was at Cambridge, in 1836, my father suddenly proposed to me that I should go to Australia with Sir John Franklin, the great Arctic explorer, who was about to sail as Governor of V.D.L., as Tasmania was then called. He recommended me to Sir J. F., one of the finest characters that ever lived, who on the passage appointed me his civil A.D.C. and, about a year later, his private secretary, thus bringing me into real work, keeping me in his home all the time, and treating me in every respect as if I had been his own son.

From Melbourne Lady Franklin journeyed to Sydney. After encamping upon the right bank of the Murrumbidgee, they reached Yass, and thence diverged to the beautiful and luxuriant district of Illawarra" ; camping out in the bush, and returning by Campbelltown and Liverpool, they arrived at Sydney just six weeks after leaving Melbourne.

A most important part of the Governor's work was the setting up in the new colony of a system of education, and in this Sir John played an active and beneficial part. It was a period of awakening interest in the cause of education, and one of the earliest projects which engaged the mind of the new Governor was that of founding a colonial college.

The first step taken by Franklin towards the realisation of his project was to seek the advice of Dr. Arnold.

" The charge " (he wrote) " which I wish to impose on you is to select for me a well-qualified person to be head-master or principal of a public school of the highest class, which we are preparing to establish in Hobart Town, and which is to be primarily adapted to the present limited wants of the colony, but capable of expanding into a more liberal institution when the developed energies and increased population of the colony shall demand it."

These quotations are from Mr. Traill's book,* and he gives a considerable portion of Sir John's admirable letter, explaining the situation with much shrewdness. " Dr. Arnold's response to this appeal was most gratifying, and the mission entrusted to him admirably executed. For the principal of the contemplated college his choice fell upon the Rev. J. P. Gell, sometime a pupil of his own, who, after a successful career of seven years both as organiser and teacher, and, in truth, pioneer of the higher education in the colony, returned to England, to become, in 1849, the husband of Sir John Franklin's daughter and only child, Eleanor."

Dr. Arnold chose an admirable man for principal of the college, but when, as will be seen in a subsequent letter, he proceeded, at Lord John Russell's request, to draft a charter for the college, the result was a scheme so impractical and fantastic, appointing an Anglican and Presbyterian as principal, turn and turn about, that Sir John and Lady Franklin and all interested in the new college were obliged to say that such a plan would be simply self-destruction.

Besides the college which Sir John wishes to found, Lady Franklin takes in hand a high school for girls,

* *Life of Sir John Franklin.*

83

and writes admirable letters on the kind of education she purposes. The following letter to her sister will shew how wise she was, and how capable in mastering details :—

" . . . . April, 1840.   Hobarton.
" I do not recollect whether in my last hasty letter I mentioned Mrs. Bracebridge and the school-master and mistress she has procured for me. They will be extremely welcome, but I much fear that, owing to the lowness of the salary suggested by her, and to their going first to Sydney and Port Phillip—which if they go *free* they must do, they will be taken up and detained at one of the latter places. One hundred pounds a year might safely be promised to such people as she describes. A single woman would not perhaps get more than fifty pounds ; but in the free schools or district schools of the colony a married couple is always required.

" I shall probably be induced to resign my idea of a school at the Huon in favour of other more populous parts, where they will be more useful. Mrs. Bracebridge need not fear to send out several more couples of the same kind as those she describes. They are much wanted and would be sure to find employment. Pray thank her for kind remembrance of me in this instance and tell her I shall be eagerly expecting the other letter she promises me.

" Our district schools have lately been reorganised somewhat on the British and Foreign School system.   The Bible is read, but no creed or catechism taught.   One day in the week, however, is given up to the clergy to instruct the children in the peculiar tenets of the churches to which they belong.

" Tell Mrs. Bracebridge that the next time I write to her it will be to ask her help in procuring me the means of forming a female institution—school, college, or what not—to be acting on the female part of our upper classes, as Mr. Gell will be working on the other half.   I want people just like herself talented, benevolent, energetic, not daunted by difficulties, not easily disgusted, hopeful, fervent, and steadfast. They must not come to make a fortune (though I dare say they will make one), but must come in a really missionary spirit, to do good. And a noble task it will be, to *regenerate* (for nothing far short of a new birth *can* do it) the race of girls in this colony. Their frivolity, emptiness, and ignorance and boldness of manner are deplorable—at least in this town. However naturally shy and reserved, they lose it all as soon as they go into society. And yet they are sharp-witted and pretty, and no doubt have as much moral aptitude for good things as the generations from which they sprang.

" I have thought that a very excellent and sensible and talented clergyman and his wife, such people as were Mr. and Mrs. Penrose* (the parents of John's Rugby friends), only younger, would be just the sort of people required for such work. They must have one mind in the same cause. The man must not be above directing the studies and forming the minds and manners of the girls, even though the wife were sufficient for this. As a clergyman, he might be on the ecclesiastical establishment of the colony, and act as being so, having a church, and receiving salary as a colonial chaplain.

" In addition to these two, there should be an accomplished foreigner—a French, Swiss, or German lady, a Protestant and of high character. Such accomplishments as are not found amongst these three might be indifferently supplied here—sufficient to furnish a *show* of accomplishments to please the parents of the girls themselves, and to enable them to digest better the more solid food which would be their indispensable regimen.

" A great proportion of the women of this country live in much seclusion. They ought to have a love of reading and of improving study. Their time is divided between housekeeping and their children and the being able to read with enjoyment and profit the best works of the wise and good would be of inestimable advantage to them. At present it may be said of the girls generally that they do nothing.

* Relatives of Mrs. Arnold.

85

LIFE OF LADY FRANKLIN

" I wish such a school as I am thinking of to give a more solid and manly education than girls get at home, where the facilities for learning *handy-works* and show accomplishments are so numerous and so attractive.

" The institution should be a few miles out of Hobarton, but near enough for me to visit very frequently ; not from a desire to interfere, but with the hope of establishing the most intimate intercourse between Government House and the school. I would have the older girls continually with me by turns, or together, so as to introduce them gradually into society and give them a taste for better things than they are accustomed to, and I should wish to be on the most friendly terms of fellowship and sympathy with the heads of the house. Such an institution, if it contained only twelve or twenty girls, would gradually leaven the whole mass. It would be a normal school for imitation, a pattern for manners, and those who never entered it would be influenced by it. The heads of it would be benefactors to the whole community and would meet with their reward.

" I would receive them all three into Government House till they could be settled. I cannot help thinking such an institution might meet with Government support (such as the rent of a house), but I cannot answer for this, and perhaps it would be better not, for if the Government give money, they would give laws also."

.   .   .   .   .   .

" I received your letters by Mr. Gell at the beginning of April, at Launceston. He landed at Hobarton, and finding us absent, stayed only one day with the archdeacon (the only person in the colony he knew), and came up to Launceston, where we took him in, and he accompanied us (as I have already said elsewhere) in our wild coast tour ; and since our return to headquarters, has continued to live with us.

" I cannot tell you how much I like him ; he has a profound and original mind and pure and noble feelings. It does me good to be with him, though I am exceedingly and even painfully anxious as to his success.

" There are certain things he thinks essential for this purpose,

86

and they are precisely the things which are most doubtful of attainment. The first of these is a charter of incorporation for the college, to enable it to receive endowments and to give it a legal and independent existence, instead of existing solely by the yearly votes of the Legislative Councils. This must be procured from home, and Mr. Gell writes to Dr. Arnold, and Sir John to the Secretary of State about it.

" In the meantime, Mr. Gell opens the " Queen's School " in connexion with the college ; a house having been taken for the purpose by Government for three years while the college is building. He desires the latter to be out of town, and so does everybody who cares for the morals and discipline of the scholars, but the townspeople like it in the town, as more available for their sons as day scholars. Mr. Gell is responsible to the Governor alone and the Governor alone has taken every step hitherto, but he can do nothing if the Legislative Council do not vote the money, and thus things are in a state of abeyance.

" If we do not get the charter from home for the college, I much fear Mr. Gell will leave us. He will never remain (and ought not to remain) to keep a boarding and day school in Macquarie Street."

In August, 1840, she writes :—

To Mrs. Simpkinson.

" Government House, Hobarton, 18th August, 1840.

" . . . . . . The *Terror*, Captain Crozier, came in on Saturday last, the 17th, having parted company with the *Erebus*, Captain Ross, seventeen days before. Yesterday brought her also, all in high spirits and well ; but the *Erebus* had lost her boatswain, who fell overboard in a gale of wind between this and Kerguelen Land, which they left the 20th July, after a prolonged stay of ten weeks. They and Henry Kay will live altogether with us. They have all just returned from looking out for the site of the observatory, which is to be, I believe, in the ' Dormain ' so called."

Later, in September, she says :—

" Mr. Gell is not living with us now, but is hard at work with his boys in a house hired for the Queen's School, at a rent of £300 a year in the street adjoining. The vote for the college buildings and masters' salaries, and also £2,500 for exhibitions, has passed in Council.

" The college would now be on a right basis if it were only established that a member of the Church of England should always be at the head. It is the church of a vast majority of the inhabitants, but the main reason is that the head of the insitution should always be of the same religion. It is easy to conceive the disorder and strife which might otherwise ensue. I do hope if Dr. Arnold has anything to do with the making of the charter that he will establish this principle." *

Sir John and Mr. Gell were both great admirers of Dr. Arnold. But what might be called a "naïve suggestion" for getting the Doctor out as Bishop of Van Dieman's Land, as a fact had its origin in a letter from Dr. Arnold himself, written in July, 1836, in response to Sir John's offer to find some Colonial employment for two of the Doctor's sons.

Dr. Arnold had two months before written, on hearing of Sir John's appointment :—

" I am not so sure how far this appointment may be a subject of congratulation to yourself, as I am sure that it is to the settlement and to public service ; and feeling, as I do, the immense importance of infusing good elements into an infant society, it is to me a matter of most sincere rejoicing that a growing settlement like Van Dieman's Land will have the benefit of your management and character."

" And now," he writes, in July, " let me thank you most heartily for your truly kind offer with regard to my boys. If either

* The Doctor's plan was, in fact, the very reverse of this, as will be seen later.

of my boys, as they grow up, were disposed to try his fortune in a new settlement, it would be an unspeakable comfort to be able to send him to Van Dieman's Land while you were Governor and to recommend him to your kindness and to Lady Franklin's. But I sometimes think that if the Government would make me a Bishop or the principal of a college or school, or both together, in such a place as Van Dieman's Land, during your government, I would be tempted to emigrate with all my family for good and all.

" There can be, I think, no more useful, no more sacred task than assisting in forming the moral and intellectual character of a new society. It is the most and best kind of missionary labour. . . . .

" Forgive me for all this, but it really is a happiness to me to think of you in Van Dieman's Land, where you will be, I know, not in name nor in form, but in deed and in spirit, the best and chief missionary. My wife joins me in kindest, may I venture to say in most affectionate, good wishes to yourself and Lady Franklin."

In January, 1841, Lady Franklin, with Mr. Gell, was visiting Mr. Gell's brother, in South Australia. There she induced Colonel Gawler, the Governor, to set apart a plot of ground on Stamford Hill, overlooking Port Lincoln, in Spencer Gulf, on which she undertook to get a monument set up in memory of the splendid work done by Captain Matthew Flinders, early in the nineteenth century. In February she is back in Hobart Town, but is soon off again, having been offered a passage in the sloop of war *Favourite*, to New Zealand.

At Port Nicholson she again received a deputation, who made her a complimentary address, and invited her to a public banquet. She spent a month at Auckland, and her impressions of the country are thus given in a letter to her sister.

" The next day Colonel Gawler took us to Mount Lofty, and gave us a dinner at a small inn there ; on two other days he invited company to meet me, and by this time we had arranged and prepared for an excursion into the interior, which occupied us a week, and which we enjoyed all the more as feeling what a relief it must be to our kind hosts. Mr. Frome, the Surveyor General, a clever and agreeable man, was requested to accompany us, and with tents and stores provided by his department, we went over a space of 170 miles, visiting as our extremest point Encounter Bay and the mouth of the Murray as it issues from Lake Alexandria and opens to the sea. Here are those tremendous breakers which caused the destruction of poor Sir John Jeffcote and his companions, and which will ever, I should fear, render this inlet of commuuication from the sea to the interior altogether unavailable. The marine surveyor, under favourable circumstances, has twice entered this passage, but the last time he saved himself (having been dashed out by the breakers) only by the clinging to an oar.

" A great part of the country we passed through was exceedingly pretty; in some parts not unlike an English park, grassy and lightly timbered, and quite free from scrub and underwood. I saw no river whatever that was anything better than a string of water holes, the intervals between the little pools being dry ground. In winter there is sometimes a continual stream. The Torrens at Adelaide is a river (so called) of this description.

" With the exception of three consecutive days of rain, the climate of Adelaide was very sultry and disagreeable. The night was nearly as hot as the day and prevented sleep to a degree that made me suffer much. It is free, however, or very nearly so, from mosquitoes, which is a great blessing. Now and then the dust hides everything from view beyond a few yards ; not only the hills a few miles off, but the shrubs close to the eye, the very pathway that passes under the house is annihilated. A poor emigrant who has come from thence to this colony to save his life says, he thinks the painful weight he carries about at his chest is a peck of dust which has been accumulating there during a year's residence. After all, I think my impressions of the Adelaide climate are not so bad as my description, and as to the climate in the interior, after passing the Mount Lofty range, I found it most pure and beautiful.

" We had no experience of any of the *hot winds*, although it was the season in which they sometimes blow for several days together with great intenseness.

" The mountains are tame and monotonous compared with ours ; indeed Van Dieman's Land is beyond all comparison the most picturesque in its scenery, though there is a species of dressy or park-like scenery in S. Australia, as at Port Phillip (in Victoria) of which we can scarcely boast, and which contrasts strangely with the fact that there is neither dwelling nor occupant in such scenery, and that in spots fitted to surround a mansion you are obliged to pitch your tents as you would with us, in the most rugged and wildest spots of the bush and the mountain."

The Flinders monument was set up in the autumn. Meantime, Lady Franklin had carried on a long correspondence with Miss Elizabeth Fry on the subject of female convicts. In April, Sir John and Lady Franklin made an excursion together up the West Coast of Tasmania.

Whilst they are absent, Eleanor writes to Sir James Ross.

" You will be glad to hear that the Government House is in progress and that the college will also be begun in about a month. A piece of the second stone is to be reserved for you—at present the stones remain precisely as the thief left them. Mr. Gell has had the inscription engraved on a copper plate, which is to be deposited and built round immediately, that there may be no chance of a second theft. It was found necessary to alter the plans of the college, the former being too expensive. It is to be completed in fifteen months after it is commenced. The charter is not yet arrived, but it is said that Drs. Arnold and Peacock have been engaged to draw it up. Dr. Arnold, as you will probably hear from other quarters, has been appointed Professor of History at Oxford, so that there is now no chance of his coming here as bishop. We are now anxiously looking forward to the nomination of a bishop for this colony. On the 16th of last month, Papa laid the foundation stone of the Tasmanian Museum at Ancanthe. You may recollect that in the road to Mama's garden we passed a wooden cottage with some pillars in front, which is a very pretty object from the road, having the mountains in the background—it is almost that very spot which is chosen for the site of the museum, Mama having just bought about ten acres there for the purpose, to be called Lower Ancanthe.

" Mr. Gell's boys were at the ceremony and were required to sign their names to the inscription with the rest of the company present. I am sorry that I have not a copy of the inscription here or I would send it to you. It was in six languages, English, French, Italian, German, Latin and Greek. . . Few persons were present besides those concerned in it, and those only by invitation. Mama desired me to send you a card having a drawing of the front of the museum upon it, but she took it away with her, as also that for Captain Crozier. Every person invited had one of these cards sent to them. I am afraid that neither Papa or Mama will be able to write this time, but you may be quite sure that they will if they can.

" It is getting near post time and I must, therefore, conclude,
" Believe me, my dear Sir, yours very sincerely,
"ELEANOR J. FRANKLIN."

With Mr. Gell's help as editor, a scientific journal was now started, connected with the museum.

In 1843, Lord Stanley, the Colonial Secretary, recalled Sir John,'whose term of six years was more than up. The despatch was not at all courteously worded, and so badly did the Colonial Office manage things, that it did not reach Hobart Town until his successor was already there. Not wishing to land in England during the winter, Sir John and Lady Franklin delayed their sailing until the end of the year. But they left Tasmania for New Zealand. From Hobart Town he had a magnificent and most affectionate send off. His passage to the harbour and from the harbour to the *Flying Fish* which lay in the stream, was one long triumphant procession by land and water, and was described at the time as " a tribute of affection paid by a loyal and generous people to a truly good man with whom their destinies had been bound up for six-and-a-half years ; and as true and upright a ruler as ever the interests of a British Colony had been entrusted to."

From New Zealand they went to Melbourne, to join the *Rajah*, in which they had proposed to take their passages to England ; but finding that there would be a delay of a month before the *Rajah* sailed, with characteristic energy they made an excursion into the bush.

The following is from Lady Franklin's diary :—

" We left our hotel on the morning of an Australian summer, in all the glory of an unclouded sky and the exquisite freshness of its early hours, on the 18th of December, 1843.

" I may here mention that, although no great coward, I should, in Australia, invariably protest against being driven by anyone unaccustomed to the ' bush.' The difficulties of ' navigation ' upon any but the really magnificent and well kept roads which are here and there to be found in all the colonies, are not trifling

to those who unlike the friend in whose care we had placed ourselves, have made but slight acquaintances with the natural bush
tracks which serve the purpose of ' a road ' in the ordinary accept-
ation of the term.

" In alluding to the few regularly made roads which do exist,
I may mention that none of the Australian Colonies can boast of
one on the whole so magnificent as that (in Van Dieman's Land)
between Hobarton and Launceston ; carried a hundred and twenty
miles in nearly a straight line, and which passes through country
offering in many parts natural impediments of an apparently
almost insurmountable character. Art has, however, triumphed,
and the colonists may well boast of this and similar works of labour.

" But to return to the day of our departure from Melbourne.
We travelled through country possessing the characteristics of
ordinary Australian scenery, of which, on looking back upon it,
I think the most remarkable to the eye is the absence of enclo-
sures. This in itself produces a sense of freedom which must be
felt to be conceived, but cannot perhaps be adequately appreciated until one has returned to the hedges of Old England. Dear
as these must be to all her children, they yet take away the feeling
of unfettered liberty which belongs to the traveller in Australia.

" To the eye of a new comer, the colour and form of the foliage
is very remarkable ; it is difficult to realize the effect of its almost
unvarying sombre hue. The cherry tree is an exception, being
of a bright, rich, though not pale, green, and when the sun shines
brightly upon its tufted foliage—for it cannot be said to have
leaves—the relief to the eye is great. The fruit of this tree is
that, the description of which has so often tried the faith of those
who doubt traveller's tales ; the cherry with the stone growing
on the outside. The mimosa or wattle-tree offers in the spring
an agreeable liveliness of colour when the young shoots are put
forth ; and soon after its golden branches of lovely flowers, the
effect of which is most beautiful. But in Australian scenery the
gum tree or eucalyptus, in great variety, always predominates, and
it neither refreshes the eye nor cools the heated wayfarer, who may
long in vain for the shade which such forests would seem to

BUSH CAMPING IN 1843

promise, for the long flat leaves hang down edgeways, and offer as little shade as can be conceived. . . . . . .

" A lady accustomed to ride only in England may be excused for feeling nervous in making her way through ' the bush,' especially if her companions possess more experience than herself. She has to watch for the lower branches of the trees possibly swinging about broken, but not detached ; if firm, not less dangerous, for she must bend her head over her horse's neck if she cannot turn him aside in time to avoid being carried beneath. Then again, neither an Australian horse nor probably any of the lady's companions feel it necessary to keep to the tracks in the parts where the bush is ' open ' and as the said track has been cleared mainly, if not solely, by the felling of the trees which interposed, in most cases the trunks lie where they were cut down, by the side of the path. The horses are trained to jump over these, and a firm seat and a steady eye are not the least necessary acquirements for the comfort, not to say safety, of a horsewoman. . . . . .

" I look back upon many nights spent in the bush with much pleasure, thanks to the beauty of the climate, and the effects produced by the usual arrangements of an encamping party, and especially by its sub-divisions. Ours was of a somewhat mixed character, and grouped itself into small knots, each having its own fire. This seems the ordinary, if not invariable, practice, and as the solitary wayfarer is generally thankful to join others who may be going his way, encampments often include individuals not belonging to the original party. This evening, although it was evident that a hot wind was coming on, five or six fires were soon blazing near to each other; one, however, the ladies' fire, being the most distant, and simply within hail of the rest.

" The light cart was brought within a few feet of the chief fire, the ladies' fire beside which we had been sitting. The back was turned towards it, with the shafts resting upon the ground. Between these a blanket was fastened so as to form a back to the bed ; the wheels were interlaced with boughs to shelter us from any passing breeze ; on the earth were spread our cloaks and a

95

kangaroo skin rug, and finally our carpet bags were to serve as pillows. . . . .

" The excessive and parching heat of a hot wind kept us close prisoners until after sunset, when we went out to witness a corobbery or native dance, for which preparation among the natives had been going on all the afternoon. All our party had at different times, and in other parts of Australia, seen this extraordinary exhibition, and I can never forget the impression produced the first time I saw this dance. I believe that undefined horror and dread predominated, and on witnessing it again, although the former astonishment was not renewed, I yet could hardly get rid of a sense of fear. The gestures and countenances of the dancers are all that one conceives to be demoniacal, and the unusual character of their agility is at once startling and unpleasing. The flickering and unsteady light of the fires, deepening by contrast the surrounding obscurity—for the darkest nights are preferred for this exhibition—the monotonous chant of the single musician, if one can afford such a term for one whose only instrument consists of two flat sticks struck together, the almost wailing accompaniment of the women's voices, except when they are excited into admiration by the efforts of the dancers, and the hearty exclamation, ' merrijig ' (very good) is heard on all sides, all contribute to make this spectacle an almost bewildering one.

" On this occasion we were struck by the deportment of some of the women. They were seated among the rest in the circle always formed by them near the chief fires ; but these were completely covered by their kangaroo skin rugs, and thus, with their backs to the dancers, they remained the whole time, not raising their eyes nor indeed uncovering their faces. They were the same who had been observed earlier in the day by some of our party, as crouching and sidling along while passing some men of their tribe, not permitting their faces to be seen. We only learned the explanation of all this, after our return to Melbourne, from the Chief Protector of Aborigines, a very good authority. He informed us that these are the mothers of girls betrothed, and that their concealment continues during the period of betrothment, until their daughters' marriage.

" The remainder of the women took their usual parts in the ceremonial of the corobbery by beating time on their folded rugs, and in this way producing a hollow sound by way of accompaniment to the chant of the old man who officiates as leader of the orchestra. This man is usually the oldest of the tribe, but on this occasion the most aged appeared to be unequal to the task of keeping up the usual song for the required time, and his place was supplied by one apparently less infirm. All the dancers also have flat sticks, which have been mentioned, but their being used depends upon their gestures, the arms being often completely extended."

They got back to Melbourne on Christmas Day, 1843, and started on their homeward voyage on January 12th, reaching England at the beginning of June, 1844.

They were met on landing by Sir James Ross, who presented to Lady Franklin a beautiful gold bracelet, the gift of the Tasmanian Philosophical Society, which Mr. Gell had asked Sir James to get made with an inscription and appropriate designs—the Kangaroo, the Emu, and the Wattle as well as the English Oak—there being at that time no goldsmith capable of such work in Tasmania.

Lady Franklin wrote the following letter to Sir James Ross :—

" July, 1844.
" My dear Sir James,
" Though I have already expressed to you personally the feelings of great pleasure and gratitude with which I received the beautiful and most unexpected gift of the Tasmanian Society, yet it remains for me still to request that you will convey these senti-

ments to V.D. Land and assure the members of the Society how deeply I feel this mark of their kind feelings towards me. The inscription it bears and your own kind letter entitles me to regard it not merely as an acknowledgment of the cordial interest I have always felt in the objects of an institution of which my husband, as I am kindly reminded, was the founder, but as a tribute of personal friendship, esteem and attachment. In this light it becomes as precious to me as it is honourable.

" I am glad to find that you are going to send out to Tasmania a drawing of the medallion as it will enable my friends there to admire the taste and judgment with which you have executed their commission, and I beg once more, dear Sir James, to assure you that the manner in which you have conveyed to me the sentiments of the Tasmanian Society (of which I do not forget that you yourself are an honorary and most honoured member) has still enhanced its value in my eyes and calls for an expression of my especial obligation.

" Believe me, my dear Sir James, with great esteem and regard,
" Ever yours, JANE FRANKLIN."

The medallion is the size of a florin, and exhibits figures of the Kangaroo and the Emu on either side of a flagpole displaying the Union Jack. The whole is upheld by the British Oak and the Tasmanian Wattle, and the obverse of the medallion bears the following inscription.

To LADY FRANKLIN

AS A TOKEN OF THE GRATITUDE, ATTACHMENT, AND RESPECT OF THE MEMBERS OF

THE TASMANIAN PHILOSOPHICAL SOCIETY,

FOUNDED BY CAPTAIN SIR JOHN FRANKLIN, R.N.,

1839.

SIR JOHN'S LAST VOYAGE

The bracelet has been presented by Miss J. Lefroy to the writer.

In 1844, the Admiralty being urged by the Geographical Society, amongst whom were such authorities on Arctic affairs as Sir Francis Beaufort, Sir Roderick Murchison, Sir Edward Parry, Sir James Ross, Captain Sabine and Sir John Franklin, to complete Sir John's fine work in exploring the North American coast, and finally to discover the North-West Passage, gave, not unnaturally, a favourable response. Sir James Ross had no desire to command the proposed expedition, and urged Franklin to put in his claim as senior Arctic explorer. This he did, and in spite of his age, only two months short of sixty, the first Lord offered him the command. Sir Sherard Osborn wrote: " His sensitive and generous spirit chafed under the unmerited treatment he had experienced from the Secretary of State for the Colonies, and sick of civil employment, he naturally turned again to his profession as a better field for the ability and devotion he had wasted on a thankless office."

His wife shared her husband's delight at his being again at sea.

The expedition left England on the 19th of May. The old ships in which Ross had visited the Antarctic, the *Erebus* and *Terror*, were thoroughly overhauled and again made use of. Sir John flew his pennant on the *Erebus* and Captain Crozier again commanded his old ship the *Terror*. Commander James FitzJames was appointed second in command under Franklin. The officers and crew of 138 souls were all picked men.

99

They were victualled for three years, but with ordinary luck they might reasonably expect to achieve their aim and be back in the following year.

Before setting out on his last voyage, Sir John Franklin made a round of visits to all his Lincolnshire relatives, and on March 23rd he visited his niece, Catherine, and her husband, the Rev. Drummond Rawnsley, at Little Hadham, in Hertfordshire, in order to stand godfather to their infant son, the present writer, to whom he then gave a prayer book and bible in one volume, handsomely bound and with double clasps, in which he had written :

WILLINGHAM FRANKLIN RAWNSLEY.

From his affectionate Uncle and Godfather, on the day of his babtism,* 23rd March, 1845.

JOHN FRANKLIN.

Search the scriptures. Pray with the spirit and pray with the understanding also.

In the last letter written before he sailed, dated H.M.S. *Erebus*, Greenhithe, 18th May, 1845, he says to his father-in-law :

" I wish you could see the ship now ; she is almost as clean as she will be at sea, and quite ready for sailing. The officers and the crew all fine men and in excellent spirits. This day we had the happiness of joining together on board in Divine worship to praise God for past mercies and to implore His guiding and

---

* Sir John was not a Greek scholar, and the spelling of "babtism" with a "b" was as he always pronounced it.

protecting providence. In this spirit we all hope to begin, continue and end our voyage."

From Stromness he writes to his wife on 1st June, 1845, in which he wishes he could write to each of his home circle, "to assure them of the happiness I feel in my officers, my crew and in my ship." The last letter he wrote to her was a very long one of sixteen quarto pages, when thirty miles distant from the coast of Greenland.

Lady Franklin went to Madeira and then to the West Indies, in order to escape the English winter, taking Eleanor with her, by the advice of the doctors. Next year she went to America, and in 1847, no news having been brought by whalers, people began to be anxious about Sir John and Captain Crozier and their expedition.

It was in this year 1847 that Dr. King made earnest and repeated appeals to the Admiralty and to the Colonial Office to send a relief party down the Great Fish River and pointed out quite correctly where the *Erebus* and *Terror* had been beset.* His letters were not even answered; for Sir James Ross and others told them there was no need for anxiety. The rest concurred, and *that sealed their fate.* Admiral Beechey alone voted with Dr. King.

He ought to have been listened to ; none knew the locality better; for as far back as February, 1833, Dr. King with Lieutenant Back (who had been with Sir John Franklin in 1821) were sent down the Great Fish River from the Great Slave Lake to look for the

* *The Land of Silence*, by Sir C. Markham, page 248.

Rosses, but hearing that they had reached safety soon came back.

Lady Franklin now goes to Italy, and is soon in correspondence with the Admiralty about a search expedition, and now for the next six years she is perpetually occupied in getting ships sent out either by the Admiralty or at her own expense, but all in vain.

She writes to Lord Palmerston, and to Napoleon, and the Czar and the President of the U.S.A., who responds warmly and aids Mr. H. Grinnel, a New York merchant, who was indefatigable in fitting out exploring ships—he equipped and sent out two expeditions in 1850 and 1853—and kept up a continual correspondence with Lady Franklin for many years. Part of this will be found in the appendix to this volume.

TASMANIAN MVSEVM

MARCH XVI MDCCCXLII

Part IV

LAST ARCTIC EXPEDITION AND AFTER

CHAPTER VIII

1845-1875

SEARCH FOR THE MISSING SHIPS

THE search expeditions, which should have begun in 1847 and should have gone to the south of the Arctic regions, where Dr. King had rightly judged that the missing ships would be found, did not set out in real earnest until 1850, and all made for the northern part of the Arctic regions.

Captain Ommaney had found in 1850 the place where Sir John wintered in 1845, near Beechey Island, at the entrance of Wellington Channel, and noticed that at least seven hundred tins of preserved meat labelled " Goldner's patent " had been opened and left, showing that the meat was uneatable, a great and deadly infamy.

When it was all too late, the Admiralty offered £20,000 for the discovery of the ships, and Lady Franklin added £3,000 for any real information as to the fate of the crews. The colonists in Van Dieman's Land sent her £1,700 to aid her search fund; for when

LIFE OF LADY FRANKLIN

in 1855 the Admiralty gave up the cause as hopeless, they having already spent £60,000 on it, Lady Franklin, though she too had taken to widow's weeds and sent out a tombstone to be erected to the memory of the officers and crews, still hoped to find some journal or papers which would tell of their doings and their ultimate fate. And so of her own resources, with the aid of her friends, she in 1857 sent out her fourth vessel, under Captain M'Clintock. This was the screw yacht *Fox*, 124 feet long, 24 feet broad, 13 feet deep and 177 tons burthen.

The following appeared in a paper of 17th July, 1857 :—

LADY FRANKLIN'S FINAL SEARCH FUND

A paragraph in a letter of Captain M'Clintock, which was published in the *Times*, having led many persons to imagine that funds sufficient to cover the whole expense of the Final Franklin Search had been collected, the following statement is made by those friends of Lady Franklin who have made an appeal to the public with a view of correcting that erroneous impression and to shew the liabilities for which that lady has made herself responsible.

	£	s.	d.
Cost of the *Fox*—provisions, etc.	6636	6	5
Amount of two years' pay to officers and men ...	3798	4	0
Total amount	10434	10'	5
Subscriptions received up to July 17th	2667	7	0
Lady Franklin's liabilities	7767	3	5

LETTER FROM RESCUE PARTY

1857

Although the *Fox* was purchased at a bargain, the estimate given above by Captain M'Clintock seems to the uninitiated a large one ; but when a vessel has to spend an extra winter in the ice, the cost of wages and provisions and coal almost doubles the expenditure, as may be seen from this notice when compared with Captain M'Clintock's original estimate.

In the Winter of 1857 and Spring of 1858, M'Clintock was greatly disappointed at being carried, frozen fast in the pack, a distance of 1194 miles south from Melville Bay, thus losing all chance of sledgework for that spring. The following letter gives an account of the Christmas day festivities on board the *Fox* in 1857, showing that they kept up their spirits in spite of their ill luck.

"*Fox*, Holsteinborg.   6th May, 1858 ; closed 7th May.
" My dear Miss Cracroft,

" Hitherto our voyage has proved to be a failure, and a whole year has been lost, but a well-grounded hope of better success this year comes to the rescue, so that however much we must all deplore the past, we cannot but be most sanguine for the future. I have written but briefly to Lady Franklin, well knowing how keenly she will feel the disappointment of her most anxious hopes ; but have supplied all the necessary information in an account of our ' Proceedings,' accompanied by a track chart.

" You will, I am sure, present the most cheering side of the picture to her, and such sympathy and consolation as I fear she will be sadly in need of.   For another year you will suffer delay, but not, as heretofore, I trust, *anxious suspense.*   Our greatest enemy has been *ennui* ; the want of occupation and change. Hobson, Young, Walker and myself for eight long months shut up in our very small messroom ! After winter set in my own

105

immediate anxieties were at an end, but the hopes and fears and final disappointment in Melville Bay, for one long month, were most wearying. But again as spring advanced all this was revived, and until we were fairly in ' blue water ' on the evening of the 25th April, I could not get rid of the apprehension that we might be too late in getting free, or too much injured or debilitated to renew the search.

" It has pleased a merciful Providence to be gracious to us ; to relieve us of all these fears, and I devoutly trust that He will yet grant us an ample measure of success. We have come here to refit and send home letters, rather than recruit, for really we are all in excellent health. My crew are glorious fellows, real men-of-war's men ; always willing, cheerful, and ready to look at the sunny side of everything.

" How rejoiced I am at having so many followers and old Arctic cruisers amongst them.

" *On Christmas Night,* 1857, when I thought the festivities of the day were over, our chief quartermaster, old Harvey (a mulatto), came to say that the crew would take it as a great favour if I would go down for one moment to the lower deck, as the officers were there and ' all-hands ' enjoying themselves very much. I found the doctor in the middle of his song (' The Lifeboat ') ; all were evidently in high enjoyment, pleased with themselves and everybody else ; Hobson and Young, almost obscured with tobacco smoke, reclining in corners, and taking in with great satisfaction the novel scene. When the song and cheers it elicited were over, I drank the health of the crew, wishing them many happy returns of the day, but (with great emphasis) ' not stuck fast in the Floe.' I praised their spirits in making the best of our position, which next year would be more suitable for our purpose. I said I was glad to have seen them enjoying themselves so much, and so rationally, as I could the better describe it to Lady Franklin, who was so deeply interested in everything relating to their comfort ; she was indeed the Sailor's Friend. They immediately expressed their desire to drink her health ; I therefore proposed it, coupling with it that of ' her adorable niece,' as suggested by Harvey

STEAMING AMONG ICE-PACKS

(I have not altered his words) ; and it was drunk amid the loudest acclamations. Before they ceased I was back in my cabin, more happy and cheered by what I had seen than can easily be imagined. They are so loyal and devoted to the cause. One remark I noticed was ' Never mind, Sir, a bad beginning makes a good ending.'

" Last evening our men landed for the first time ; they took a fiddle and flutes in order to get up a dance. Soon all the native population, from the Governor downwards, were squeezed together in a large shed, and Harvey, perched up above all, presided over the entertainment and led the orchestra with his flute.

" F. L. M'CLINTOCK."

Writing to Collinson on May 3rd, 1858, M'Clintock says :—

" We are thoroughly efficient, but rather shorthanded. Our chief quartermaster, Ransom Unthank, was left behind at Aberdeen ; McLewis, cook, sent home invalided ; and I am sorry to add one other name, Robert Scott, leading stoker, who died on 4th December, 1857. You will therefore look after his allotment. The sale of his effects realized £12 6s. 6d. I sent you home last year a list of our crew, with their ratings, etc., etc. I took on board an Esquimaux, Anton Christian, at Disco, and have promised him A.B.'s pay (single only). He is our dog driver, and a very useful fellow. This year I hope to pick up a couple of good young hands out of the whalers, and also another Greenlander. If I get these three, we shall muster twenty-seven all told.

" Poor Scott was a sad loss to us, as he was an engine-driver; now Mr. Brand has to drive the engines himself. But as we are reduced to one, we could not have a better man than Mr. Brand ; he is first rate. I never saw in ice work anything equal to our escape from the pack, steaming out against an ocean swell and heavy close-packed ice; and then Mr. Brand worked the engines for eighteen hours. I do not think that a full bowed ship could have accomplished it ; I never saw a sharper sea-going vessel than

107

the *Fox*. She would make a beautiful little clipper barque. Our steaming speed is not great ; the most we have gone is 5-2 knots, but it is quite enough for us.

" We have now forty tons of coal on board, and will take in as much more at the Waigat. Our annual consumption, exclusive of the engine room, amounts to about eleven or twelve tons only.

" As for provisions, all we have are excellent in quality. I give you some of the principal items from a survey taken 18th March last.

" Salt Beef, 1lb. ration if used every 3rd day will last 15 months (lunar).

" Salt Pork, 1lb. ration if used every 3rd day will last 34 months (lunar).

" *Preserved Meats, 1lb. ration if used every 3rd day will last 12 months (lunar).

" *Pemmican, 1lb. ration if used daily will last 8 months.

" Hence we have of salt meats exclusively 17 months ; preserved meats and pemmican 13 months. *Vegetables in tins, or dried cabbage, or dried potatoes, used *daily*, 16½ months. *Biscuit and flour in lieu, 25 months. Also 9ozs. per man of flour every 2nd day. *Split peas, a proportion equal to that of salt pork. *Chocolate and coffee, 26 months. *Tea, 24 months. Lemon juice, 15 months. Beer, 6 weeks. *Sugar, abundance. Dried apples and gooseberries, used weekly, 25 months. Pickles, 24 months. Currants or suet, 19 months. *Soup, 26 months Rum, 14 months. Tobacco 13 months. Mustard or Pepper, 24 months.

" All those marked thus—* can be obtained at either Beechey Island or Port Leopold, perhaps at both. At the former place we can also obtain clothing. I am uncertain about the quantity of rum and lemon juice left at Beechey Island. The Blue Book (p. 62) says, ' supplies for 60 men for one year.' From this you will see how well provided we are, and how easily we can complete ourselves for a third winter at Beechey Island, and this I purpose doing. The above scale is calculated for 25 *mouths*, and for lunar months. We do not consume our allowance.

DISCOVERY OF NORTH-WEST PASSAGE

" No venison has yet come in, but we get fish, ptarmigan, hares and a few ducks and I may run into Port Dundas in the hope of getting a walrus for the dogs."*

In another letter to Collinson, dated July 3rd, 1858, he tells how :—

" On 7th June, ran on the rock near Buchan Island (the Cone Island of the Admiralty chart) and stuck fast, as the tide was ebbing. The water fell about four feet, and left the poor *Fox* with a rock under her foremast, six fathoms of water under her stern ; she heeled over to starboard 35°, and laid the starboard gunwhale abreast the mainmast under water ! I greatly feared that she would tumble over altogether, or that the loose ice which lay all round us would drift down upon the ship and complete the catastrophe. Altogether my cogitations, when balancing myself upon the weather gunwale, whilst the water steadily rose above the lee, were *not agreeable*. Had anything fetched way on deck or in the hold, I think she must have tumbled over. I did not allow the fellows even to move along the deck. Three steam whalers were in sight, but as they could not have helped me, I did not make any signal to them. As the tide rose the vessel regained her upright position and came off quite easily, after having been eleven hours upon the rocks."

After all these disappointments the success came in the Spring of 1859, when, by some wonderful sledge journeys, M'Clintock and his Lieutenant Hobson found the record of the missing ships on King William Island and learnt that Sir John had died on board ; but not before he knew they had discovered the long sought North West Passage by the route he had said they

* The dogs are fed once in two days, 60lbs. for 30 dogs is cut up small and spread out on the snow before they are allowed to rush upon it; in 42 seconds it is all gone.

would do. They learnt, further, that the ships had been abandoned in 1848, and knew that none of the 110 men who started on that terrible journey for the Fish River survived.

Two officers and six men had left the ships on Friday, May 24th, 1847. They had taken four days to reach Point Victory, and no doubt pushed on to Cape Herschell, where they would sight the American coast, and know that from thence " it was all plain sailing to the westward." After this they would return at once to the ships, and no doubt would reach them a week before Sir John's death, for the record goes on to tell us that " He died on June 11th, 1847, and it is pleasant to think that Sir John, before his death, would be made happy in knowing that they had at last solved the question of the North West Passage. We, too, are made happy in the knowledge that he had died before Captains Crozier and Fitzjames had, as the record also tells us, left the ships, and were about to start, on April 26th, 1848 " for Back's Fish River." " The total loss by deaths in the expedition being up to this date nine officers and fifteen men." Graham Gore being one, he having died on board the *Erebus* in the winter of 1847. " Thus," says Markham, " died Sir John Franklin—a man of great force of character, one of indomitable energy and courage ; an ardent geographer ; an enthusiastic devotee of science, a good officer and seaman, and above all a sincere and true Christian."

Nothing can be more apt than his quotation of Spenser's lines from *The Faerie Queen.*

LADY FRANKLIN VISITS ALGERIA

" Is not short payne well borne that brings long ease,
And lays the soul to sleep in quiet grave ?
Sleepe after toyle, port after stormie seas,
Ease after warre, death after life does greatly please."

F.Q. IX. 40.

The *Fox* was back in England by September, 1859.
But Lady Franklin had not waited for this. She now
begins and continues for fourteen years a regular
system of world-travel, in which she is accompanied by
her niece, Miss Sophy Cracroft, and a faithful maid,
though the maid, not being of such tough material as
her mistress, had to be replaced more than once.

Miss Cracroft took pencil notes of all they did, and
with amazing industry wrote these out and amplified
them in long, closely written letters to her mother and
sisters. These letters are sometimes forty-eight pages
long, from which the following extracts have been taken.

" Hotel de Paris, Algiers. 22nd April, Thursday night ;
closed April 27th, 1858.

" We have reached this strange and interesting land, after an
uncomfortable voyage of rather more than forty-eight hours,
mostly passed by me in my berth, in my usual misery.

" Our vessel, a very large one, was excessively crowded, chiefly
with soldiers, some of the line, some Zouaves. There were some
wretched-looking families of the colonists, and one Arab, who
served as a sort of introduction to the many of the race we were
so soon to see. I took him at first for an old woman with a
dingy brown cloak—there is no describing the dress well—on the
head, a sort of dirty white woollen shawl, kept upon the head by
a rope of black camel's hair twisted round it, which makes the
edges gather round the face into something like a big frill. There
is a garment beneath of dirty white cotton, which forms something
like drawers closing below the knee, showing the brown lanky

LIFE OF LADY FRANKLIN

legs beneath, an old brown woollen cloak over all—feet with sandals only—all looked squalid in the extreme—and now that I have since seen hundreds of them, the one description, indifferent as it is, will serve for all. Soldiers, colonists and Arab lived and slept on deck ; such a motley group as they were ! There were several French officers with their wives and families, and a Polish count and countess with maid and courier.

" This morning proved very miserable, and the dulness of the weather took away much of the beauty of approach for which Algiers is famed. Still it was very striking—in form like a great triangle with the base resting upon the sea—the upper part distinctly forming the Moorish part of the town. The difference between the French and Moorish habitations (all white together) lay in the absence of the windows from the latter ; these have only narrow slits in the outside walls, for fear of curious eyes wandering into the apartments of their women.

" Immediately after anchoring, a party of brawny Moors came on board and shouldered the great leather cases containing the mails, and we quickly followed, and landed amidst a horde of people of every garb, kept off, however, by a policeman.

" It had been raining heavily, and the mud was intolerable as we toiled up after our guide from the quay, between rows of baskets of oranges, snails and tortoises (the two last considered very good food) and many other less remarkable eatables exposed for sale beside a fine mosque, which I hope to go into some day without my shoes.

" We had trouble to get rooms, but I need not dwell on this, for a French hotel is no novelty, but go on to tell you how delighted I am with the singular appearance of everything. It has been raining heavily almost all the afternoon, but we have been out. First I went with Drummond* about the luggage, and saw plenty of curious people—amongst them two Moorish women in long robes to the feet, of white woollen stuff, the full trousers appearing below, veiled of course, i.e. leaving only the eyes exposed. Jews, richly dressed, with long beards ; one was

* Father of the Editor.

112

MAP SHOWING THE NORTH WEST PASSAGE DISCOVERED BY FRANKLIN.
Being a chart published in 1857 with the 2nd edition of a Letter to Viscount Palmerston, K.G., from Lady Franklin.

The material originally positioned here is too large for reproduction in this reissue. A PDF can be downloaded from the web address given on page iv of this book, by clicking on 'Resources Available'.

in violet with a crimson sash; noble-looking Moors, wretched looking Arabs, a very tall, fine negro, quite black (the only black creature we saw).

" But the drive was the best, for we went to deliver some letters of introduction—one to the English Consul, Mr. Bell, who lives in the Moorish quarter, in the most beautiful Moorish house you ever heard of, except in a fairy tale. The getting into it was not the least curious part of the matter. We drove along a narrow street and stopped at the foot of an ascent, partly steps, partly stony ground between walls, which after a few yards became the sides of houses, which again, a few yards further on, closed over your head. The pathway was never more than five or six feet wide ; beneath one doorway, which was really only an arched hole in the wall, there sat an old negro woman making baskets. All kinds of people were passing up and down, and at last we reached the door of the Consulate in a street which really *was open* to the sky, though not more than four feet wide. We entered by an arched and carved Moorish doorway, into a little vestibule, then into a larger one lined with sedilia, all paved and lined with glazed tiles, the walls only being gayer than the floor ; then up a few steps which led into a small quadrangle, in the centre of which grew a banana. We stood under a gallery which ran round the first floor, supported upon columns, and were conducted upwards into this gallery where we were met at the door of the drawing room by Mr. Bell, the Consul. All the first floor rooms in a Moorish house open into this gallery, from which again you ascend to the upper floor, upon which is the flat roof. However, we did not see all this then, but only the general and lovely effect of the whole. At each column not *within* the gallery, but facing the quadrangle, was a pot of brilliant geraniums in full flower ; and in the centre rose a slender and beautifully formed cypress. Above was an open balustrade, surmounted by pots of brilliant flowers. It was a perfect picture.

" Mr. Bell recommended us to some apartments in one of the Faubourgs, which we immediately went to, and engaged from the following Saturday, when they were to be vacated by an English family named Hawkins, who had been there four months. We went into them late on Saturday evening, thankful to escape from the noise of the city. It was almost incessant during the twenty-four hours, for the heavy carts begin to come in before daylight, and the noises made by these Arabs are perfectly unearthly. We are in one of the two principal streets. The square below is called the Place Royal, in which is a statue of the poor young Duc d'Orleans. These two streets are entirely modern, built by the French in humble imitation of the Rue de Rivoli with its Arcades ; but the streets are very narrow and the houses high, so that one seems to live upon the sides of a narrow funnel with all the sounds ascending.

" *Monday, April 26th.*—The experience of every day does not wear out the effect of the singular country we are in. The population is so varied, as well as so densely crowded. It is a perfect morning panorama to walk in the town ; but we are most thankful to be, comparatively speaking, in the country. It is everything to sleep in peace. My room opens upon a balcony, roofed with an open trellis, which the rapid growth of a vine is covering with its leaves. We overlook the Bay of Algiers, and can hear in the evening stillness the distant moan of the waves, concerning which it is singular to see that they are always in the same place. You know there is no tide in the Mediterranean (Why ? Can Ben tell us ?) So there is the same unbroken curve within the bay of shining, dancing blue water, washing a low coast, behind which rise luxuriant hills dotted with white mansions, the landscape backed by the very noble range of the Lower Atlas Mountains. The scenery is very charming. But after all, it is the people that are the most wonderful.

" The Jews are a very dominant race here, and they look as if they knew it. On Saturday last (their Sabbath) they appeared in holiday and generally beautiful costume. Drummond happened to go into the quarter where many reside and, saw their women at the doors, richly dressed. We saw later in the day many of them in magnificent shawls of crimson, yellow or scarlet, over rich silk or satin gowns (they are greatly to be distinguished by the absence of crinoline, or any approach even to a substitute). **The** front of the dress sometimes covered by a stomacher of sparkling and massive gold embroidery, a rich handkerchief fastened at the back of the head and falling down behind. They have one almost *invariable* adjunct, viz., a white handkerchief drawn across the chin and falling a little below it, the ends fastened to the hair behind and falling below. Whatever the degree, a Jewess is hardly ever seen without this partial concealment of the face. They are generally very ugly—at least those we have seen ; not so the men. Their dress, when clean, as it is on their Sabbath, is often quite beautiful. They wear the full trousers, fastened below the knee, generally of white cotton, stockings and well-made shoes, sometimes ascending high over the instep. Above is an open jacket, with open and slashed-up sleeves, generally embroidered— the white shirt sleeve fitting close to the wrist ; the cap is a simple one. The beauty of the dress consists much in the richness and harmony of colour. For instance, white trousers, a broad crimson silk sash, and a deep violet jacket embroidered in gold. The young men affect bright colours. You see jackets of the loveliest crimson, bright green, pale olive, blue, violet. They are frequently tall and elegant, though perhaps rather lanky. But later in life they are often magnificent men, with black, grey and white beards. We saw one stately man of perhaps sixty, dressed entirely in black, with a grey beard (they are very rarely long), most gentleman-like in appearance. We saw some whose dress was altogether violet. But enough of their dress.

" The Jews are among the chief shopkeepers of the place, and seem to know their own importance.

" Then there are the bazaars, in which the men work as well as sell. They sit, or rather squat, in little niches hung round within and without with their wares. Tobacco, for instance in every form, and pipes of every shape ; at another embroidery and jewellery ; at another shawls and carpets ; slippers at another ; in a larger division are to be seen the men busily employed in embroidering the leather or silk ; and all the while as you look on, you are being passed and nearly hustled, by dirty Arabs, negroes,

Kabyles, Jews, and every kind of human being one has seen, except a John Bull.

"But the narrow streets are wonderful indeed. They are perhaps six feet wide, excessively steep (Algiers is built on the side of a very steep hill), and lined with shops—such shops ! Often only holes in the wall, and, at best, little slits of rooms which a Christian would certainly shrink from entering. In one was a barber at work upon a man in a great turban, others seated waiting for their turn ; butchers' shops, in which the meat was strangely cut up, fruit shops, vegetables, bakers, millers, confectioners, Moorish coffee houses, chalk shops (which are always kept by negroes, who sell the chalk in little lumps to the Moorish women, who use it in their houses), leather sellers ; in fact one might greatly lengthen the list. Between these shops the population swarms to and fro. The veiled Moorish women make their purchases in a noiseless sort of way. We saw one with an attendant (veiled like herself), who received things selected by her mistress and followed her. Drummond saw one man trying to cheat, and the seller resisting. At another hole men were playing cards ; in another some game like draughts. In the fruit and flower shops we saw strings of orange flowers and orange buds hanging, and were told that these were wound into the hair of the women. I saw a fine looking young Jew, well dressed, carrying a particularly pretty wreath of this kind, and I was tempted to admire it to him in French.

" Strange to say, a great number of these people speak French, and well. The other day in a mosque, a Mahommedan attendant addressed us in very good French.

" And now about the mosques. We have been in two beautiful ones. One consisted of a succession of fine wide aisles formed of circular arches, all white, the floors spread with matting and here and there with carpets ; upon these last we were not allowed to tread. In various parts were men at their devotions—sometimes squatted on the floor, then they would bend forward, resting on their hands and knees, and repeatedly touch the floor with their foreheads. At the entrance of every mosque is a fountain in which the faithful wash their hands and feet before going to prayers, and we saw some thus busily engaged. In a distant part of the mosque several men were seated cross-legged, listening to two men who were reading aloud alternately in sing-song tone.

" This mosque was entered from the Rue de la Marine through two or three courts, into one of which there opened three small chambers, in which were men engaged in writing. In one a European was also seated. The whole place was shining white and the coolness and repose were delightful.

" The second mosque we have seen has an interesting history. It was designed by a Christian slave. When the building was completed the Bey was told that he had designed it in the form of a cross. Whereupon the architect was immediately put to death. It really is in the form of a Latin cross with circular arches.

"Now a few words about the climate. We have come at the most beautiful season of all, and the rain has made all the short-lived vegetation lovely. The sun is hot when you stand exposed to it, but the air is quite cool ; indeed, sometimes almost chilly. Day after day is bright, the sea and sky blue, though by no means cloudless, and the houses shining white.

" To-morrow we go off to Blidah and Medeah for three days. Don't address any more letters to Algiers, but to Marseilles.

" Drummond has not been well, and is very fidgety about Catherine and little Margaret. Catherine reports so ill of herself that I believe that he will go back at the beginning of next week. Her letter of yesterday quite unhinged him.

" We shall go on Monday to Philippeville, a port to the East-ward, whence the ancient city of Constantine is reached, return to Algiers, and then probably go to Oran and thence back to Marseilles, without returning here.

" Yours affectionately,

" S.C."

" Medeah,

" April 30th, 1858.

" It is a great pleasure to begin my next letter to you in this interesting place. We are between three and four thousand feet

117

above the sea, and have passed the Lesser Atlas Mountains. Three days' journey would carry us to the desert, but this we must not think of.

" This is a walled town, with a number of French troops, and a General commanding the district, which is a very important one for the peace of Algeria. We came all the way yesterday from Blidah over a most wonderful road, entirely cut out of the sides of the mountains—and here we find a French hotel with all the civilisation which *Frenchmen* require. When we had fixed on our rooms, the mistress, a stirring Frenchwoman, who seems to be very popular and to enjoy life, asked if we would like to go to the opera ! It was too much, to resist the Opera Comique beyond the Atlas Mouutains, and my aunt said we would go. It was Auber's Opera of Haidée, and we stayed out the first act, which was all that the heat permitted to us. This is not a thing which is very likely to occur a second time in one's life. On coming out, we passed a *Café Arabe chantant*, and went in. This scene was more curious than the other, and the audience exclusively Arab. The singing so-called was monotonous in the extreme.

" On our way to and from Medeah, we saw the black tents of the Arabs for the first time—standing near to fields cultivated by themselves—with their cattle and goats around. The women in this part do not merely wear the usual veil over the nose and beneath, but cover their faces completely, leaving only a peep hole for one eye. The men are a very fine race, and are said to dislike the foreign yoke laid upon them.

" Blidah is a famous place for oranges, and the air is perfumed with the blossoms—rather too heavily to be agreeable. We do not, however, consider them to bear out their reputation, except that they are very sweet.

" Yours affectionately,
" S.C."

CHAPTER IX.

ON EACH SIDE OF THE MEDITERRANEAN

" Malta,

" May 26th, 1858.

" My last letter will have warned you of our change of route ; that instead of going back to Marseilles in order to take boat for Athens, we were to go to Malta by way of Tunis. And here we are, after the most delightful visit to *real* Africa you can conceive. I am afraid if I had been able to write from thence, you would have thought me somewhat overcome and demented by the charm of the novelty we were surrounded by. Now perhaps I am some-what sobered by a sea voyage hither, and the return to European civilisation ; but I shall always look back upon that first visit to Tunis (I have very nearly set my heart upon a second !) as one of the most delightful episodes possible.

" You may see by the map that the city of Tunis lies upon a lake near the sea. The lake is entered at the Port of Goletta, by a very narrow channel, in which boats only can pass. From this port we drove to Tunis round the lake, the only European characteristic of the journey (of two leagues) being the cranky cabriolets in which were stowed my aunt and myself in one, Foster and bags in the other. We were on a sandy plain—Arabs and black men in various kinds of eastern dresses, flocks of goats, cattle, and camels and sheep, the black tents of the Bedouins, the trees, olives, with here and there a palm, the only permanent dwelling a café by a well, at which we stopped to water. Then the white city surrounded by a wall bristling with guns ; and lastly, the city itself, intersected with a black sewer (of which every writer speaks with loathing), and streets so narrow that no carriage can pass except along the suburbs, an irregular kind of street (such

119

LIFE OF LADY FRANKLIN

a street !) running between the inner and outer walls, and so narrow
that in many places the wheels all but scrape along.

" Then we got to a French hotel (there are two), where, in
spite of decent cleanliness, the vermin was intolerable, with the
dreadful addition of fierce mosquitoes.

" We had soon visitors, there being an English Consul-General
(Mr. Wood) and consuls of most other nations. We found, on
anchoring, that the pennant was flying on board a small vessel,
the *Harpy*, and learned that it had been sent to Tunis by Lord
Lyons, in order to be at the disposal of Mr. Davis, who is engaged
by our Government in excavating among the ruins of Carthage.
Perhaps you do not know any more precisely than we did, how
very near to Tunis is the site of this famed place. It is about
twelve miles from Tunis, upon the Bay of Tunis, and stretches
close up to the Goletta. Of course we were anxious to know
Mr. Davis, who was said to be living in the country, near Carthage ;
so you may imagine our satisfaction on hearing him announced
on the second day, with Mrs. Davis, the commander of the *Harpy*,
and some other people. We found them heartily kind, and we
thankfully accepted their invitation to go and stay with them at
Ghamart, where they have a house, to be described presently.

"Meanwhile, when Mrs. Wood called, I had openly spoken of
my great desire to see some of the interiors of first class Moorish
houses. Her reply was not encouraging. She was obliged to visit
them sometimes and must shortly do so on the occasion of the
Bairam (the great Mahommedan festival, which closes the Fast of
the Ramadan) but she disliked these visits very much. Of course,
as she did not offer to take us, there was no more to be said. She
afterwards explained to the vice-consul that our mourning was an
insuperable objection. I can't say we believed her, but rather concluded (and justly) that she did not care to take any trouble about it.

" Knowing that the Davises had been long in the country, I
put forward my own wish when they called. It was most kindly
met by Mrs. Davis, who said she ought to pay her respects to
the Bey's wives (he has two) and proposed that we should accompany her to his palace in the country, where is his harem.

120

GUESTS IN THE BEY'S HAREM

" I should also say that we had enquired of Mr. Wood whether it was possible to witness (from any corner) the ceremony of presentations to the Bey (at another of his palaces, the Bardo, which answers all the purposes of our St. James's), just for the sake of seeing the Bey, who receives during the first three hours of the first three days of the Bairam all and any of his subjects who wish to kiss his hand. The consuls and persons of rank are more privately received. This our desire was pronounced unattainable, and you must bear this fact in mind in order to understand the good fortune which followed.

" On Saturday morning, then, we left Tunis very early, for Morsa (where is the Bey's usual residence, and around which are the country houses of most of his ministers) and met Mrs. Davis, who was accompanied by her five children and a young lady friend, Miss Rosenberg.

" Just as we were entering the court-yard we saw that the Bey had returned with his ministers and court for his early reception at the Bardo, and at the entrance to the harem we saw some gentlemen standing about, one of whom was the Hasnadar, or Prime Minister Sidi (my lord) Mustafa. They wore European dresses, uniform frock coats with gold lace down the trousers, collar and cuffs, and white turbans round the usual red cap with blue tassel.

" The Hasnadar bowed to Mrs. Davis, whom he knew, and looked curiously at us as we passed. After passing three or four of the usual guards to the harem upon the staircase, we came suddenly through a little dark passage, into a Moorish court, where we were met by a young woman whom Mrs. Davis (after being cordially welcomed and kissed on both cheeks) introduced to us as one of the Bey's daughters. She was amongst children and others, evidently of the class of servants, and was gorgeously dressed as far as magnificent jewels went ; but, oh ! what a queer dress. As it is the type for all, I will at once describe it. Her legs were clothed in tight fitting drawers, which came down to the ankles ; they were of silk, but covered with massive gold embroidery from the knee downward. Above was a garment

121

of brocade of the form of a chemise, exceedingly short, i.e. not quite, I think, reaching the knee. As you may suppose, the effect is somewhat wide of the mark of decency according to our notions. When they sit down, i.e. squat cross-legged on a sofa, they draw the said chemise over the knees, and you see that the width only just suffices ! Transparent sleeves cover the arm to the elbow ; an embroidered handkerchief is tied round the head with the ends standing up at the top ; a veil hangs down behind, slippers on the naked feet, and the lady is dressed all but her jewels, which are, of course, confined to the highest ranks. The costume I have described is, *in form*, common to all the Moorish ladies we have seen (now a great many). It varies only in richness of material, and embroidery ; but we saw none, even among the attendants who crowded the rooms, who wore anything less rich than silk, generally brocaded ; but these had no jewels—only gold and silver armlets and perhaps anklets. There are said to be eight hundred women (including of course all the servants) in the Bey's harem ! The hair is combed flat on each side of the forehead and cheeks, and then cut off in a straight line to the ears. They wear no sash ; slippers, plain or massively embroidered in gold and silver. Some are a little rouged, but all have the eyelids and eyebrows painted and the nails stained with henna, which some carry up to the first joint of each finger.

" The young lady whom we met led Mrs. Davis across the court to pay the first visit she had before her, viz., to the Lilla (Lady) Kabira, the first wife of the Bey. He has a second, but the elder wife holds the first place in the harem. Our visit had been announced by Mrs. Davis, who had also explained that we should be in mourning, because black is not liked upon the occasion of a high festival like the Bairam. The ladies quite understood that in our case it was not a matter of choice, and were very kind about it, Mrs. D. said.

" We found the Lilla seated cross legged on a sofa with her sister, in a sort of large recess from the first room we entered from the court. She received us very graciously, and began eagerly talking of us to her sister. She asked Mrs. Davis (who speaks

THE FAVOURITE WIFE

Arabic) many questions about my aunt, and desired she might be told she was very happy to receive our visit. She is no longer young nor handsome, but is very stout (a chief personal attraction), with a thick complexion. We were all seated around upon sofas, and presently some pleasant drink (sherbet, I believe,) was handed round. These ladies were magnificently dressed, and their diamonds were splendid, large sprays on their heads ; ear-rings, bracelets, rings in profusion. As we were sitting and observing we were amazed by the entrance of two gentlemen in uniform, who went up to the two ladies and kissed them on both cheeks ! They were relations, and on this account only are privileged to enter the harem—one a son of the Bey, the other the sister's husband. After a very few words, they went off, leaving two little boys dressed in miniature uniforms, children of the Lilla Kabira's sister.

" Mrs. Davis gave the signal for retiring, and we made our curtseys, the Lilla shaking hands with two or three of us.

" Our next visit was to the second and favourite wife, the Lilla Jenina, a very clever woman, who is said to have much influence over the Bey. In all I describe of the harem you must take for granted that women are passing in and out, and standing and squatting in crowds everywhere, especially in the apartments of the Lilla Jenina, the finest in the harem, and where they seem to amuse themselves very much. Mrs. Davis says that she always finds life and cheerfulness in this quarter.

" After poking our way through various passages and stair-cases, we entered a long and richly ornamented room, and came full upon the Lilla Jenina seated in a corner of a sofa with her feet down, in close confab with the Prime Minister, who was on a chair. (N.B. The Prime Minister has married a sister of the Bey.) Our notions of the seclusion of the harem were being strangely dissipated. Mrs. Davis presented my aunt and myself to the Lilla, who was exceedingly gracious. No sooner had the Prime Minister heard my aunt named than he rose, asked if she spoke Italian, and they exchanged a few sentences, and made a profound bow, and would not resume his seat until we were all seated—my aunt on the sofa by the Lilla ; Mrs. Davis and I having to exercise some agility in placing ourselves on the top of a very high sofa in front of her.   I assure you the getting up was a feat which belonged to tender years, rather than to my sober age. However, it was done, and then, after a few compliments, the Hasnadar (Prime Minister) began questioning Mrs. Davis in Arabic about my uncle, and the expedition, and what had been done and was doing in way of search.   This habit of questioning about a person in their presence is an Arab fashion, and as there were necessarily some Italian words introduced, we perceived the drift of the conversation, which for a moment quite overset my aunt, on account of the eager manner of the Hasnadar, and the excessive interest shewn by the Lilla, and also the other women who crowded round in earnest attention, and you saw how they sympathized with the story and with my aunt.   What a topic for such a place ! Poor Mrs. Davis felt most painfully the having to tell it all to my aunt's very face, but there was no escape—and then the Hasnadar turned to me and exclaimed, ' *E son morto* ? ' to which I replied, ' *Credo che si—ma non lo so ancora,*' to which he warmly assented. You can imagine how much my aunt felt all this scene, which I really cannot recall without burning cheeks, so painfully interesting was it.   The Hasnadar is a very clever man, and quite able to enter into what he heard.

    " This over, coffee came as a seasonable diversion, and Mrs. Davis began to talk to the Lilla, who let us admire her splendid dress.   She is not handsome according to our notions of beauty, her features being thick and heavy, after the Moorish type, with a thick, pasty complexion ; but she looks clever, as the history of her elevation (too long to tell here) proves.   Her diamonds were magnificent—besides head ornament, ear-rings, and bracelets, she wore immense rings upon every finger and thumb ; on one hand all alike, i.e. a great emerald surrounded by big diamonds. On our noticing all this splendour, she said to Mrs. Davis that she knew our ways were very different ; the English put their money into a bank, the Moorish ladies invest theirs in fine clothes and jewels.

THE BEY "EN FAMILLE"

" Two other gentlemen came in and talked and looked—one
was a son of the Bey, whom we soon missed, and almost directly
after the Bey himself came in with him. Mrs. Davis exclaimed
that it was the Bey, and of course we stood up. The Prime
Minister presented us, and immediately told him (as we evidently
saw) all about my aunt. He looked very much interested, and
desired she might be told how glad he was to see her. He is a
tall, fair man with grey reddish hair and rather prominent features,
and was in the Arab dress, a beautiful pale grey burnous.

" Now, don't you think we were exceedingly fortunate in
seeing the Sovereign in this way, rather than from behind a lattice
receiving in public ? Here he was *en famille* (a pretty large family
party !), and we spoke to him face to face. After a few minutes
conversation he again bowed to us and went into his private
apartments. What surprised me was that the Lilla Jenina sat
still in the corner of her sofa all the time, without shewing any
respect to her lord and master.

"Several children came in and out ; one, a little son of the
Bey's, about three years old, like him, with red hair. I made
friends with him by means of my glass. At last our visit ended,
the Hasnadar shaking hands with us as we went out. We went
off to another Lilla, a sister of the Bey, married to one of his
ministers, a nice looking woman. Her apartments looked over
the great entrance to the palace, and in the road below there was
music and dancing going on. Such music ! and such dancing !
It was amusement, however, for the poor ladies immured in the
harem, who crowded all the closely latticed windows looking that
way. The last lady, I forget her name, showed us how they
painted their eyes, and Mrs. Davis's young friend went through
the process. She has very fine eyes, and the effect was excellent.
We went into this lady's bedroom ; all the upper bedclothes were
folded up, and the pillows exposed. There are quantities of pillows
of all sizes, down to little ones as small as one's hand.

" But I must cut short my story and tell you only one more
incident. As we were leaving the last mentioned lady we found
ourselves again in the square hall, from which we had passed into

the Lilla Jenina's apartments, and while taking a last look at the stage-like effect of the scene, we saw coming in from one of the passages Sidi Ismain (whom we had seen before) with one arm thrown round the shoulders of a gentleman (in the same uniform as himself) the other hand over his eyes, so as to blindfold him. This was the only way in which, not being a relation, he could be conducted to the presence of the Bey through the hundreds of women thronging about everywhere. He might hear them shuffling along in their slippers, and the rustle of their silk chemises, but not one might he behold ! He disappeared into the apartments of the Lilla Jenina, through which were those of the Bey. Often as Mrs. Davis has visited the harem, she never saw such a sight as this.

" On leaving the palace we saw the Bey at a window from which the lattice had been raised, with his little boy on his knee, watching the music and dancing.

" After one more visit to the wife of the Hasnadar (who looked vexed when Mrs. Davis told her that we had seen her husband in the Bey's harem) we drove on to Ghamart, to the house of Mr. and Mrs. Davis, with whom we stopped nine days ; visiting Tunis, however, most days from various causes.

" This is indeed a charming house, purely Moorish, and so beautiful, the rooms are entered from a large open quadrangle, in which is a large tank ; the effect by moonlight was beyond description charming. From my window at the back I looked down upon the garden of an adjoining Moorish house, with beautiful palm trees, and a well from which a camel drew water by working a wheel ; beyond are the sand hills which conceal a part of the ruins of Carthage, and the blue sea beyond that, such blue !

" I could fill sheets with the history of those days up to Monday last, the 24th, when we left our hospitable friends ; but I must content myself with only a part of what we did. Mr. Davis has been for some months employed by the Government to excavate among the enormously extensive ruins of Carthage, among them a vast amphitheatre, with the marble columns broken and lying about, and he has sent home to the British Museum some most

THE SITE OF CARTHAGE

valuable mosaics and inscriptions of the various eras during which Carthage existed—Carthaginian, Roman and Christian; and how we longed to be able to see it excavated !

" For the history of Carthage and Utica, vide G. B. A. Lefroy. Who would ever have thought that I should ever sit upon the precious fragments of that once mighty city ! Columns of the richest marble lie upon the shore, with the waves breaking over them ; portions of mosaic are scattered around ; the sites of temples visible and *traceable.* Vast cisterns in almost perfect preservation—and in other spots corn growing over buried heaps of ruins. Of course, we took the excavating fever, and it was only chilled by the stern necessity of returning to Tunis in order to take our passage to Malta and Athens.

" Yours affectionately,

" S.C."

The diary which Miss Cracroft kept at Athens is made to do duty for home letters on June 5th, June 21st, and July 6th, 1858. I take from these letters the following extracts.

" . . . The Greek dress is so beautiful (men's dress) and they move along grandly, with a sort of swinging gait which is very peculiar, some are magnificent men. The dress is white, except a small embroidered jacket with sleeves, which open down the front of the arm and can be closed or not, as the wearer pleases. On very hot days the sleeves fall behind, and you see only the white under sleeve over the close fitting shirt sleeve. Below the waist is the fustanella, that wonderful petticoat three quarters of a yard deep, and about a mile-and-a-half in length or width, of snowy white cotton. Gaiters to match the jacket (or not) and the red cap with long tassel.

" As for Athens itself, I am more and more astonished at it. Its present condition shews an expansive power in the Greeks which is perfectly marvellous, considering the terrible disadvantages they labour under from bad government   Nowhere in the civilized world is education so largely provided, and upon so

127

LIFE OF LADY FRANKLIN

complete a scale, especially for girls. There is a single institution here (intended partly for the training of teachers) in which there are no less than five hundred girls receiving education upon the most enlarged scale. The examinations are now going on, conducted by a Board of Education. The Queen and several of the Ministers attended on the opening day, and grieved were we not to hear of it in time to be present also.

" *Wednesday, June 23rd.*—A note came early yesterday from Mdlle. de Pluskon, announcing to my aunt that the Queen, " *Sera charmée de la voir, ainsi que Mademoiselle sa niece, a deux heures et demie.'*

" We were received in an ante-room by Mdlle. de Pluskon, a very nice old lady, and conducted to the Queen. She was standing up, and came forward nearly to the door to meet us with much cordiality, and made my aunt sit beside her on the sofa, I near her on a chair. She is a handsome, fresh coloured and most agreeable looking woman, in her fortieth year. Very lively and intelligent, and eager even, in conversation, which was, of course, in French. She knew my aunt had been here before, and seemed much pleased to shew her that she knew she had a piece of land here, and gratified at my aunt's most freely expressed admiration and surprise at the progress of Athens. She knew of my uncle's having served in the Greek war, and was much interested by my aunt's telling her that he had been presented to the King at Nauplia, and had the honour of being a Chevalier of the Greek Order of the Saviour of Greece. In reply to her enquiries if we liked travelling so far, my aunt told her that we had both been at the antipodes, at which she exclaimed with surprise, and made my aunt tell her everything about Australia. Then came the Arctic subject, and she made my aunt describe her own expedition and its objects. We paid quite a long visit, for the Queen was plainly as much interested as possible, and excited my aunt to go on unquestioned, contrary to the etiquette of courts, which prescribes that the royal personage shall lead in conversation, and be followed only. The Queen, however, has an *eveillée* look, which, together with her questionings, makes one see that she is not only ready, but anxious

128

to hear all you can tell her. She spoke to me several times most pleasantly, and my aunt asked me one or two things about the Expeditions in reply to something the Queen asked. The interview was closed, as usual, by the Queen rising and curtseying to each of us, and expressing in a very kind way to my aunt the great pleasure she had in seeing her. She then left the room. I am told that everyone expresses astonishment at her freedom from all pretension ; and yet it is also said that she might do incalculable political good, if she would reside at least a part of the year in Athens."

.　　　.　　　.　　　.　　　.

The next extract is dated July 6th.

" My last will have announced to you our departure from Athens, and that the Minister of Marine had very handsomely placed a vessel of war entirely at my aunt's disposal. We sailed in one of the King's steamers, on the evening of Thursday, the 25th June, and arrived next morning at Chalchis, in the Island of Eubœa or Negropont, a town placed at the very narrowest point of the channel between the island and the main land. It is so narrow that a bridge of only two arches spans it, and it is deep enough (or will be rather) for the passage of large vessels. The bridge opens in the middle to admit them ; but, after all seemed finished, it was found that the excavation at one spot had not been sufficient, so they have closed the bridge until the work is finished. We were therefore to find here another vessel, which had come down the channel from the north to meet us. The *Nautilus* ship of war was accordingly waiting for us. She is a large schooner, with a number of officers and men which we should think enough for a very much larger vessel ; but the Greek navy is small enough as yet, and this is one of the very best and largest vessels, commanded, too, by a commander with two lieutenants, etc.

" We were, however, to pay a visit at Chalchis to M. Boudouri, one of the Deputies (the same as our M.P.'s), a Greek of good family and fortune with a large house. So now we saw something of the

family life of the Greeks. M. Boudouri came on board the steamer
to take us to his house, close to the shore, and just out of the town.
He is a great fat man (a rare thing among them), with a red but
honest face. He speaks French well, and was in England many
years ago on a political mission. They came in a Greek ship, and
on their way home were wrecked on Alderney, and spent four
months in Guernsey—this was in 1824. His wife is a very ladylike woman, silent and melancholy looking, with handsome features.
Her dress was in Greek fashion—light sleeves, with body open
in front and shewing a square of white chemisette. Her head
covered (in an indescribable way) with a silk handkerchief which
completely covered it, passing from the forehead behind. There
was a young married daughter with her husband, who is a
judge and also speaks French, which none of the ladies did.

" This family has a wonderful history. Scarcely two years
ago the house was entered by a band of twenty-five robbers one
evening, while it was still quite light. The father was in Athens
for the session ; the elder daughter, married, and living in the
house with her husband, who is the son of a man of large fortune.
This gentleman and his then only intended brother-in-law, the
judge, were playing at cards. The robbers tied up everyone
while they ransacked the house, half smothering the poor children
with pillows, etc. Not finding Mme. Boudouri's jewels, they
tried to make her give them up, which she refused, and they proceeded to boil oil to pour down her bosom as a torture—a barbarity
they did not, however, effect. The chief of the band absolutely
insisted on the judge trying his luck at cards. First his life was
the fearful stake, and he won ; next, his liberty, and he won again ;
thirdly, the house, which they had already set fire to, and again
he won ! Meanwhile they sent off as prisoners the elder son-in-law,
the young lady, now the judge's wife, and a younger son, then
about six years old, and carried them up into the mountains,
themselves following with all the booty they could carry away.
You will hardly believe it when I add that, although the house is
close to the town, not twenty yards from other houses, a French
ship of war lying under the very window, troops in the barracks,

FAMILY LIFE IN GREECE

and the daylight still amply sufficient, these wretches spent *an hour-and-a-half* in the house, and finally got off with their prisoners before assistance arrived. It is not attempted to be denied that there was connivance and deliberate delay on the part of some. For twelve days the wretched parents knew nothing of their children ; at the end of that time a letter reached Mons. Boudouri, telling him they were safe and might be ransomed for some enormous sum, which was finally reduced to an amount which he could and did pay, viz. 60,000 drachmas (8½d. is a drachma) for his children and 40,000 for the son-in-law, by his parents. At the end of forty-nine days they were restored. You can well understand why the mother looked so melancholy, and how the father's hair had turned from black to silver grey during those dreadful days. After the restoration of the prisoners, Government made vigorous and successful search for the brigands, who were mostly, if not all, taken and generally executed.

" The house is large and handsome in some respects, but, oh, the vermin. We endured two nights, owing to the want of wind for getting away. We lived quite Greek fashion ; thus, the day began by a servant bringing in a glass vase of sweetmeat (preserve), another vase containing tea spoons, flanked by tumblers of water. You are expected to eat one spoonful of the preserve and then drink some water. Almost immediately after comes the coffee, *à la Turque*, which means that it is very thick, the sugar boiled in it, the grounds, or rather mud, filling one-third of the tiny cup. I have come to like the coffee, not the mud, which I reject, unlike a Greek or Turk. Breakfast from ten to eleven, just like a dinner. Dinner again at four, five, six, seven or eight ; coffee again, and then we had excellent ices. I ought to have said that M. Boudouri wears the Greek dress, but instead of the fustanella, he wears the enormous Turkish trousers, with a very rich Albanian scarf as sash ; his youngest little girl is very handsome, with most magnificent eyes, and he expects that she may one day be a maid of honour to the Queen. It was very vexatious to be unable to speak to the ladies, who understand nothing but Greek—the gentlemen interpreted for us.

131

LIFE OF LADY FRANKLIN

" We have a very good courier, by name Dimitri, who speaks French extremely well. The captain (Theraki) also speaks French perfectly, but not one of his officers.

" Early one morning the captain sent to say that the wind was fair and we must be off up the channel, but it soon fell calm, or nearly so, and we did not get to Edipso until early the next morning—a Greek village beautifully situated in Eubœa. Here we slept one night in a single room, and then got two at the hot springs close by—a most curious earthquaky looking promontory, out of which bubble and spout several boiling springs. The earth is a sort of rocky crust, which is uncomfortably hot in many places. Some of the springs are petrifying, and cover things placed in the water with a white crust. Some are iron and turn the earth around perfectly red. My aunt had a wish to try these baths, which have a great reputation ; but the accommodation is very miserable and at the best we could have passed only three or four days, so we left the day after arrival, on hearing that the wind was fair, for the Bay of Zeitun, on the shore of which stand Mount Aeta and Thermopylæ. As usual the wind, or rather the want of it, troubled and detained us for hours, but we were at the right spot by the next morning, and my aunt and I landed with Dimitri, got horses and ascended to a spot under Mount Aeta, and above the defile of Thermopylæ, on which stands the remains of a most ancient monument to the noble Greeks who laid down their lives here. The ruins of the monument are seldom seen by the travellers, and my aunt when here before searched about in vain, so we were particularly pleased with our success. The view from this point is lovely, and we had a beautiful ride through country which was in many parts a perfect garden of flowering shrubs (especially on the borders of the streams), among which the oleander shone magnificently—such splendid flowers of the deepest rose colour !—pomegranates, and many I had never seen before.

" On returning to the vessel we went by very slow degrees into a port on the north of the Island of Eubœa, from whence we rode first to a Greek village, where we spent the night, and then to Kastaniotissa (where I began this sheet), the estate and house of

THE SALONICA DISTRICT

Mrs. Leeves,* in a beautiful situation in the mountains. Here we spent two days quietly (including Sunday), and should have enjoyed it, but for the horrid associations with the spot, for it was here that her son and daughter were murdered in bed. I can't write about this fearful tragedy. The village is very pretty and quite secluded. The women dress mostly in white cotton, sometimes embroidered round the sleeves and hem with crimson sashes—the head also covered with white drapery. The men in Greek dress I described from Athens. In the evening they dance the Romaika, which is simple enough as they dance it.

" On the third day we again mounted our horses and rejoined our ship for the last time. We soon entered the Gulf of Volo (to the north) and were invited on shore at the little town of Volo, to the house of the English vice-consul, Mr. Borrell, who has married a pretty Smyrniote lady, the first cousin of the Mr. Chasseaud who wrote a book on Syria and dedicated it to my aunt. They proposed to us an excursion which could be accomplished in the interval of three days before the arrival of the Constantinople steamer, and I wish I could describe this excursion very fully, it was so very pleasant, setting aside the fatigue of the first day.

" I should explain, indeed you will see it on the map, that the town of Volo (in Turkey) lies at the foot of Mount Pelion, which is about 6,000 feet high. This range runs nearly N. and S. between the Gulfs of Volo and Salonica, forming one of the long narrow promontories of this part of Europe. This range is lovely, and there are scattered over it no less than twenty-four of the most picturesque villages, each quite distinct (though often quite near to each other) and containing each a population varying between 700 and 5,000. The plan proposed to us was to visit the mining establishment of Messrs. Leahy, near the village of Zaghora (the largest of all the villages) on the other side of Mount Pelion, and most beautifully situated.

" It was to be a seven or eight hours' ride on mules over difficult road. We set off with Mr. Borrell and Dimitri, with a guard of

* Mr. and Mrs. Leeves were friends of whom they had seen a great deal when they were in Greece with the *Rainbow*.

six Albanians, part of the corps of a chief who has five hundred men under him and guards the frontier. He wished much to accompany us, but was detained in Volo by business; a very nice young man of about twenty-five, gorgeously dressed ; his men were habited in the dirtiest possible edition of this costume, which I need not describe again. We had two baggage mules and muleteers to each.

" The first day we stopped at the newly-built house of a Greek merchant of Volo, in one of the villages in the mountains. He is very rich, and spares no expense, so the upper storey of his house (where the family rooms are) is painted outside a bright gold colour, with intensely green shutters ; below, the sober stonework is relieved by colouring the mortar a vivid blue ! Here we rested for three hours, and were visited by the mother and family of the Albanian chief I have alluded to. They are Turks, and came in their Yashmaks, and the whole person enveloped in dark woollen robes. They could not speak to us, nor we to them, except through Mr. Borrell, and after they had looked at us enough they were fain to go into an inner room and relieve themselves of the heavy covering, which must have oppressed them grievously, but which the presence of the gentlemen obliged them to retain.

" On leaving this village, we were joined by a Greek family, travelling also to Zaghora—a most comical party. You must know that it is the fashion of the country for ladies to ride astride, and even poor Foster had been compelled to follow it upon this excursion, as there were but two side saddles. (She ended by being quite reconciled to this, the really safest way of riding in mountainous parts). The Greek party was composed of a fat nurse with a little girl on her lap, a very fat Mama, and a fatter still Papa. As to the Mama, she was a sight. She wore a dress with tight body and sleeves (N.B. Greek ladies even don't wear stays), the last open and shewing the arms to the elbow, a man's round straw hat inclined to turn up rather than down, bright blue boots, a small rose-coloured parasol of late fashion, and rose-coloured gloves of very open net work, and there she sat (after the fashion I have alluded to) upon the top of a huge pack saddle, at a temperature of 86° in *the shade!* Papa might have been a trifle the heaviest, but he was not put upon the baggage.

" I assure you we felt it very nervous work to follow this ponderous family up the rocky side of Pelion, and at last we managed to pass them, but not until the worst of the ascent was over. Our highest point was 5,800 feet. The descent to Zaghora on the other side was *exceedingly* difficult. Nothing but a mule could have accomplished it.

" We had a most hearty welcome from the Messrs. Leahy, who have hired a Turkish house near their mines and their smelting works. Theirs has indeed been a wonderful work, which makes me proud that they are Englishmen ; but you must know and see the country to estimate what has been done. Mr. Leahy is a civil engineer and discovered the enormous wealth of the ore of Mount Pelion in lead and silver. He obtained a firman from the Sultan, opened a mine of lead, got his machinery from England, and at the end of four years is working it most profitably, the lead being uncommonly rich, and having a very large proportion of silver, which they carefully extract, as well as gold. They employ near one thousand men, of which about six are English and German, *whom they can trust.* But they have an armed guard in their pay, who watch continually at the smelting place, with loaded arms, so that no precious metal can be carried away. They melted down and refined some of the finest silver in our presence, in commemoration of our visit, and gave each of us a valuable and weighty specimen. Nothing can be more beautiful and romantic than the position of these works, and our ride to and from them was a singular mixture of the wild and the civilised ; a party of ladies and gentlemen scrambling up the sides of a ravine upon mules, escorted by eight or ten Albanian guards (until lately a positively *necessary* precaution), who now and then planted themselves upon a rocky prominence and fired off their long thin guns (which they loaded again instantly), as a signal to the works below that we were getting on safely. We spent one whole day at Zaghora, and returned to Volo on the third day (Saturday). The evening before, Mr. Leahy requested the Albanian guard to dance for our amusement, and here we saw the Romaika executed with wonderful grace. They are like a set of ballet dancers in their fustanellas (the short white petticoat of such enormous width) and their movements are really beautiful, so varied, so agile, so graceful, notwithstanding that their floor was a rough stony place which it was unpleasant even to walk upon."

Next month Foster, the maid, had quite broken down, Eventually they took boat from Volo for Constantinople, having spent all of June and half of July in Greece, during which, though the maid was knocked up, Lady Franklin was all the better for her out-of-door life, in spite of the heat, and for her comparative freedom from letter-writing, as all the chronicling of their daily doings was handed over to her niece, who not only wrote frequent and amusing letters home, but, at Athens, under the influence of an American Greek Professor, became an ardent Philhellene.

They now took the steamer from Volo to Constantinople, and thence made an excursion to the Crimea, of which we have the following very interesting account.

H.M.S. "TERROR" LYING IN THE MEDWAY AT CHATHAM, 1836

CHAPTER X

NEWS OF THE "FOX"

From Miss Cracroft.

" On Board the Austrian steamer *Progressa*, from Trebizonde to Constantinople. Begun September 15th, 1858.

" Before I tell you anything of what we have done since my last, sent off from Constantinople just before we started for Odessa, I must tell you that I rather think this will be the last letter you receive from me out of England, as we intend getting off as quickly as possible from Constantinople, and shall travel pretty fast. We take the route by the Danube to Vienna, as being the only way to escape quarantine now that the plague, or something very like it, has appeared in Tripoli. The quarantine at the Dardanelles saves the Black Sea ports from the infliction of quarantine over again, so we go up to Galatz and then up the Danube by steam to Vienna, and thence homewards, without stopping more than a day anywhere, and very seldom even that.

" We are destined to receive Arctic news suddenly and un-expectedly, and so we see in a file of Galignanis received by the consul at Trebizonde, McClintock's letter to Captain Collinson, detailing his singular—nay, unexampled—bad fortune in not having got across Baffin's Bay even last season. We shall find our letter at Constantinople ; though we already know the actual facts of the case. How little can we, or anyone, calculate confi-dently upon what may occur in Arctic service. The absence of the Expedition is now, of course, prolonged by another year.

" My aunt says, will you kindly make all possible enquiry in likely quarters for a successor to poor dear Foster. She ought to know the ordinary duties of a lady's maid and be able to execute them readily and quickly, but hairdressing is not required. She ought to know that my aunt has bad health, and that much of her attendance will have the character of nursing; good health and good temper are as indispensable as trustworthiness. We can never hope to get a second Foster in many important requisites. We engaged a sort of substitute on leaving Constantinople, but she proves quite unsuited, and, of course, we do not take her home. We have a fair courier, but as he does not speak German, we cannot take him for the homeward journey; though, as we like him, my aunt would gladly do so. He is a Greek, and speaks Turkish, Italian, French, and English.

" And now to our late trip which has lasted longer than we anticipated. The steamer from Constantinople to Odessa made so long a passage that the steamer for Sevastopol had started the day before, and as it only goes once a week, my aunt determined to go by land rather than remain eight days in Odessa to be smothered with dust, which is worse there than in any other place in the world. She had a letter from the Russian Ambassador at Constantinople (in consequence of one we took him from Baron Brunnow) to Count Strogonoff, the Governor-General of New (i.e. Southern) Russia, which includes the Crimea, and possessing great power, and he gave my aunt letters to the Governors of all the towns we passed through, within his dominions, and besides orders to all the post stations (where we changed horses), so that for the first three days we found the horses ready harnessed for us. This special order was over and above one which we carried, which commanded the post-masters to give a certain number of horses. We had five; three driven by hand by a coachman, and two in front with a postillion. You would often have laughed at the turn-out; we had all sorts and sizes both of men and horses, which took us often at a great rate over those dreary steppes. It was necessary to buy a carriage—we got a secondhand one, which carried us all the way from Odessa to Kertch and is there left to be sold—an open one, holding four inside and two on the box, with great room for luggage; by name a Tarantasse, a really comfortable and easy carriage. This mode of travel being adopted, it became necessary to have someone who could speak

THE KARAIM JEWS

Russian, and a young man was engaged for us, who accompanied us to Sevastopol only.

" We started on Monday and arrived at Sevastopol on Tuesday in the following week, travelling by the regular post road, sometimes spending the night in the towns, but more often at the Government post stations, where two rooms are provided for travellers ; the furniture consists of a table, chairs and sofas on which to sleep, sometimes clean, sometimes dirty, but I must say generally pretty clean.

" We passed through the towns of Nicolaieff (formerly the chief naval arsenal and dockyard of Russia), Cherson, Perekop, Simpheropol the *modern* capital of the Crimea, and Bakshiscrai, the ancient and Tartar capital ; a most curious place, entirely Tartar, with no Russians whatever, except a very few officials. No hotel, of course, and we were lodged in the ancient palace of the Khans of Crim Tartary. At this singular place we remained a day in order to visit a still more singular town inhabited solely by Karaim Jews.

" The Karaim Jews are descended from the tribes who separated from those upon whose head lies the curse of having crucified the Messiah. Not only have they no antipathy to Christians, but they are without the superstitions of the Talmud, and live strictly according to the Law given through Moses.

" The probity of the Karaim Jew is a by-word among all nations where they are found, and they have the advantage of others of their race in other respects also. We went to the house of their Chief Rabbi, a very learned man, who was most kind and interesting, with a very handsome wife, whose hair of crimson auburn hung down to her waist in a profusion of little platted strings as wide as my pen.

" We were somewhat inconvenienced by the fact that the Grand Duke Michael was going the same road as ourselves to the Crimea, and for two days the post horses were wanted for him, as he travelled day and night. In consequence, we had to go on one short stage on Sunday, contrary to my aunt's practice. We travelled on the whole very fast over those dreary steppes, sometimes not seeing a tree during the whole day ; the road usually very good. Nevertheless we managed to injure one of the wheels, and had to leave the carriage behind at a station, to catch us up by travelling all night. We left the servants with it, and my aunt and I went on with the Russian interpreter in the common Russian post carriage (or cart), which is the usual conveyance for people who have no private carriage.

" All the Governors were excessively kind, four of them are admirals. One (now Governor of Nicolaieff) was distinguished during the war. He (Admiral Bontikoff) shewed us over the dockyards, etc., and we really pitied him on seeing how entirely the place had been shorn of its former importance. He told us the terms of the Treaty, which utterly cripples Russian supremacy in the Black Sea. We particularly liked Admiral Bontikoff.

" Immediately after passing the Isthmus of Perekop, we came upon the original Tartar population, distinguished by their round caps of black, white or grey curly lambskin, and the very peculiar Tartar physiognomy—sometimes they were our coachmen, but more often we had Russians clad in a cotton shirt (generally of bright rose colour), and a grey or black cloth overcoat very full in the petticoat, and tied round the waist by a crimson sash, wide trousers tucked into high boots nearly reaching the knee. Away they drove, screaming and calling out to their horses as if they were mad, and no matter how unpromising the appearance of the said horses, they carried us over stages of from fifteen to twenty miles at a pace which was often much too fast to please us. As for the gear, that is an indescribable mixture of rope, leather, sheepskin with the wool on, and wood, the whole surmounted by a bell, which is fastened to a great arched wooden collar(?) rising high above the head of the middle horse.

" You will say you have had enough of the details of our travelling (the same as in all parts of Russia), when there is so much more interesting matter to write you. But I do not think the real interest of the site of the war *can* be conveyed ; it must be felt. We drove in to Sevastopol through the valley of the Belbec—over the Tchernaya—across the field of Inkerman and

RUINED SEVASTOPOL

down by the Woronzow road—every name teeming with associations. The city has the singular appearance of being utterly
in ruins, without any perceptible cause—at least, it is only in
a few cases that you see the traces of fire—it has been *battered*
into ruins. The shells of very fine stone houses remain, white and
sharp against the clear sky—balustrades, columns, terraces,
flights of steps—all shewing the character of the former city.
About five hundred houses in all have as yet been re-built. But
I think nothing surprised us more than to see how close to the very
heart of the town were the most renowned points of resistance.
We had but to walk a few yards from our hotel to see the Malakoff
and the Redan, and to realise that the city was ours from the
hour that we attained those positions. How any creature survived destruction, or one stone remained upon the other, seems
wonderful.

"Besides the letter of Count Strogonoff to the Governor,
Admiral Messer, we had another to Captain Portnaff, a young
Russian officer of engineers, who kindly undertook to guide us
everywhere. He was in Sevastopol during the entire siege, as
were his mother and sister, and, strange to say, not one of them was
wounded. They were all among the last to cross the bridge when
the city was evacuated by the Russians. He says that everyone
got quite used to having shot and shell flying about, and to the
incessant roar of the artillery, which was for ever in their ears
during nearly eighteen months—and all the time they were living
under fire ! The day after our arrival he accompanied us over the
country which forms the site of the war. We visited the Redan
and entered it ; looked at the Malakoff and Mamelon ; visited
the headquarters of the English and of the French ; entered the
room in which poor Lord Raglan died ; went to Cathcart's Hill
and other cemeteries; examined the monuments we have erected
upon the chief battle-fields to the memory of *all* who fell in that
deadly strife ; also the dock basin, etc., which were destroyed after
we got into the city.

"All our cemeteries are excellently kept by the Russians;
the walls around them perfect, no sign of decay or want of care.

LIFE OF LADY FRANKLIN

The grass grows long and thin, but there are no weeds nor anything to offend one's feelings. You will be amazed when I tell you that the several places (all I believe walled in) where our poor people lie buried, amount in number to 192! They could not be carried far from where they fell.

" The French, with characteristic irreverence and want of feeling, abandoned their cemeteries to desecration; our own and the Sardinians are a standing reproach to them.

" One day we went to Balaklava, which is entered by the road made by the English ; a monument of their skill. Side by side with it are the traces of the railway, which was taken up after the war was over and carried to Turkey. We rowed about the harbour in a boat, and seemed to see the crowd of ships where now there is *not one*, beneath the high cliffs on which you read in huge black letters upon a white ground ' Cossack Bay,' ' Leander Bay,' ' Castle Point,' all fresh as in 1855. Then we ascended the heights and looked down upon those walls of rock against which the *Prince* beat herself to atoms within a few yards only of the harbour she was bound for. We descended by the site of the hospital (the wooden joists are still lying on the ground, waiting, I suppose, to be carried away) and saw (only at a distance I grieve to say) the cemetery, which we could not visit on account of the approaching darkness. Our guide in these researches was an officer who was eleven months in England as a prisoner at Plymouth ; a very nice person, Captain Seraphim, speaking English well.

" Another day we went to St. George's Monastery, where the telegraph was during the war. To me, the being at Sevastopol was like a dream ; the battle-fields around seemed peopled with our brave and suffering men, and I found myself wondering that the earth was no longer blood-stained.

" We saw a good deal during our stay of Mr. and Mrs. Gowen—Americans. He is the person who is raising the ships which the Russians sunk, to the number of eighty, in the harbour. He has raised several, and our subsequent voyage from Kertch to Trebizonde was performed in one of them, originally built at Glasgow.

142

THE ITALY OF RUSSIA

The Gowens are very nice people, and most kind in lending us their carriage almost daily. Their house was close to our hotel. On leaving Sevastopol to go by the south coast of the Crimea to Kertch, Mrs. Gowen and her cousin, Miss Foster, accompanied us two days' journey, through the most beautiful scenery, in their carriage. This country is truly magnificent ; after passing through the valley of Baidar you get upon the coast between a range of precipitous rocks and the sea, the interval being clothed with pine trees and vineyards. It is called the Italy of Russia, and here are the residences of some of the wealthy Russian nobility, as well as the palace of the Dowager Empress, where the Grand Duke Michael was stopping, and that of Prince Woronzow. The latter has an extravagant reputation for magnificence ; but we found a bad style of architecture—Gothic and Moorish all mixed up together. Here we were so fortunate as to find a friend of Mrs. Gowen's, Mr. Graves, an Englishman who was adopted when a child by the late Prince, whom he served as private secretary and librarian. We liked him much and hope to see him in England this winter.

" I must not spin out my story, but tell you that by the end of the week we were in Kertch, having travelled the whole road from Odessa from one end of the Crimea to the other. We arrived late on Saturday evening, and on the following Tuesday evening we embarked for Trebizonde. We had a very quiet passage along the coast of the Caucasus, stopping four times at towns where the Russians have a *pied à terre* ; namely, at Soukhoum Kaleh, Redoubt Kaleh, Poti and Batoum. At the first place was the Governor-General of the Caucasus, Prince Bariatinsky, just going to embark in the steamer sent to enable him to meet the Russian Grand Dukes. He heard my aunt was on board, but thought it incredible ; and sent his A.D.C. off to our captain to enquire. The next morning she had a message to say that but for the necessity for his immediate embarkation, he would have gone on board our steamer to pay his respects to her. We had on board the wife of the Russian Governor of Princess Damian's Territory.

" We landed at Soukhoum Kaleh. Here the Russians keep 2,000 soldiers, and here the army of Omar Pasha remained for some time. You may remember that the Russians blew up and abandoned all their forts on the seaboard of the Caucasus during the war.

" We reached Trebizonde on Saturday evening, and were most kindly received by the English Consul, Mr. Stevens, into his house, where we remained until yesterday (Wednesday) morning, when we embarked in the Austrian steamer. We get on very slowly, on account of stopping at many places, so that we cannot get in before Saturday or Sunday ; to-morrow we hope to land at Sinope, the scene of the massacre and destruction of Turkish ships by the Russians. Everywhere and from all nations we have had the greatest possible kindness and attention, and we shall never forget this most interesting trip, which must stand quite alone from all others.

" *September 22nd, Constantinople.*—We leave this to-day for the Danube, and hope to be in England very shortly, i.e. in perhaps three weeks, in Albany Street."

1859

Captain M'Clintock to Lady Franklin, on his return with the *Fox*.

" U.S. Club, London.
" 21st September, 10 p.m.

" My dear Lady Franklin,

" Hoping to find you in Town, I did not write any letters for you, and now have only time to say we have returned all well. I am sure you entertained no high hopes of survivors being found, and, this understood, you will, I think, receive our news as good news. Brief records have been found, but they tell us the Expedition wintered at Beechey Island after ascending Wellington Channel to Lat. 77 N., that they were beset in September, 1846, off the North West Coast of King William Island.

" Sir John Franklin died on 11th June, 1847. The ships were

The above is carved out of a solid panel of oak measuring 27 inches by 16, and 4 inches thick. It was found in a shop in Exeter just before the war, by Sir Drummond Chaplin, who left it with me whilst he went out as Administrator of Rhodesia. The shrouds had been coated with some sparkling white powder to represent ice ; this was nearly worn off. The pennant is coloured red. Sir Clements Markham, to whom I sent a photograph of it, was greatly interested, and intended to come and see it, but the sad accident which proved fatal to him prevented this. I had asked him whether he thought it might have been carved by the ship's carpenter when the " Erebus " and " Terror " went to the Antarctic under Sir James Ross during the long Polar winter, but he was inclined to think it was the work of some " Dockyard Maties."—W.F.R.

SIR JOHN FRANKLIN'S DEATH
SIR JOHN FRANKLIN'S DEATH

abandoned nearly in the same place on 22nd April, 1848. The survivors, under Crozier and Fitzjames, numbered in all 105 ; they proceeded with boats on sledges to the Great Fish River. One of their boats was found by us, untouched by the Esquimaux, and many relics brought from her, as also obtained from the natives of Boothia and east shore of King William Island. We found them most friendly. The west shore of the island is not inhabited.

" I carefully explored Montreal Island and its vicinity without success, beyond a few scraps of copper and iron, and on my return came up the west shore of King William Island, along the line of retreat of the lost crews.

" The whole of the shores which remained unexplored or unknown were discovered and searched by our three parties— Hobson, Young and myself, with men and dogs. It is almost certain that the *Erebus* and *Terror* passed down Peel Strait, but no records have anywhere been found, except one at Port Victory, only two shore miles from the ' Point Jane Franklin ' of Sir James Ross, and another a few miles further southward along the coast.

" We did not give up the attempt to pass south of Bellot Strait until 27th September.

" I first went down Peel Strait until stopped by fast ice, after penetrating only twenty-five miles. The tablet was placed at Beechey Island, near Bellot's, and the cenotaph put up in 1854. We got through Bellot Strait, but were stopped by ice across its western outlet. Our spring journeys commenced in February, and were continued until the end of June. All on board have behaved admirably. I left the ship off Ventnor at one o'clock to-day, and have just arrived here.

" The *Fox* is proceeding to the East India Dock.

" I fortunately got letters from Miss Cracroft and yourself at Disco, although none arrived for the ship's company. We left Brentford Bay on the 9th August and Disco on 1st September.

" Pray excuse this very hasty scrawl, and
" Believe me ever very sincerely yours,
" F. L. M'Clintock."

K   145

" P.S. I cannot help remarking to you what instantly occurred
to me on reading the records. That Sir John Franklin was not
harassed by either want of success or forebodings of evil. It was
the summer of 1847 which proved fatal to the hopes of the Expedition."

Captain M'Clintock to the Admiralty on the return of the *Fox*.

" Yacht *Fox*, R.Y.S. September, 1859.

" Sir,

"I beg you will inform the Lords Commissioners of the
Admiralty of the safe return to this Country of Lady Franklin's
' Final Searching Expedition,' which I have had the honour to
conduct.

" Their Lordships will rejoice to hear that our endeavours to
ascertain the fate of the ' Franklin Expedition ' have met with
complete success.

At Point Victory, upon the N.W. coast of King William's
Island, a record has been found, dated 25th April, 1848, and
signed by Captains Crozier and Fitzjames ; by it we were informed
that H.M. Ships *Erebus* and *Terror* were abandoned on 22nd
April, '48, in the ice, five leagues to the N.N.W., and that the
survivors—in all amounting to 105 souls, under the command of
Captain Crozier—were proceeding to the Great Fish River. Sir
John Franklin had died on the 11th June, 1847.

Many deeply interesting relics of our lost countrymen have
been picked up upon the western shore of King William's Island,
and others obtained from the Esquimaux, by whom we were
informed that (subsequent to their abandonment) one ship was
crushed and sunk by the ice, and the other forced on shore, where
she has ever since remained, affording them an almost inexhaus-
tible mine of wealth.

"Being unable to penetrate beyond Bellot Strait, the *Fox*
wintered in Brentford Bay ; and the search including the estuary
of the Great Fish River, and the discovery of 800 miles of coast-
line—by which we have united the explorations of the former

searching expeditions to the north and west of our position with those of James Ross, Dease, and Simpson, and Rae to the South— has been performed by sledge journey this Spring, conducted by Lieutenant Hobson, R. N., Captain Allen Young and myself.

" As a somewhat detailed report of our proceedings will doubt- less be interesting to their Lordships, it is herewith enclosed, together with a chart of our discoveries and explorations ; and at the earliest opportunity I will present myself at the Admiralty to afford further information, and lay before their Lordships the record found at Point Victory,

" I have the honour to be, Sir,

" Your obedient Servant,

" F. L. M'Clintock, Captain R.N."

" To the Secretary to the Admiralty.

Sir John Richardson to Lady Franklin.

" Lancrigg, Grasmere, 11th October, 1859.

" My dear Lady Franklin,

" Knowing that you were on the Continent I did not write to you on hearing news of the *Fox*, from ignorance of your address, and I learnt that you had returned to England only a few days ago. The result of the voyage has shewn that you made an admir- able choice in Captain M'Clintock, and nobly have he and his officers and crew redeemed the trust you placed in them. The touching and mournful intelligence they brought carries with it one consolatory fact to you personally and to all the relations and friends of dear Franklin, in that it pleased Providence to remove him at a time when he must have been rejoicing in the prospect of a successful solution of the great North-West problem and enjoying the satisfaction of having already accomplished much in the way of discovery.

" We know now that on the opening of the navigation after his first winter of 1845-6 he ascended the previously unexplored Wellington Channel to the 77th parallel and then took a westerly course along the north side of Cornwallis Island, when doubtless finding the westward route barred by ice, he turned to the south down Byam Martin Channel, thus anticipating the discoveries of Lieutenant de Haven and Captain Penny in Wellington Channel and of much coast line now existing on our charts, through the perseverance and great exertions of the sledge parties sent out in successive years by Captains Austin, Kellett, and Sir Edward Belcher. Had the journals or charts of the *Erebus* and *Terror* been recovered, we should moreover have had additional information respecting the channel north of Cornwallis Island in the direction of Finlay Land.

.   .   .   .   .   .

" The spot where the ships were beset on the 12th September, 1846, is about twelve miles from King William Island, and within sixty miles of the open channel traversed some thirty years previously by Dease and Simpson, which the officers might with some confidence expect to reach on the anticipated breaking up of the ice in the summer of 1847. These fond anticipations which were doubtless entertained were fatally disappointed ; the summer passed and the ships were still fast, while the provisions were ebbing away. A third winter, and the short allowance which, as a precaution, would be resorted to, brought on scurvy, the never failing concomitant of such privations in that rigid climate ; and the large proportion of officers among the deaths that ensued tells a glorious tale of self-denial, and of the strict distribution of private stores among the crew at large.

" Your husband and those who died in the winter were spared that sad and toilsome march over the ice, on which I fear to let the imagination dwell. The incidents of men dropping and dying on the march are but too familiar to those who have read of the voyages of the early explorers in any country, and in the Arctic is to be attributed to the ravages of scurvy, the certain effect of three winters in that rigid climate on short allowance of food. The greater proportion of deaths among the officers tells a tale of heroism ; they must have given over their private stock of provisions to the sick, and were less able than the men to digest the salt provisions. We may conjecture that before the party had gone far many of the wasted men would be benumbed by cold, and as the number of draggers fell away it would be necessary to abandon one of the boats ; that this was taken to the nearest shore, two sick men disposed in it as warmly as circumstances admitted, and all the provisions left with them which the party could afford. I cannot dwell further on the fatal march over the ice, except to add that there can be no reasonable doubt of as many of the party as were competent to drag one boat having reached the estuary of the Great Fish River. The boat which the Eskimos broke up on Montreal Island, and the researches of Mr. Anderson on the spot are convincing proofs of the fact. The Eskimos would never have taken the trouble of dragging a boat thither, but would break it up for the wood and nails wherever they found it.

" The information which Captain M'Clintock got from the Eskimos is most valuable, as testifying to abandonment of the ships, their subsequent drifting on shore, and the tracing of the route of our ill-fated countrymen by the bodies that lay on the way as they had fallen, being from direct observation of the reporters. One of the parties also seen by him had got their wood from the boat on Montreal Island.

" The intelligence procured by Dr. Rae was less reliable, as coming from a tribe who had seen neither the wrecks nor the crews themselves, alive or dead, but had got their information and the European articles they possessed through an intervening party. Some of their reports therefore are to be regarded merely as the habitual exaggerations of a rude people in repeating a story.

" On the strength of the first intelligence of the loss of the ships brought by Dr. Rae, I formally wrote a letter to the *Times*, claiming for the survivors of the crews of the *Erebus* and *Terror* priority in the discovery of a North-West Passage, a portion of which, though a small one, was obstructed by ice. This may be done on still stronger grounds, and the passage may be said to have been traced *by open water* through Victoria Strait by the conjoined efforts of several parties. For Dr. Rae in his boat passed to the northward of the position of the *Erebus* and *Terror* when first beset, and Captain Collinson traced the coast line some miles beyond Rae.

LIFE OF LADY FRANKLIN

" I ought perhaps to apologise for addressing these details to you who already know them well, but as I am aware that your husband's hard-earned fame, and that of the officers and men who stood so gallantly by him and perished in carrying the flag of their country through scenes of peril and death, are most dear to you, I felt desirous of stating to you my view of the case. Though the devotion of your energies for twelve years, and the expenditure of your means have not been crowned with the saving of life, yet the world has seen what the affection of a wife can accomplish, and your efforts have not terminated without bringing a reward, in the increase of Franklin's already widely extended reputation. To us who know how well prepared he was for entering into his rest, it is a satisfaction to know that the work he desired to accomplish is done.

" I remain, dear Lady Franklin,
" Faithfully yours,
" JOHN RICHARDSON."

Mr. Henry Grinnell to Lady Franklin.

" New York,
" 12th October, 1859.

" My dear Lady,
" The information, which reached us on the 8th instant, of the return to England of Captain M'Clintock, and of the consummation of his object, has caused intense interest and excitement in this country ; perhaps quite as much as in old England. It is the general subject of conversation—the political affairs of Europe and this country are insignificant in comparison. I can truly say I thank the Great Disposer of events for the result attained by *your Expedition* under the command of that most able and excellent officer, Captain M'Clintock. He has acquired a just fame for himself, which the pages of history will never allow to be obliterated.

" For yourself, it is better I should say nothing, for I have not the command of words to define the estimate I entertain of your character. I am not alone in this ; the whole community are

150

ROYAL CONGRATULATIONS.

with me. I am from all quarters congratulated on the event, as though I had a part in bringing it about ; it is you, however, that is intended, through me.

" I suppose now there can be no question as to your husband's Expedition being the first to ascertain the water communication with the Atlantic and Pacific, north of the American Continent, or otherwise the North-West Passage.

" Again with my kind regards to you and Miss Sophia, believe me to remain truly

" Your friend,
" HENRY GRINNELL."

E. Becher to Major General E. Sabine.

" Windsor Castle,
" October 26th, 1859."

" My dear Sir,

" I have received your note of the 24th and have laid before the Queen the box with the interesting relics which Lady Franklin was kind enough to send for Her Majesty's inspection. Obtained as they were only by the unremitting and praiseworthy efforts of Lady Franklin, they have been of the greatest possible interest to Her Majesty, and in returning them now, the Queen requests you to convey Her best thanks to Lady Franklin for allowing Her to see these documents which, although sad in their tenor, must have relieved her of very painful and continued anxiety.

" I remain, my dear Sir,
" Yours very truly,
" E. BECHER."

Captain M'Clintock was welcomed with all sorts of honours. The Queen knighted him. The freedom of the City of London was conferred on him and the Universities in England and Ireland bestowed on him honorary degrees, whilst the Royal Geographical Society awarded him the Patron's Gold Medal.

151

The sum of £5,000 was voted to M'Clintock and his officers and men and £2,000 for the erection of the Franklin monument in Waterloo Place. Only one other (that of Charles I.) had ever been put up as the gift of the nation. The inscription on it is :—

FRANKLIN.

TO THE GREAT NAVIGATOR
AND HIS BRAVE COMPANIONS
WHO SACRIFICED THEIR LIVES IN
COMPLETING THE DISCOVERY OF
THE NORTH WEST PASSAGE
A.D. 1847-48

ERECTED BY THE UNANIMOUS VOTE OF PARLIAMENT.

On this occasion the Founders' Gold Medal was, by exceptional favour, but with admirable justice, awarded to Lady Franklin, in the following terms.

" Desirous of commemorating in an especial manner the Arctic researches of our associate, the late Sir John Franklin, and of testifying to the fact that his expedition was the first to discover a North-West passage, the Council of the Royal Geographical Society have awarded the Founders' Gold Medal to his widow, Lady Franklin, in token of their admiration of the noble and self-sacrificing perseverance in sending out at her own cost several Expeditions until at length the fate of her husband has been ascertained."

Sir John, it may be noted, was promoted to the rank of Rear Admiral in his regular place of seniority on the Navy List on 26th October, 1852, and his name

STATUE IN WATERLOO PLACE

MEMORIALS TO FRANKLIN.

was kept on the Navy List until the actual date of
his death was known from the record discovered by
M'Clintock.

A copy of the statue in Waterloo Place was soon
after this cast and sent out to be erected in Hobart
Town. But it has not got the admirable bas relief on
the pedestal, representing the funeral of Sir John in
the frozen ocean, which is the most attractive feature
of the London statue by Noble.

Another statue and always considered a good
likeness, by Bacon, had already been set up in the
market place of Sir John's native town, Spilsby, in
Lincolnshire, where it was unveiled by his old friend,
Sir John Richardson. He is described on this as the
discoverer of the North West Passage, and the touching
words are added. " They forged the last link with
their lives."

CHAPTER XI

1860.

NEW YORK AND HONOLULU

Lady Franklin's great struggle against what, to most people, would have often seemed insuperable difficulties had come to an end, and she was now in possession of all the facts we shall ever obtain. A complete rest and change was necessary for her, and she determined to be absent from England for at least eighteen months.

The following letters refer to a beautiful silver model of the *Fox*, which Lady Franklin presented to M'Clintock. He showed it to us once with much pride. It was a yard long and a really lovely model, in the drawing-room it stood under a glass case, whilst in the hall was the actual sleigh on which he had made so many hundred miles in his search. It was so light you might lift it with one hand, but was the result of much thought and experiment, and was to me quite the most interesting thing he could possibly have shown us.

The reference to " Justitia " in the following is to a letter written by a lady to the *Athenæum*, showing a great deal of ignorance of Arctic matters and intended to belittle Sir John Franklin and his discoveries.

M'CLINTOCK'S RECEPTION IN IRELAND

M'Clintock wrote an excellent rejoinder, but did not send it, as so many others had taken up the cudgels.

From Captain M'Clintock to Lady Franklin.

"48 Hardwick Street, Dublin.

"Saturday, 22nd January, 1860.

" My dear Lady Franklin,

"By this post I send you the drawing of the masts of the *Fox*, which Captain Young tells me you require in order to have your model of that celebrated vessel properly rigged. Mr. Whiteside will have much pleasure in calling upon you when he goes to London, but I don't think he will go until Monday week. I am to dine with him on this day week. He has a solemn *plain* face which effectually masks the liveliest imagination ; he is too rash a person, I am told, to start a measure, but a good man to back up one, and of course is most eloquent ; he requires to be made up on the subject and takes this sort of *cramming* very quickly. The only fact I have mentioned to him which may not have occurred to you, is that the money value of the aid in stores, pemmican, etc., supplied by the Government to your Expedition, amounted to between £600 and £700. Of course, this is only my estimate. I have told Mr. Whiteside that I thought the Government people should be the first to introduce the subject of a reward to the crew of the *Fox* and that I did not wish it to be started by anyone known to me. In the propriety of this view he fully concurred. I hope they will direct a sum of money equivalent to the expenses incurred by you in the *Fox* Expedition, to be devoted to the erection of a National tribute to the lost crews. The good people here are trying to make me believe that I am not the *same* individual that I was before I sailed in the *Fox*. I dined at the Lord Lieutenant's banquet yesterday: 102 persons sat down together in St. Patrick's Hall ; it was really a splendid sight. The Lord Lieutenant introduced me to some of the grandees and said ' We are quite proud of him ! He has wonderful tact in "gammoning" *us* over here.' I often meet Mr. Napier ; you may know that Mrs. Whiteside is his sister. Poor ' Justitia ' has been quite swamped with

155

indignant replies to that absurd letter. I hope you continue in good health and spirits. Will you be kind enough to send me an autograph of Mr. Grinnell's, for Mrs. Coote, Sir Edward Parry's eldest daughter ?

" Most sincerely yours,
" F. L. M'CLINTOCK."

It was not till the Summer of 1860 that Lady Franklin with her niece and a maid started for a prolonged trip to America and the Sandwich Islands. It was during the War, and for that very reason the time had attractions for her, for she loved to be at the centre of things, and so great was the admiration and sympathy caused by her heroic struggles to find out what had been the fate of her husband, now definitely revealed by M'Clintock, that wherever she went she was welcomed with enthusiasm and treated with the utmost consideration.

Apparently she sailed in the *Adriatic*, on June 20th, and so was not able to meet the Queen when she visited the *Fox* in July, as described below.

Captain Allen Young to Miss Cracroft.

" S.S. *Fox*, Cowes, July 19th, 1860.

" My dear Miss Cracroft,

" I wrote to Lady Franklin this afternoon as I went to Southampton by steamer to say that the Queen has been on board our ship, and I only wish you could have been with us to hear how very kindly she spoke of Lady Franklin and the great interest she seemed to take in everything relating to the Arctic voyage of the *Fox*.

" We commenced preparations at 3 a.m., and we had just finished laying down red carpet fore and aft and rigging gangways, etc., when the royal barge came alongside from the *Fairy* ; the

THE SPILSBY STATUE

royal party were received by all the officers, and I had the honor of presenting them one by one to Her Majesty, who put several questions to each of them. We then had up some of the sounding apparatus and other instruments which were explained as well as we were able. I fortunately had one of M'Clintock's own sledges on deck, and this seemed to be very much admired for its simple construction ; in fact the Arctic voyaging was, of course, the main topic of conversation, and Her Majesty seemed anxious to express sympathy for those who are missing and asked several times if we had come to the sad conclusion that none of the crew of the *Erebus* and *Terror* were yet alive.

" The Prince was below for some time with Mr. Davis examining the instruments and charts and asking information about our route.

" After remaining on board, three-quarters of an hour, the Queen returned to the *Fairy*, and we manned rigging and cheered her. The weather was beautifully fine until they landed.

" I must now say good-bye, and I am sure you will excuse my writing any more, as I must write all night and I dare say you will be tired of hearing about this cruise.

" Believe me, Yours very truly,
" ALLEN YOUNG."

From the dates and places endorsed on such letters as we have, we make out that Lady Franklin was with Mr. Henry Grinnell, in New York, early in July, 1860 ; In September, at Niagara Falls ; in November, at Baltimore with Captain Kennedy, and starting at the end of November from New York to go down the Pacific coast, stopping at Rio de Janeiro.

The paper which announces her departure says that " the best wishes and sympathies of the American people will go with her." In March, 1861, she was at Victoria and in Vancouver Island ; in April, at San Francisco ; and in October, in Nevada and California.

But between April and October she had been for a visit to the Sandwich Islands, where she made acquaintance with King Kamehamaha and Queen Emma, returning in June from Honolulu to San Francisco again, whence also, after visits to Carson City and Victoria in Nevada, she set out for her homeward journey in October, 1861.

Whilst at Niagara Falls she received a letter from her sister Fanny, Mrs. Majendie, with the sad news of Mrs. Gell's death, at Tredunnoc, Monmouthshire.

The following extracts from two letters, each of forty-eight large and closely-written pages, will give some idea of the indefatigable way in which Lady Franklin always carried out her intentions of seeing what was most remarkable in all the countries she visited, and of the extraordinary industry of her niece in recording what they accomplished.

" Honolulu, Sandwich Isles,
" April 22nd, 1861.

" We had some difficulty in framing our plan of action, so as to combine the visit to the volcano and that to the scene of Captain Cook's death, with returning to Honolulu by the next trip of the steamer. After much consultation it was decided that the steamer should meet us on the following Thursday (a week hence) in Kalekeakua Bay (the scene of the Cook tragedy) on the opposite side of the Island to Hilo. Meanwhile we were to travel round by the south part, from the volcano, to a place called Minoli, where the King's boat was to meet us, and carry us up to Kalekeakua Bay.

" Colonel Kalakaua (the A.D.C.) had, of course, full powers from the King as to preparations, and he was hard at work all day arranging for our departure on the following day (Thursday), it being our particular desire to spend Sunday at the volcano, rather than anywhere else on the road. My aunt and I were to have litters and a horse besides for me (I need hardly say that anything like a carriage, or even cart, was wholly out of the question), with another for Buckland, who was to ride the whole way. We also carried a tent, though we were to depend upon the native houses on the road.

" It was intended that we should stop at Hilo, in the house of the Governess of Hawaii, who resides here, this being the capital of the Island. She is the King's half sister (older than himself), and she succeeded on the death of her husband, who was like herself of the highest rank, to the Government. She has great power and is entitled to a seat in the House of Nobles. She is just now away and Mr. Austin performs her functions, but we may hope to see her during our journey.

" We were, however, not unwillingly prevailed upon to stop for the night in Mr. Coan's house, and after dinner, went down to the Governess's house in order to explain to Mr. Kalakaua, our only cause of compunction being that he had taken great pains to arrange the house comfortably. Having to cross a very little stream at its mouth, we for the first time found ourselves in the canoe common to the islands of the Pacific, with the invariable outrigger which balances the frail bark. It is wide enough only for one person to sit, and the seats are placed almost on a level with the gunwale—this was a very small one, but my aunt, Mr. Pitman and myself managed to get in, and we were pushed across the tiny stream. Starting early, by the end of the second day we reached the region of pure lava. Vegetation grew on it, but mostly low scrub and scarcely anything worthy to be called a tree. One shrub was particularly abundant and bore a singular flower, slender thread-like petals of bright crimson ; the young shoots of a low bush were of the same colour—stalks as well as the leaves. I asked Mr. Kalakaua to desire one of the men to pick me one of the flowers—he hesitated, and laughed a little and explained that it was one of the many superstitions still associated with the volcano, that Pelé (the goddess supposed to reside within its depths) did not like anyone to pluck flowers by the way—something was sure to happen if this was done. He picked one for me

159

LIFE OF LADY FRANKLIN

however, and turned to one of his own men bidding him remark it and see if any misfortune happened in consequence. It was very curious that our ascent should be so really imperceptible, as the volcano lies 4000 feet above the sea. The latter part of our journey of sixteen miles was over thick, coarse grass, from which only here and there a block of lava projected. We were not now upon a lava stream, and turning the corner of a slight elevation about 2 o'clock, we overlooked the crater and were at the end of our ride for the week.

" We were, however, not upon the edge of the crater, but upon the highest of three narrow ridges or plateaux to be descended into one after the other, by perpendicular rocky paths, the last, leading down upon the crater—an enormous area of lava enclosed in a wall of rock which is interrupted only in the part where the path is formed over a perfect saddle. At the lower side (opposite to where we stood) of the crater, there rose clouds of smoke from the burning lake of lava which is always more or less in activity, and from which issue the floods of molten stuff which forms the bed of the crater. Smoke was also issuing from a new place, but on the whole, Pelé was very quiet, more so than we at all desired she should be. It was evident that the *visible* fire was confined to the lake. In every direction, however, both in the bed of the crater and even on a part of the ridge above, clouds of steam arose from the fissures which rent it in all directions—and on the level of the plateau next below us, was a great bank of sulphur smoking away with all its might. We could see a similar bank rising out of the crater, some four miles off on the lower side.

" Our quarters for the next two nights did not promise much comfort, and the tent being of simple cotton, without lining, was pronounced by the gentlemen to be too cold for us. The former house of reception for travellers was no more, from old age, or some other cause, and the framework only of the new one was completed ; so we were reduced to making the best of by far the worst native hut we had seen anywhere, standing on the brink of the topmost ridge. It was in fact a mere shed, in which we could not stand upright even under the centre ridge pole. It was made

160

MRS. ASHURST MAJENDIE
When past 70 years old

of the coarsest grass and leaves, one half had no front wall (!) ; the other, which was in some sort enclosed, was given up to us ladies, the gentlemen screening themselves off with a waterproof sheet, and their share served as dining and drawing room in which we one and all reclined to eat our food, the servants squatting themselves in front. Our floor was strewn with fresh ferns and had a bit of matting over part of it, on which were placed the iron bed and the litters alongside of which there was just room for the water calabashes for washing, and our carpet bags. In the evening heavy mist and even rain swept round our exposed position, and it is wonderful we did not suffer seriously from cold, but we certainly did not. Of course, we were free from mosquitoes.

" After a glance at our habitation, we set off to the sulphur bed close at hand, the wind fortunately favouring our approach. It was a dangerous path owing to the fissures which lay everywhere, half concealed by rank grass, but which are of immense depth— some said to be bottomless !—and as we approached the bank, we *crunched* over a mixture of fine lava and sulphur, which was warm and felt like a thin crust. The crystals of sulphur were beautiful and we scrambled a few steps up the bank with our handkerchiefs to our noses, in order to break some off—I brought away those which overhung a tiny cavern, and nothing could be more exquisite than these specimens, but we were without the means of packing such delicate objects, and I very much fear they will be crumbled to dust before you see them. I ought to have said of the above mentioned fissures, that steam issues from many of them, so that you could hardly bear it on your hand.

" Returning to our hut, we witnessed a characteristic pro- ceeding. You will infer that what with litter bearers, horse keepers, bullock drivers and servants, our party required a good deal of food, so a pig was bought and being killed, was cooked native fashion. For this due preparation had been made by lighting a fire in which great lava stones were heated ; the body was then drawn backwards and forwards through the ashes until all the hair was singed off. Its now vacant stomach was crammed with the hot stones which were stuffed into every corner—it was wrapped in many folds of huge fern leaves called (I think) the *ti* plant,—a pail of water poured over and into every cranny. More hot stones piled around and above the body with a layer of fern leaves above all. Thus was piggy cooked! I must say that we had our misgivings of the result, and were not surprised when after two hours stewing, the little square lumps of pork (cut from the best parts though they doubtless were) put upon our tin platters were wholly uneatable—so whilst others feasted daintily after their own fashion, we made but a sorry meal.

"Our party of hangers-on was increased this evening by a few stragglers, one of whom was an old man with grey hair and a peculiar countenance, who is one of the very few professed heathens left, and who is a priest of the goddess Pelé. I believe he had many stories about her, and said that she was angry with men nowadays, and therefore seldom shewed herself—a sort of confusion appearing to exist on this point, i.e. whether Pelé shews approval or rage by an eruption. It is many years since this crater of Kilauea has overflowed.

"And now, as the brief twilight left us, we realised the vicinity of the fiery caldron by the lurid glow which flamed where we had seen smoke in the daylight—presently the clouds of mist which rushed past us hid all from us, and there appeared in its place the reflection of the flaming abyss upon the clouds above—it was a very singular effect, and was seen only when the mist shut out the lake. The brightest spot of light from the flaming lava changed its place and gave us the idea that the fire spouted up in various spots. You can imagine how my speculations and anxiety were excited by such a sight—there it was, all night long. I had only to raise myself in my litter, and it was in sight.

"*Sunday, April 28th.*—We spent a quiet morning, and a short service (in Hawaiian, of course) was held in and around the other portion of our hut. After this we set off to the crater, and found less difficulty than we had been led to expect, in getting down the steep rocks—wherever flat ground occurred, we got into the litters which saved us a great deal. At last we were on the bed of the crater, and here the men fastened on sandals made of wisps of

A LAKE OF FIRE

grass, the lava being uncomfortably warm. During a part of the road to the lake, which lay over a rather recent overflow, it lay so black and shiny, that you could fancy it had rolled itself sluggishly along within the last hour. Then we got upon an older formation, in which were rents in the crust, which was in some places not more than six inches thick. Some movement beneath, had made it crack, when one part would sink perhaps only a few inches, perhaps several feet ; looking beneath, you saw only chaos. In other spots the surging mass had been convulsed and tossed about—then you came to a seemingly fathomless chasm, over which our bearers sprung without difficulty or danger, but there were two at which we preferred to trust only to ourselves. Clouds of steam puffed out in every direction, and on coming to a somewhat higher mass our guide made us stuff our handkerchiefs to our noses, and look for a moment over the side of a furnace steaming with sulphur and glowing intensely with fire from a narrow chasm. Near here we left our litters and scrambled over masses of broken lava and stones of every size, with no little fatigue, but this led us up to the mighty scene of the lake, which I certainly can never fail to remember in all its vividness. Walking to a ridge of broken piled-up lava, we came upon the edge of a vast surging caldron of molten lava, looking like lead in colour, except when an unclouded sun turned the mass to silver. Out of this spouted fountains of blood-red lava, which cast itself in fiery spray upon the black rock enclosing it like a wall. As we gazed, the heavy centre began to change—a fiery streak extended along the shore beneath where we stood, which gurgled and bubbled and seemed to struggle to burst itself upwards, but instead of this other spots became intensely brilliant and fresh fountains arose and tossed themselves on high. The heat was awful and we were compelled to turn away our faces every minute, notwithstanding the fascination which kept us watching where the fiery mass would next break forth, more especially as Mr. Austin told us that we might expect to see, as he had, the entire lake glowing and spouting as one sheet of fire ! We were, however, less fortunate, having but little time to stay.

163

" As our party sat around, we observed a remarkable looking man seated on the very edge of the cliff, who began a sort of monotonous recitation, and we were told that he was another of Pelé's priests, who had followed us down. Like a cunning man as he was, he watched the signs in order to begin, and presently just as our time was expiring, a splendid fountain rose from the very centre of the lake (with others playing also at the edge beneath the cliffs), which, after spouting for a few seconds sunk down, and the entire mass became of the hue of lead. With this, the finest display we had witnessed, we closed our visit to the grandest volcano in the world." . . . . . .

The first part of the coast they passed along in returning from Hawaii to Honolulu was all composed of blocks of black lava, which had poured from the volcano into the sea and lay piled in fantastic shapes, often precipitous, with caves and blowholes through which the sea spouted up to a great height. In their canoe they took two days and a night to make the journey to the bay in which Captain Cook was murdered.

" By six in the morning we were in the well-known Kaleakakua Bay, running into Kaavaloa, the village where Cook was killed. Here a clean little house was given up to us, and we were able to rest as well as breakfast, after which we went to the spot on the beach where he fell and died, and then up the hill to the place where his body was burned and partly eaten and where a sort of monument was set up by Lord Byron in the *Blonde*, in 1825. On a mound of lava stones stands a pole with a flat piece of wood at the top, on which is fastened a copper plate recording the event. A rough wall of lava blocks surrounds the mound, and within this wall is inscribed in large white letters, the name of ' B. Boyd—1856.' He passed many years in the Pacific, cruising in his delightful yacht the *Wanderer* and came to V.D. Land before we left—we went on board and had luncheon. The poor man had a wretched, but for some time, an unknown fate. At last it was ascertained beyond a doubt that he was murdered by the natives on one of the Navigator Islands. It is proposed to erect a worthy monument to Cook, and some steps have been in progress for some time among the English in this country. On descending, we went to the stump of a cocoanut tree connected with the above tragedy, and which is covered with copper sheathing, inscribed with the names of different ships of war which have visited this spot, so deeply interesting to Englishmen.

" This over, we crossed the bay in a canoe, to the village of Kaleakakua, the largest, except Hilo, we had seen in Hawaii. The whole population were assembled at the landing place and a great number assisted in running the canoe high and dry on the shore, that we might spring out on dry land.". . . .

They next called on the King's aunt, who governed the natives of Kailua, and the whole province of Hawaii, and the journal continues as follows :—

" And now to Kailua. As we neared the beach, we saw two very good stone houses of two stories, and from the larger one we observed several people issue and walk along the beach to the landing place—the foremost a lady with an umbrella. This was the governess, who had come to meet my aunt. She was dressed Hawaiian fashion so far as the shape of her dress went, but it was of some handsome texture. She wore shoes and stockings, but nothing on her head, her dark wavy hair being gathered up behind. She was of the usual dark brown complexion, but certainly the ugliest as well as the fattest woman we have seen in the land. As to size, she is perfectly enormous with fat, and her gait is a mixture of waddle and stately swing, quite remarkable to behold. She is a very great lady and looks (or walks at least) as if fully conscious of it. She was attended by six or eight women (of whom one appeared to be of higher position than the rest), all dressed alike in lilac cotton. Her own residence was close to the landing place (a tiny cove), and we rested under the awning before going on to the other house (also her own property), which the King occupies when here, and which was given up entirely to us, and where she accompanied us. It is a large house with excellent rooms, and standing, with a grassy enclosure, close upon the shore and faced to the sea by a wall of lava blocks. Above this wall there is a sort of open shed thatched lightly with the great palm leaves, under which were chairs and a sofa, a shady resort at all hours of the day. In describing her dress I ought to have mentioned a double necklace of the feathers we had already noticed in the cloaks, yellow, crimson and green—this, of course, shewed her high rank, none but the ' high chiefs ' having the right to wear these feathers. Having shewed us the rooms we were expected to use, she left us for the shady bower I have mentioned, where she spent the rest of the day with her maidens.

" Having refreshed ourselves a little, we enjoyed that greatest of Hawaiian luxuries, a ' lomi lomi ' or shampooing, which I cannot but declare to be the most wonderful restorative possible. You are thumped and pinched and pulled and rubbed, until every sensation of strain is removed. Two of the governess's women are expressly devoted to this service and they certainly shine in their vocation.

" At twelve, we started in our litters to a bay, a little way below this, to see some surf riding, and seeing the Roman Catholic church open, we looked in. The priest invited us in, but we declined, stopping only long enough to observe that it was large, very well kept, and without any of the usual nonsense and frippery—only one picture was over the altar. There were several natives there praying—i.e. on their knees, and this made us regret that this act of outward homage does not prevail in the Presbyterian Church. We were quite a cavalcade of horsemen and walkers, men, women and children, some of whom accompanied us the whole way, some three miles, our bearers often running along merrily. We alighted at a very nice native house, belonging to a chief of the lower grade, a very good-looking man, whom Mr. Kalakaua had introduced to us yesterday. He is an excellent surf rider, and joined in the succeeding sport, which was also witnessed by a great number of people belonging to the village.

who clustered all round the house. I fear I can hardly give you a correct idea of surf riding, but I must try.

" A man (or woman) swims out to the line of breakers, having before him a thin board from four to six feet long and about fifteeen inches wide, this in swimming he carries before with one arm, swimming with the other. The curling waves are nothing to these wonderful swimmers ; they either dive under them, or rise up the face of the liquid wall and appear on the top of or behind it. They choose their wave according to its height and the direction it will take in reaching the shore, and then, instead of facing it, they turn about, place the surf board immediately in front, rise to the crest of the wave, and literally ride upon it with extended limbs, until it has spent itself upon the beach. But if they perceive that it will cast itself against the rocks ; then they turn round again and stop short. It is a really wonderful sight, and some are so expert that during their flying progress, they can spring upright on the surf board and come in erect ! We saw one man do this.

" All here, living on the coast, are as much at home in the water as on land, and seem to enjoy it thoroughly. The children begin from tender youth—three or four years old—you see them run into the edge of the water and out again ; a little older and they go farther and dance in the outer edge of the spent waves, throwing themselves down that the water may pass over them. Older still and they have their tiny surf boards, already being good swimmers. Morning and noon time you see them here by the dozen in the water, shouting, playing, jumping in from the rocks head foremost, or straight upright, diving, standing on their heads and dashing their legs in the air—in fact their antics are innumerable.

" As we were watching the sport, who should come up with a goodly train, all on horseback, but the governess with eight female attendants and probably at least as many men. She wore a bright yellow petticoat, after their fashion, of which I intend to learn the mysteries, but cannot describe at present, farther than to say that being astride, it falls in front on each side in sweeping folds and is kept down by going over the foot into the stirrup. All the ladies wore black cloth capes—the petticoats were either yellow or bright red, and the hats black or straw colour. Unfortunately, we did not see them dismount, nor would they mount until after we started to return. We would have given a good deal to see that enormous woman get into the saddle ! We saw something of the secret of her fat to-day—she is very fond of English bottled ale, and absolutely drank three tumblers quite full without eating anything solid.

" We are thoroughly enjoying the fruit. I never tasted such oranges in my life, so perfectly ripe and teeming with juice. We have had a most extraordinary surf. For two days it has been terrific, and the waves have dashed up this sheltered bay in a manner never seen before and very alarming to the people. It was fine fun for the boys, but their mothers were alarmed and every now and then we saw them screaming and beckoning them to come in from the surf into which they had dashed with their boards at high romps. Two men were actually thrown down under the surf (for want of expertness) and nearly killed. At the outer point of the bay the waves broke with tremendous fury, shooting up great mountains of spray. At night these spray masses turned from snowy white to black and gave one the idea of a volcano flinging forth its dense clouds of smoke. nothing could be more magnificent than to watch the huge wall of pale translucent green as it advanced towards the shore, ever increasing in height and volume, and then breaking over with a voice of thunder.

" *Thursday, May* 16*th.*—Finding that the steamer had gone on without picking us up, we embarked at 4 a.m. in a canoe with six natives to paddle and reached Kawaihae (pronounced Quihi) at 4 p.m. Here Mr. Lowe, a young clerk at the village store, described to us the wonderful and awful circumstances of the last eruption, only two years ago, which he witnessed continually from a distance and visited repeatedly. This fearful outburst did not proceed from the crater we visited (Kilanea) but from a new one on the side of Mowna Loa. Out of this issued a stupen-

RELIEF FOR THE NATIONAL MEMORIAL TO SIR JOHN FRANKLIN

[M. Noble, Sc.

dous column of fire and lava which spouted up continually during a month and then ceased, only, however, to break forth again with fresh fury. The lava poured out and down the side of the mountain, a molten stream which at night gave out such intense light, that at Kawaihae, fifteen miles distant, you could see to read the smallest print with the same ease as in daylight. This outpouring of the inner life of Mother Earth lasted continually for a whole year ! During that time the stream was flowing red hot into the sea, hissing and spouting, keeping the water at boiling point to a distance of 300 yards from the shore ; numbers of fish floating about not only dead but ready cooked for eating. Mr. Lowe approached as near as possible to the junction of the molten stream with the sea, but the heat was so intense that it was unendurable, even at 300 yards, beyond a few minutes. The heat of the water loosened the seams of the boat or canoe, and safety compelled him to move off. The stream was forty miles in length from the crater to the sea, and it was a fortnight in getting to the sea. The eruption destroyed only one village, but it filled up a bay and made a new promontory.

" *Friday, May* 17*th.*—The steamer arrived this morning, and as it was to stop all day, we started to visit a Heian, or temple built by the first Kamchamcha, and the last on which human sacrifice was offered. It stands on a steep hill rising from the beach. We were on our litters, Colonel Kalakaua riding. On the beach we met a small party of natives on horseback, one of whom greeted Kalakaua with extreme cordiality and was at once presented by him as Mr. Isaac Davis, grandson of the Isaac Davis who, with John Young, was the first white who settled on the islands. He is an exceedingly handsome, gentlemanlike looking man, six feet two in height, with well cut features, wavy hair and dark complexion. This young man is the second husband of the governess of Hawaii, and he is actually older than she is, for she is only thirty-two ! a thing almost incomprehensible to us.

" The Heian, standing upon a lofty point running down to the sea, consists of a semi-circular wall of rough stones about twenty feet high. The area is roughly paved, and within it are the places used for sacrifice; that in the middle, a cavity filled in with loose stones, was for the human sacrifices; in front of it for beasts ; to the left for fruits. Immediately in front, and a little below the level, of this sacrificing area, was a more closely paved terrace on which the highest chiefs placed themselves— lower still, was another for the inferior chiefs, and lowest of all, the common people assembled.

" The last sacrifice was brought about by treachery in which the grandfather of Colonel Kalakaua was the chief agent. The first Kamchamcha had conquered the whole of this island except the territory of a single chief, the Lord of Kani. This brave man could be vanquished only by stratagem, by which he was induced to trust himself on a visit to Kamchamcha. On approaching the great chief, he found himself in the hands of an army. He was seized, carried up to the Heian, and was the last human victim ever offered. This is one of the few Heians still left on any of the islands, and we were fortunate in having an opportunity to examine it.

" *Saturday, May* 18*th.*—We left our anchorage about 10 a.m. with additional lady passengers, and reached Lahania about 2 p.m. The King had given orders that the means should be provided for taking us up to the seminary at Lahania Luva, on the hill above Lahania, and we were driven thither by Mr. Bartow, who is the post-master, etc. Then we drove to the house of Dr. Hutchinson, an Englishman, whom the King has lately made district judge here. He is a medical man, and went out to Van Dieman's Land as doctor to an emigrant ship, the *Henry*, while we were there, he says. He has married an Englishwoman, on which ground we were anxious to meet their wish that my aunt should call on her. She comes from near Gillingham in Kent, and knows something of Mrs. Turner, widow of the purser of the *Erebus*.* Many of the crew having lived in that part, she has been in the habit of hearing of the Expedition and of feeling unusual interest in it.

---

* M'Clintock, on May 25, 1859, came at midnight, near Cape Herschell on the W. coast of King William's Island, on a human skeleton lying face downward with its head towards the Great Fish River, and judged from the dress that it was that of a steward or purser.

HAWAIIAN EDUCATION

" *Sunday, May* 19*th*.—We arrived early at Honolulu, and found
the Queen's carriage waiting to take us back to Mr. Wyllie's
house.   Fortunately there was time to breakfast and return into
the town for church.

" I shall here close this letter—at the end of what may be calle d
the first episode in our deeply interesting visit of three weeks to
this kingdom.   My next will tell of Honolulu and the people.

" Your very affectionate,

"SOPHIA CRACROFT."

In Honolulu they became very intimate with the
King and Queen, of whom they saw a great deal, and
no people could have been more friendly.

The King helped them in every way to make excur-
sions to the hills and to all places of interest or natural
beauty.   Miss Cracroft dwells especially on the fine
views, the wonderful wooded ravines, the waterfalls
and also on the variety of the tropical fruits and flowers,
and the fine presence of the natives and their skill in
riding and in swimming ; a distance of fifteen or twenty
miles not being too much.   One woman had lately
landed on the beach, decorated by a fringe of dried fish.
She explained this curious petticoat by saying that the
schooner she was in having gone down eight miles off
land, as she did not know how far she would have to
swim for safety or how long she might have to be in
the water, she had tied food for several days round her
waist as a wise precaution.   One other thing which
struck them as remarkable was the excellent system
of education for boys and girls of every class, and the
personal interest which both King and Queen took in
all the schools.   One place which they made a point

of visiting was Waimea, the spot where Captain Cook first landed on his discovering the island in 1773. He sighted the island of Kunai, spent a few days off Waimea, and then went off to Bering's Strait, whence he returned in December of the same year, and sighted the island of Mani ; thence he sailed round Hawaii and eventually in the following February met his death. Waimea is now a missionary station, the village spreading along the beach under a range of hills.

CHAPTER XII

LAST TRAVELS OF LADY FRANKLIN

In 1862, on their voyage all round South America, both the ladies suffered much from the heat and from the mosquitoes. At Rio Lady Franklin had a long interview with the Emperor of Brazil—a most enlightened monarch and with an unusual knowledge of all that had been done in Arctic research. She was happy in being able to give him M'Clintock's book. They passed through the Straits of Magellan, the name was spelt by the dwellers on the spot Magalyaents and pronounced Magalhaens. Miss Cracroft notes the singular difference between the Patagonians on one side of the Strait and the Tierra-del-Fuegians on the other. The former tall, and all horsemen, and possesssing no boats or canoes, the latter short, and living in their canoes and possessing no horses at all ; both clad like savages in skins of that curious Patagonian animal the guanaco. The natives looked on the English ladies as curious animals ; they had never seen a white woman before. After passing through the Straits they were attracted by the beauty of Concepcion in Chile, also of Acapulco in Mexico, and the strange history of independence exhibited by the Araucanian Indians in Chile between the Andes and the sea. Their ship was large and roomy, with very few passengers, and they had a wonderfully good stewardess, who had, with her former captain, made in ten years one hundred and one voyages across the Atlantic. She was at once a nurse, a doctor, a carpenter, a mechanic, and the Captain said of her, "If you want to get the topmast down just let her know and she will have it done."

They arrived at San Francisco to find that the rivers from the Rockies had flooded that town and Sacramento, so they took advantage of a good steamer going to the Sandwich Islands, and at Honolulu they made great friends with King Kamehameha and Queen Emma, both highly cultivated people, and after spending some time with them and visiting Hawaii and the great volcano they left for Japan, where Lady Franklin was the first English lady traveller who had been seen. The King actually appointed her "his special ambassadress and plenipotentiary" at the Court of "His Imperial Majesty the Tycoon of Japan," and deputed her to thank him for the presents he had lately sent to the King of Hawaii. On her return, I remember her visit to my parents and the paper pocket handkerchiefs she presented to us children, and the funny description she gave of the custom which had rather shocked her, of the children, with their parents and grandparents, all taking their afternoon or evening tub together by the roadside in front of their houses.

Ninety days from December to March were spent by the travellers in sailing from San Francisco to Japan, and on landing at Yokohama, in March, they received the sad news, just communicated to the Consul, of the death of the Prince Consort, which had taken place on December 14th, 1861.

During her visit of two months to the Sandwich Isles Lady Franklin became very friendly with the King and Queen,* and also with Mr. R. C. Wyllie who was, for many years, and under three kings, if not four, the Minister of Foreign Affairs. He had a beautiful sugar estate, called Prince-Ville, on one of the smaller islands, where he usually lived at a house called " Rose Bank," and being the highest authority under the King on all matters of state, etc., he had much on his hands ; but he found time to keep up a brisk correspondence with Lady Franklin. In 1861, an Ayrshire paper claimed that Queen Emma was a daughter of Mr. Wyllie, who was an Ayrshire man, and hence an Ayrshire village claimed to have a reigning queen on its parish roll. Mr. Wyllie was never married ; but Queen Emma *was* descended from a Lancashire man named John Young, who married a high chieftainess, Kaoanaeha, in the reign of Kamehameha I., at the beginning of the century. She was a daughter of Kalikokolami and a direct descendant of Neawe, the ancestor of the royal line of Kamehameha. The daughter of John Young was called Kakela, and she married the chief Naea, a lineal descendant of the ancient kings of Hawaii, and their daughter was Emma, who was adopted by Dr. Rooke and brought up as his own child, receiving an excellent education, so that she was fitted both by lineage and upbringing to add lustre to the throne to which she was raised by the King.

* Queen Emma and her husband.

LIFE OF LADY FRANKLIN

1865

After a visit to Spain, Lady Franklin hurried back to England to make preparations for receiving Queen Emma of the Sandwich Islands in her little house at Kensington Gore. The Queen, since Lady Franklin had parted with her at Honolulu, had lost her husband as well as her son, and when my aunt asked me to come and be introduced to the Queen, I found a tall, handsome, rather big-limbed lady of stately presence ; she was dark and with a somewhat brown colour, with an extremely pleasant smile, lively manner, talking fairly good English and full of enthusiasm for all the people she was seeing, and whom she managed to interest in her scheme for raising funds for a cathedral to be built at Honolulu for the lately appointed bishop. My aunt found her at times a little *difficile*, but when you consider that her people were but three generations back the savages who killed Captain Cook and that she was herself a native and had never till now been beyond the group of islands which she ruled, it must be conceded that she conducted herself with extraordinary propriety and *savoir faire*, and never once offended by word or action during the months that she visited in one great house after another. My aunt asked her lord-in-waiting, a huge Hawaiian warrior, to sing to us, and the softness of the language with its crooning, 'u' and double 'o' preponderating, was what struck me most.

In 1866 Lady Franklin was at home and had some correspondence with the Board of Works about the position of the national statue to Sir John.

HAWAIIAN QUEEN VISITS ENGLAND

1867-73

The year 1867 was spent by Lady Franklin and her niece in travelling over Europe. Their aim was to avoid the English winter, but they did more than that, for Lady Franklin had an ardent desire to see all parts of the habitable globe, and she was afraid of no fatigue or heat or rough accommodation in her determination to miss nothing which was worth seeing. Wherever she went her name was a passport, and ensured her every attention, and she always had introductions to the right people in every place she visited.

April and May of 1867 was spent in Dalmatia, which they traversed from south to north. They were delighted with Cettaro, Ragusa, Spolatro, Zora, Pola, and Fiume, and with several of the islands along the coast, and they penetrated into the mountains to see the waterfalls; whilst the Venetian buildings at the sea ports, and still more the considerable Roman remains at Ragusa, Spolatro and Pola interested them enormously.

In June, 1868, Mr. H. Grinnell presses them to pay a visit to his family in New York; this they did in 1870.

There are few letters during this " wander-lust." But there is a pleasant note from Charles Tennyson Turner, the poet's brother. Charles and Alfred had married sisters, nieces of Sir John Franklin, so he calls her "aunt."

To Lady Franklin.   " Grasby Vicarage, near Brigg,
                                     " November 14th, 1868.
" My dear Aunt,
    " I got your very kind note on the 10th, and I ought to have answered it before this. I have dwelt on it with no common

M   177

satisfaction for the affectionate expressions as well as the literary praise. Indeed, it is much to tell me that you have relished my music for years. The 'Last Sweep of the Scythe' I am glad you like, but I don't know that I have singled any of my children out for special favourites, being ridiculously fond of them all, as an author should be—thus exemplifying poor Cowper's line—' fancy's fondness for the child she bears.'

"Thank you, too, for patronizing my 'buzzers.'* It has been objected that Memnon is too august a parallel for the little animals so soon to be made housemaids sweepings of, but they and the son of Aurora may, I think, be allowed to meet on the common ground of affection for the daylight. I am a good deal better of late in my health, thank you. We both hope to have an opportunity of accepting your kind and cordial invitation, but at present, I fear it is out of the question. Next summer, if it bring about our meeting, will be marked with a white stone.

" Will you give our kind love to Sophy and accept it for yourself,

" And believe me, My dear Aunt, Your affectionate nephew,
" CHARLES TURNER.'

" We hope your winter's migration may do you both much good. You have perhaps seen in the papers the death of poor Horatio's† wife ; he is left with five children."

Spring of 1869 found them at the Azores. Miss Cracroft writes a very fully descriptive letter of sixteen closely but clearly written pages of all they did and saw on the round trip from Lisbon between April 15th and May 1st; and as the islands are still comparatively unknown to English people, extracts from the letter will not be without interest.

* Houseflies in November sunshine. *See* Sonnet 209.
† His brother Horatio Tennyson.

IN THE AZORES

" Off the Island of Terceira of the Azores.

" April 20th, 1869.

" My last was sent from Lisbon on the 15th, and we started immediately after to pay a visit to these islands (belonging to Portugal), for one week. A steamer starts monthly. We had been recommended to take this trip by our American acquaintances at Santa Cruz, the Dabneys, whose family have for two generations lived at Fayal as American consuls, and they gave us letters there, as well as to St. Michael's Terceira. We were rather more than three days making the passage, but we have a beautiful steamer, quite new, fresh from England, the company being an English one. It is commanded and manned by Portuguese, but the second mate speaks English, so does the stewardess, so we get on fairly well.

.   .   .   .   .   .

" We were off the island of St. Michael in the evening, and anchored off the chief town, Punto Delgado, about 8 p.m., April 18th. We had two letters here.

" Early next morning, Monday, April 19th, the agent of the Company to whom we were specially recommended, sent off a young gentleman from his office who speaks English, to escort us to one of the sights of the island, called in English, ' the seven towns'—a name certainly quite inapplicable. We landed at a very good quay within a little boat harbour, from where you pass under quite a handsome triple-arched gateway, into a Plaza, just out of which we found a carriage waiting—a very good one, with three horses, one of whom proved an inveterate kicker.

" We drove through a good part of the town, which is well built and very fairly clean, and through a suburb, chiefly of large houses with gardens. Our young gentleman, Senor Rangel, told us that the gardens were very fine, and some of them producing enormous quantities of the far-famed oranges ; but the season for these is just over. Our drive of nearly three hours lay near the coast and we had some fine bits of rocky scenery and passed through some very decent villages. We met no wheeled vehicles, but plenty of mules and donkeys, carrying produce, as well as

179

persons ; the men sometimes wore an enormous head gear intended to shade them from the sun—a cap, with an immense peak, and flapping sides to guard the ears and back of the neck.

.　.　.　.　.　.

" A handkerchief tied over the head is universal, and we saw quantities entirely in white, including a loose jacket—no shoes or stockings.

" After a drive of two and a half hours, we had to take to donkeys, with the country saddle ; a mere seat, with a wooden St. Andrew's cross at each end to keep you from falling off in front or behind. You sit sideways, and are in danger of dropping off backwards, or forwards ! We were to cross a lofty mountain ridge which lay before us in the clouds, and descend the other side. The road was steep and rough, but not dangerous, only very fatiguing—and within one hour we entered the thick clouds and could see nothing of any view, in fact only a few yards beyond ourselves ; and the mist was all but rain, so penetrating. It was not until we had accomplished nearly the whole descent on the other side, that we saw any portion of the lake we were to visit. The country seemed to be a mass of volcanic rock, tossed about in every variety of form, or rather of size, for the form varied little from the huge crag to the miniature ridge, rising from a rich crop of corn or lupine, the last a very common one here. This ridge is much frequented in summer by excursionists. Notice had been given of our visit and dinner ordered. It consisted entirely and solely of chicken—first boiled into strings—next roasted ; there was some cabbage, and that was the whole of our dinner.

.　.　.　.　.　.

" There is a charming house with a garden only partly redeemed from wildness, and half overgrown with weeds, but the azaleas and geraniums were all a blaze of beauty ; and the roses flourished wildly.

" After dinner we re-mounted our donkeys for a hard ride back—of course, by ' hard ' I do not mean a fast ride, but only a toilsome one of two and a half hours back to the carriage. Hap-

180

pily the clouds had dispersed, and we had a very fine view of the lake and surrounding mountains. We drove fast back to the town and embarked at once, not a little tired.

" We started at night, and were in the morning at the Island of Terceira, at the chief port of which we were to spend the day. We had a letter from an Englishman here—Mr. Dart, a resident since 1825, and married to a Portuguese lady of very good family.

. . . . . .

" The landing place here, as at Punto Delgado, is quite handsome. The stone pier has handsome flights of steps from the water and you enter the town upon a plaza with stone seats and handsome buildings around. The principal streets are of fair width, with side pavements, and are clean. Many of the houses are extremely large and handsome and the people seemed well-to-do. This island furnishes the best oranges, which, however, go under the name of St. Michael's oranges at home.

. . . . . .

" Mr. Dart proposed a drive, and we went to a country house with a charming flower garden, as well as very big orange garden. The whole was surrounded as usual by a very high wall, within which is planted a close line of a tree called the Faya, used as a screen for the oranges. But besides, the vast garden was surrounded and intersected by a lofty broad terrace having a stone parapet. These terraces are the work of years, as well they may be, as they are made of stones and lumps of rock picked out of the area of the garden.

. . . . . .

" The Domain includes one of the volcanic conical hills commanding a fine view of the coast, as well as on the landside. It is crowned by a low tower having a flat roof, and to our great surprise and interest we learned that this was the place at which the *Alabama* received her armament and equipment as a privateer. The original rendezvous was just outside the harbour, and there the vessel conveying her guns, etc., lay at first with the *Alabama*, but the wind came strongly from an unfavourable quarter, and the two vessels shifted to the other side of a very lofty promontory which forms one side of the harbour, and then began the work of transfer, carried on by night (it was full moon) as well as by day. The Portuguese authorities thought the affair very strange, and after a day or two, requested the vessels would enter the harbour, or go away, which Semmes promised to do next day, and so on, until one fine morning they had disappeared, and no one had guessed the truth ! Then came the taking of the first prizes near Fayal, which is nearly the track of American ships to all parts southward.

" We next visited the country house, on the seashore, of Mr. Dart's daughter—large and beautifully situated with a charming terrace overlooking the shore ; but absolutely without furniture, which has to be moved in and out of the town every year, on account of the excessive dampness of the climate.

.   .   .   .   .   .

" We dropped at Terceira a large proportion of our fellow-passengers, consisting of a general (about to take command in the island) his wife, and twelve of their fifteen children.

" *Wednesday, April 21st.*—We reached the island of Graciosa about 6 a.m., and remained there three or four hours discharging and taking in cargo, and then passed on to the next, St. Jorga, which we got to about one o'clock, and my aunt went on shore with Chevalier—our man—for an hour. The islands of Pico and Fayal were very near, but the fine cone of Pico was hid in the clouds. We reached Fayal before six—the harbour having the peak exactly opposite, separated only by a strait of three or four miles. Very shortly after the delivery of our letter of introduction for Mr. Dabney, the American consul, we had a visit from his son, Mr. Samuel Dabney, who urged us much to go on shore at once and remain with the family as long as the steamer was to stay. We thought, however, that we should prefer keeping our cabins, at any rate until to-morrow, as it was already dark, though our decision seemed to be regretted.

.   .   .   .   .   .

" We engaged to land the next morning, and Mr. S. Dabney kindly insisted on coming to fetch us.

NINETEENTH CENTURY PRIVATEERING

" *Thursday, April 22nd.*—We landed at mid-day, and found the elder Mr. Dabney waiting for us on the steps of the quay—an old man, the eldest of the family of which the consul at Teneriffe is the youngest, with twenty-four years between the brothers. The swell was unpleasant and the landing not very easy. This landing process is my greatest anxiety on my aunt's account, and it has been almost perpetual during the whole period of our absence this year. Whether in landing, or in getting in and out of a steamer, the boat rises and falls, sometimes most perilously. You have to stand upon the last step of the ladder, and watch the exact moment of the boat's rising, to step into it—and vice versa, on returning to the ship.

" Crossing the street from the quay, we were met by two ladies who were waiting to receive us, viz., Miss Clara Dabney, the eldest daughter, and Mrs. Samuel Dabney, and had a most cordial welcome. In a few minutes we were in their house and introduced to other members of the very large family—Mr. and Mrs. Charles Dabney, and Miss Roxana Dabney the youngest daughter, none of them being now young. We were in a large, lofty drawing-room, covered with matting, and reminding us of Indian rooms—with one great exception, the flowers which decorated it with a wealth of beauty. Besides bouquets, they were placed upon brackets in the corners, as well as on the sides of the room, with trailers of flowering creepers or ivy—the choicest flowers had separate little vases—and I never saw any room more charmingly arranged.

" It was quickly settled that we should take a drive, Miss Clara Dabney being our companion—a most intelligent, nice person, without the smallest pretension. I should have said that the house faces the sea and the beautiful peak, which is commanded from every part of the town, as it rises up the hill from the sea-shore. We found the streets very good and clean, and passing up and round the hill, we came into a valley called the 'Valley of the Flamonds,' from the fact that this valley was apportioned among the Flemish colonists. Even now the result of a mixed race is to be seen in the population, many of

LIFE OF LADY FRANKLIN

whom are fair. The mountain rises steeply from this valley, up to the edge of the great crater of the island. It is said to be a very fine ride of about seven hours, which was beyond our powers.

" From this, we drove to the first house built and inhabited by the Dabney family, called Bagatelle, the residence of the father of Mr. Dabney, who was the first American consul here. and came even before the War of Independence.

.   .   .   .   .   .

" Here we were soon persuaded to send for Chevalier and our carpet bags and engage to stop the only night which remained before commencing our voyage back, and undoubtedly we much enjoyed the luxury of cleanliness, space, fine air, quiet, the perfume of flowers and lovely scenery.

" It is indeed a spot to revel in. The ground descends abruptly from the house, which is in fact built upon the slope of a very steep hill—and the whole territory is most wisely cut into very wide terraces, supported by low, rough, stone walls. I have never anywhere seen flowers grow in such true perfection. Notwithstanding the rich luxuriant growth of roses, fuschias, geraniums, heliotrope and other hardy plants, they have not the straggling, drawn up growth that one sees in a really hot climate. The ixias, gladiolus, cactus, salvias were magnificent. The walls were hidden by roses, geraniums, fuschias. The last covered the walls and crept over the roof.

.   .   .   .   .

" But the chief floral glory of the garden is its camellias. Introduced by the first Dabney, they are now great trees from which innumerable plants of ev. ry size have been produced. There is a great wall or screen of the old trees, of the finest colours. They were nearly over when we were there, but every year it produces a perfect mass of flowers. I really enjoyed the quiet and beauty of everything, especially sitting under the verandah, having an unclouded view of the magnificent peak, which rises from the sea 7,600 feet, an uninterrupted cone, with a double head, though the highest point is considerably above the second peak at the side.

A PARADISE OF FLOWERS

" At one o'clock we drove out to see two churches, and to visit the third of these large family houses, which belongs to Mr. John Dabney, now absent. This is called the Cedars, from having, in the grounds close to the house, a magnificent thick grove of cedar-like pines. The house stands high and is very large, looking quite over the town to the peak. The garden is exceedingly large, and about half-way down the hill is connected with the Fredegonda grounds by a tunnel passing under the public road, through which we entered another of these charming territories, in which magnificent trees and flowers seemed to revel in beauty and strength and liberty. It was really a good walk between the two houses, through the grounds of both. We made our last adieux to the kind people at Fredegonda.

" Having completed our purchases of the very pretty straw embroidery upon tulle, and a sort of lace made of the fibre of the aloe, of which you will all have specimens, we dined at Bagatelle, and at six embarked for our steamer, accompanied by two of the ladies, and Mr. S. Dabney. All this day we had magnificent and ever varying views of the peak, which early this morning had a grey sprinkling of snow deposited by the clouds of yesterday. On the shore of Pico at the foot of the mountain are straggling white houses, which all but glitter in sunshine, by contrast with the dark lava mass of the hillsides. Indeed, all the houses, everywhere, are white, and are very apt to have red tiled roofs. We started late in the night and were again off the island of St. George on Saturday morning, April 24th, passing on to Graciosa, where my aunt and I landed for an hour. The little town lies on the margin of the shore, which literally bristles with low black rocks, leaving only a narrow entrance in front of the town, to a tiny beach of sand. But we had to be carried in and out of the boat. There is a high wall in front of the town, which is probably necessary to protect from the waves in bad weather. The streets were remarkably clean, and so were some of the houses which one could look into in passing. There was a large building used as a hospital, formerly a convent ; and a handsome fountain under the rock, from which the water as usual issued from several spouts.

LIFE OF LADY FRANKLIN

" *Sunday, April 25th.*—We reached Terceira early, and at a
later hour landed with kind Mr. Dart, who came off for us. We
walked up the hill to have a fine view, to a monument erected in
memory of Don Pedro's landing here, and on our return dined with
the family as before, and at six returned on board. We shall
see Mr. Dart in England in July or August, but his delicate wife
shrinks from the long journey, though the change would certainly
be of use to her health.

" On Monday, April 26th, we again reached St. Michael's,
and having made the arrangements on our previous visit, we landed
early, in order to visit the great crater and hot springs of Furnas,
rather a long day's journey.   Mr. Rangel was again our escort and
we saw a great deal of the island, passing quite across to the other
side and thence Eastward.   For the first hour we had continual
orange gardens, but when there were openings there was a good
deal of variety and much richness of vegetation, with the most
exquisite green possible.   On the whole a want of wood, but there
is some planting of young trees.   The villages mostly upon the
coast rising from a little cove between high rocks; and as the road
is exceedingly hilly, we had some beautiful points of view.   There
is no positively bad road, but the hills are often quite fearfully
steep, but we had four horses, one being ridden postillion in front
of the other three abreast, and we had the same excellent coachman, and also his kicking horse.

" In most of the villages the windows were simply wooden
shutters or panels without glass ; a very good thing for the health
of the inhabitants.   The women seem to work as hard as the men,
and some are quite handsome when young.   We saw one most
lovely girl hard at work washing linen at the tank below the
fountain.   There are no carts or trucks—everything goes on mules
or donkeys which is not carried on the head.   After five hours'
journey, we came to the upper edge of the Furnas crater, and
looked down upon it with its straggling white houses and church,
and on one side, higher up, is another crater in which is a considerable lake, the Smoking Springs, Here the well-made road
ended, to our almost consternation, as it is impossible to get at

VISITING FURNAS CRATER

the exact truth in this part of the world, and we were repeatedly assured that the carriage could go all the way, whereas a winding path lay before us, down to the bottom, and the result was that we had a walk of about a mile and a half ! We found a very decent hotel, at this season quite empty, as the baths are not taken until July. After a rest, we had donkeys to take us to the springs, as we could do no more walking, and passing through the village street we came upon a sort of small ravine, which is filled with these springs of various kinds—the only one I think which is enclosed has a long wall round a circular natural basin, in the middle of which the more-than-boiling water bursts up in a seeming agony of disturbance. It is stated that a bullock having fallen in, the bare bones were, the next moment flung up, and tossed about. The water is sulphurous, with some acid with it. It is conveyed into a bathing house near by two wooden channels, but one of which passes through a tank where the water cools, and the bath has two plugs for hot and cold water. Later in the afternoon my aunt took a bath here, but the arrangements cannot be called comfortable. We visited several other hot and cold fountains of different properties, one strongly mixed with iron (N.B. the boiling and cold springs are found within a very few feet of each other !)— and one, which flings up only boiling mud, of a dull lead colour. I forget how many there are, but we saw only a part. The ground is not only hot, but distinctly trembling, and so soft, that you can pick out pieces with your fingers—(i.e. if you do not mind the heat)—it is mostly whitish, tinged more or less with sulphur and iron. I got some very good pieces, but left them behind at a place where the scramble was difficult, thinking we should return the same way, which we did not. So I have only some specimens which are rather inferior to the others. To my mind these earth-quaky hot places are awful. One feels so terribly near the fiery centre of the earth, and the crust is really so very thin in these places. You may imagine we were tired at night, and we had to start early on our journey as the steamer was to start in the after-noon. Of course we did not repeat our walk, but had donkeys up the hill to the carriage, on joining which, we found our kicking horse in the act of a violent outbreak, which obliged him to be taken out, and pacified—after which our journey was prosperous and rapid back to Punto Delgado, where, finding that there was time, my aunt decided to visit the garden of an Azorean gentleman named De Canto, who was our fellow passenger to Fayal, and wrote to his wife here to expect us, his garden being quite celebrated for its extreme beauty and extent, and the rarity of the plants—and we found it worthy of all that could be said of it. Senor de Canto knows Kew well, and is in correspondence with the heads of all the chief public gardens in all parts of the world, and get plants from them. His is equal to any garden we have ever seen anywhere, and most beautifully kept. We were shewn through by his three ladylike daughters (the mother was too unwell to leave her room) but we could not see half, so great is the extent. He has lived fifteen years in Paris for education of his family, and has only just returned home. He speaks English, too, well, and is a most gentlemanlike man. I should think the young ladies will find Punto Delgado rather dull after fifteen years residence in Paris. They afterwards sent us a beautiful basket of oranges, lemons and flowers. I have said little or nothing of earthquakes or oranges—the wonder is that we should have escaped the former ; as slight shocks are exceedingly common, especially in Terceira. It was close to this island that, a very few years back, the island was probably saved by the bursting out, in the sea very near to it, of a volcano, which threw up five jets of water and smoke. I have a (not good) photo of this extraordinary ebullition, which lasted some months. As to the oranges—we never ate so many before, and you can have no idea of their perfection when fresh and sweet as we had them daily.

" We started this evening (Tuesday, April 27th) on our return voyage to Lisbon. We should probably have stayed longer, but that there is only monthly communication (by the steamer) between the islands, and travellers are therefore obliged to remain in one or other, for a whole month, unless they do as we did, viz., keep to the vessel for the entire trip to and from Lisbon.

" We had fine weather during the next three days, but our

DEATH OF LADY FRANKLIN

vessel has a great deal of motion, so it was an uncomfortable and idle period. The kind Dabneys lent us some books, including a novel or two, and between them and my knitting, the time was got over somehow when I could employ myself at all, which was not always.

. . . . . .

" And here ends my story of the trip.
" Ever, my dearest ones, your most affectionate
" Sophia Cracroft."

In 1870 they made a journey to Valparaiso, thence to San Francisco and Alaska, and in July visited Brigham Young at Salt Lake City.

In 1871 and 1872 they were in Spain, visited Paris, and spent the winter of 1872 in Portugal, Spain and the Pyrenees and the spring at Cannes, returning to London for the wedding in July, 1873, of Sir John's charming granddaughter Eleanor, to Mr. Wiseman, a master at Clifton School and afterwards Rector of Scrivelsby near Horncastle.

In June, 1875, the papers were publishing daily bulletins of the health of Lady Franklin, and for a time she seemed to be recovering ; prayers were offered for her in the churches both in England and America, but on Sunday, July 18th, she passed away at the ripe age of eighty-three. The *Times* next day had two columns giving a short history of her life and travels, of which the following are the first two paragraphs:—

"LADY FRANKLIN.

" We record to-day the death of one who, among the gifted women of her time, has certainly not been the least remarkable.

189

After a lifetime extended far beyond the allotted span, the widow of Franklin, the renowned Arctic seaman and explorer, died yesterday evening at 9 o'clock, at her house in Phillimore Gardens.

" Remarkable as her life had been in many respects, she is chiefly known in having taken a prominent and distinguished part in the cause of Arctic discovery. A generation has elapsed since her gallant husband, with a small band, the flower of the British Navy, under his command, sailed as the leader of a great expedition, sent to accomplish the North-West Passage, and in the cause of science to explore the unknown regions of the Pole. From that expedition no man has ever returned, but, through the long years which have followed, the widow's life has been one unceasing effort to solve the mystery of their fate, and to bring to light the details of their deeds and their sufferings. When the first of these objects had been accomplished by the little vessel fitted out expressly by herself, she clung with equal tenacity to the last. Latterly, under increasing illness, her interest was chiefly absorbed in the equipment of the *Pandora* yacht, belonging to her friend, Mr. Allen Young, whose resolve to recover any remaining records of Franklin and his companions gave her a hope of realizing the one yet unfulfilled desire of her heart."

The Daily Telegraph had a long notice ending with

" Lady Franklin sought for the missing ships in heart and spirit as passionately as the pilgrim knights of old sought for the Holy Grail. In no seaport, in no fishing town of the north country was her form unknown. Hundreds of weather-beaten veterans of the North Seas had she travelled long distances to converse with, to question, to consult on the one crucial topic, her husband's fate. Such life-long devotion, such unfaltering and unselfish love, found, not indeed an adequate, but yet some slight requital in the universal respect and admiration accorded to the widow of one of Britain's bravest and noblest sons."

and the *Guardian* in the following week had this notice of the funeral.

WESTMINSTER MEMORIAL TO SIR JOHN

" The funeral of Lady Franklin took place on Thursday afternoon, at Kensal Green Cemetery. The funeral procession, which consisted of a hearse, followed by ten mourning coaches, and nearly the same number of private carriages, started from Phillimore-gardens, where she died, shortly after one o'clock. The chief mourners occupied the first five coaches, and included Bishop Nixon, the Rev. John Gell, Miss Cracroft, Mr. Austen Lefroy, the Rev. John Simpkinson, Mr. Dixon, Mr. de Wesselow, Mr. Ferard, Mr. Charles Ferard, the Rev. Frederick Leicester, Mr. Henry Gell, the Rev. Richard Wright, the Rev. Canon Wright, Mr. Hallam Tennyson, Mr. Hardwicke Rawnsley, Mr. Price, Mr. Cane, and Mr. Edward Lefroy. In the four remaining carriages were the following friends of the late Sir John and Lady Franklin :—Admirals, Sir Leopold M'Clintock, Sir R. Collinson, Richards and Ommanney; Mr. Leigh Smith, Mr. John Barrow, Dr. Hooker (President of the Royal Society) Sir Bartle Frere, the Rev. C. Crozier, Bishop Stanley, the Rev. W. Crichton, Mr. Fuller, Dr. Merriman, Captain Reinecke, Captain Hobson, Mr. Noble, Mr. H. Wagner. The pall-bearers were Sir Leopold M'Clintock, Sir Richard Collinson, Admiral Richards, Admiral Ommanney, Mr. Leigh Smith, and Mr. John Barrow. The service was read by Bishop Nixon, assisted by the Rev. Charles Stuart, chaplain to the cemetery. The outer coffin was of plain oak with black handles : the brass plate on the lid bearing the following inscription : — ' Jane Lady Franklin, died 18th July, 1875, aged eighty-three years,' was finally deposited by the side of Lady Franklin's sister, Lady Simpkinson, in the old catacombs under the chapel. A number of immortelles were placed on the coffin on its being deposited in the recess."

Two days later, on Saturday, July 31st, there was a gathering of relatives and naval friends at Westminster Abbey to unveil the monument to Sir John which had occupied Lady Franklin's mind up to the last hour of her life.

LIFE OF LADY FRANKLIN

" The memorial has been placed in one of the chapels surrounding that of Edward the Confessor. There are also, in the same chapel, the monuments of Captain Cook, the traveller, and Captain Kempenfelt, who went down with the Royal George, and 'twice four hundred men.' Mr. Noble's admirable bust of Sir John Franklin is enshrined in an architectural design suggested by Sir Gilbert Scott, R.A., and carried out by Messrs. Farmer and Brindley. The base of the monument contains a picture in bas-relief of a ship frozen in the ice of the Polar regions, bearing above it the words :—

" ' O ye frost and cold, O ye ice and snow,
Bless ye the Lord ; praise Him and magnify
Him for ever.'

" Then follows a verse by Tennyson,* exquisitely suited to the monument, which contains no other relic of Franklin than his deathless name :

" ' Not here ! the white North has thy bones ; and thou
Heroic Sailor-Soul,
Art passing on thine happier voyage now,
Towards no Earthly Pole.'

" The selection of the fitting passage from the prayer book is due to Arthur Stanley, Dean of Westminster, whose great interest in the work induced him also to furnish the following inscriptions, which appear to right and left of the memorial bust :

" ' To the memory of Sir John Franklin, born April 16th, 1786, at Spilsby, Lincolnshire : died June 11, 1847, off Point Victory, in the Frozen Ocean, the beloved chief of the crews who perished with him in completing the discovery of the North-West Passage.'

" ' This monument is erected by Jane, his widow, who, after long waiting and sending many in search of him, herself departed to find him in the realms of Life, July 18th, 1875, aged 83 years.'

" The bust is a simple portrait, gathered from the best sources,

* Canon Wright, in 1882, published no less than 165 translations of this in Greek, Latin, Arabic, German, Italian, French, etc., by the most eminent scholars of the day.

192

MEMORIAL TO SIR JOHN FRANKLIN ERECTED IN WESTMINSTER ABBEY.

and recalling the expression of a man who was said never in all his life to have raised his voice in anger. As for the canopy, with its rich Gothic foliage, enough of praise would be spoken in the mere intimation that it is the design of Sir George Gilbert Scott, were it not, indeed, that the conscientious labour of those who have carved the warmly-coloured marble, which contrasts so well with the purity of the Carrara bust, deserves also recognition. Altogether, the work is one of which the family of Sir John Franklin may be proud, and the Abbey not ashamed."

The following, being notes from his mother's letters and his own reminiscences of Lady Franklin, are from the pen of " her grandson," Mr. Philip Lyttleton Gell, eldest son of Sir John Franklin's daughter, Eleanor.

" My mother, Sir John's sole issue, was a child of three, when Miss Jane Griffin, at the age of thirty-six, became her step-mother. (November 5th, 1828).

" My mother's youthful journals, and Lady Franklin's letters to her, disclose the incessant restlessness and Spartan indifference to hardships and discomforts which continued throughout life. She showed no desire to make a home anywhere, until the voyage to Hobart Town brought the family to an anchorage at Government House.

" Even in Tasmania, the ties of family and domestic life and of Government House responsibilities did not anchor Lady F. for long. She left family and household behind, and made prolonged journeys in New Zealand and Australia. These journeys involved weary voyages through stormy seas in little sailing ships, with what would seem nowadays miserable accommodation, but to such hardships she was indifferent. She possessed the explorer's talent. She knew where she wanted to get, and she got there.

" After the arrival of the party in England (June, 1844) until the departure of the *Erebus* and *Terror* for the North, just eleven months later,* they again had no settled home, but made their

* May 19th, 1845.

headquarters with her father, Mr. Griffin, in Bedford Place, where her sister, Lady Simpkinson, also resided with her two sons and three daughters.

"Sir John sailed in the *Erebus*, in 1845, and before long Lady F. recommenced her indefatigable travelling, taking Eleanor with her. In 1846 they visited Madeira, various West Indian islands, the United States and Canada. In 1847, they hurried through the towns of Provence and the Riviera and Tuscany to Naples, where ' Mamma's portmanteau of books ' was impounded by the Officials for Ecclesiastical Censorship, and formed a subject of controversy until, after a tour in Sicily, they recovered it on leaving the Bourbon kingdom. Then Rome in a scorching June, was followed by an unresting vetturino journey through the Eastern towns to Ravenna : from one Italian Albergo to another, back again to Florence, Mantua and Milan, through the exhausting heat of the Lombard plain in August, and finally across the Alps by the Splugen to Basle and Strasburg. Thence they steamed down the Rhine to Mayence, Bonn and Cologne, returning to England through Ghent, and came to a temporary anchorage at Folkestone in September, 1847.

"My parents were married in June, 1849. It was in 1859, when Lady Franklin brought Sir Leopold to see us after his triumphant home-coming, that she first dawns on my own recollection. Though full of kindliness to us children in later years when we began to grow up, young children did not interest her, and she never entered into our lives until after my mother's death in the following year. That disaster drew her much closer to us. My father had always been a favourite with her, from the days when they worked together and often travelled together in Tasmania. Whenever she was in London she constantly drove over to our church* on Sunday evenings, and spent an hour afterwards in our motherless home, bringing toys or keepsakes from abroad on her return from her annual journeys. In the summer she frequently joined us for a week in our holidays, wherever we happened to be. She consulted my father in particular upon her ideals of Imperial

* Notting Hill.

194

A DINNER OF CELEBRITIES

Federation (in which we boys were greatly interested), and at her request he drew up and carried through a scheme for inducing the wage-earning class to study the problem by the offer of £100 for the best essay upon it by a working man. The offer was fully justified by the results. My late brother (John Franklin) and I found Gore Lodge a paradise for young boys during the months Lady Franklin spent in her London home. She liked to have us in her big garden when we could come, and set up a fiction (which at the time we took quite literally, without any suspicion of its humorous kindliness) that we came to the garden to work there, and earned three-pence an hour and our tea. Of course, it was a pure delight to us boys to have the run of an old garden in London, cutting down dead branches, flourishing the spray of a hose, etc., and acting as *aides-de-camp* at a garden party; but when shillings were gravely handed to us on our departure, we never doubted that they were really earned by work ; and it was a very sound lesson—far kinder than the promiscuous ' tip.'

" I have a vivid recollection of an expedition arranged for us by her to witness the founding of the Statue erected to my grandfather's memory at Hobart, and again of the ceremony when the London statue in 1866 or 1867 was unveiled. The late Willingham Franklin (Lieutenant R.N.) was there as the last representative of the Spilsby family in the male line.

"Amongst the many interesting people whom I met at Gore Lodge as I grew older, the old Arctic admirals and other explorers come first, and my memories of them all centre in the little dining room looking on the garden, which was hung round with the striking series of their portraits, which Lady Franklin bequeathed to the National Gallery.

" There was also a Japanese room upstairs, reserved for her Japanese furniture and collections, gathered when Japan was little known to English travellers. Articles which are now very familiar, in the 'sixties greatly interested visitors at afternoon or evening receptions. Gore Lodge, adjacent to Lowther Lodge, Knightsbridge (which was not built till later) was an old-fashioned house of two stories, which had belonged to the notorious John

LIFE OF LADY FRANKLIN

Wilkes of the *North Briton* (1727–1797). It had a pretty and extensive garden, but the dwelling rooms were too small for Lady Franklin's social gatherings. A spacious room was added by her, and it is first associated in my memory with the attractive personality of Queen Emma of Hawaii, in graceful widow's weeds, who was Lady Franklin's guest for some time. Later in 1872, coming down from Oxford in my first year, I was staying at Gore Lodge, and it fell to me to act as host to a most interesting dinner of geographical celebrities, hastily summoned at a few hours' notice to meet Mr. H. M. Stanley, who had landed at Liverpool the same morning, bringing to England the diaries, etc., of Dr. Livingstone. A telegraphed invitation had met him on landing, and on his reply the party was rapidly gathered. After dinner, before the ladies left us, Stanley narrated very dramatically for the first time, the story of his successful search. He subsequently repeated his story in public to the British Association.

" I have no note of the date when it was known that Gore Lodge was to be demolished to make way for the present flats, and that all efforts to secure an extension of the lease had failed. It was about this time, for I remember spending many days during an Oxford vacation seeking houses which might provide a new home. Gore Lodge had been a most suitable and characteristic setting for Lady Franklin's tastes and habits, and I cannot doubt that the break up of her home at her advanced age (she was then past eighty—though I did not realize that) not only shortened her few remaining years, but also robbed them of their zest, and weakened her mental powers. I had no opportunity of seeing her during vacations in the last months of her life, and had left London for the North some time before the monument in Westminster Abbey was unveiled (July 1875), without any warning that her condition was so precarious. The news of her death so soon after I left came as a shock. It suddenly shut the door upon a relationship brimming over with kindliness, which I had come to value more and more as I grew up.

" Philip Lyttleton Gell.

" August 22nd, 1922."

SUPPLEMENT TO PART IV

AMERICAN LETTERS

1849–1859

LADY FRANKLIN'S American correspondence, especially the Grinnell letters, are of permanent as well as timely interest, and the following selection will be found a valuable contribution to the literature of Anglo-American relations.

The Lady of Sir John Franklin to the President, U.S.A.

Spring Gardens, London.
December 11th, 1849.

Sir,

I had the honor of addressing you, in the month of April last, on behalf of my husband, Sir John Franklin, his officers and crews, who were sent by Her Majesty's Government, in the spring of 1845, on a maritime expedition for the discovery of the North-West Passage, and who have never since been heard of.

Their mysterious fate has excited, I believe, the deepest interest throughout the civilized world, but nowhere more so, not even in England itself, than in the United States of America. It was under a deep conviction of this fact, and with the humble hope that an appeal to those generous sentiments would never be made altogether in vain, that I ventured to lay before you the necessities of that critical period, and to ask you to take up the cause of humanity which I pleaded, and generously make it your own.

How nobly you, sir, and the American people, responded to that appeal, how kindly and courteously that response was con-

LIFE OF LADY FRANKLIN

veyed to me, is known wherever our common language is spoken
or understood ; and though difficulties, which were mainly owing
to the advanced state of the season, presented themselves after
your official announcement had been made known to our government, and prevented the immediate execution of your intentions,
yet the generous pledge you had given was not altogether with-
drawn, and hope still remained to me that, should the necessity
for renewed measures continue to exist, I might look again across
the waters for the needed succour.

A period has now, alas ! arrived, when our dearest hopes
as to the safe return of the discovery ships this autumn are finally
crushed by the unexpected, though forced, return of Sir James
Ross, without any tidings of them, and also by the close of the
Arctic season. And not only have no tidings been brought of
their safety or of their fate, but even the very traces of their
course have yet to be discovered ; for such was the concurrence
of unfortunate and unusual circumstances attending the efforts
of the brave and able officer alluded to, that he was not able
to reach those points where indications of the course of the discovery ships would most probably be found. And thus, at the
close of a second season since the departure of the recent expedition of search we remain in nearly the same state of ignorance
respecting the missing Expedition as at the moment of its starting
from our shores. And in the meantime, our brave countrymen,
whether clinging still to their ships or dispersed in various directions, have entered upon a fifth winter in those dark and dreary
solitudes, with exhausted means of sustenance, while yet their
expected succour comes not !

It is in the time, then, of their greatest peril, in the day of
their extremest need, that I venture, encouraged by your former
kindness, to look to you again for some active efforts which may
come in aid of those of my own country, and add to the means of
search. Her Majesty's ministers have already resolved on sending an expedition to Bering's Strait, and doubtless have other
necessary measures in contemplation, supported as they are, in
every means that can be devised for this humane purpose, by the

198

sympathies of the nation and by the generous solicitude which our Queen is known to feel in the fate of her brave people imperilled in their's country's service. But, whatever be the measures contemplated by the Admiralty, they cannot be such as will leave no room or necessity for more, since it is only by the multiplication of means, and those vigorous and instant ones, that we can hope, at this last stage, and in this last hour, perhaps, of the lost navigators' existence, to snatch them from a dreary grave. And surely, till the shores and seas of those frozen regions have been swept in all directions, or until some memorial be found to attest their fate, neither England, who sent them out, nor even America, on whose shores they have been launched in a cause which has interested the world for centuries, will deem the question at rest.

May it please God so to move the hearts and wills of a great and kindred people, and of their chosen Chief Magistrate, that they may join heart and hand in the generous enterprise! The respect and admiration of the world, which watches with growing interest every movement of your great republic, will follow the chivalric and humane endeavour, and the blessing of them who were ready to perish shall come upon you!

I have the honor to be, sir, with great respect,

Your grateful and obedient servant,

JANE FRANKLIN.

To His Excellency the President of the United States.

Henry Grinnell to Lady Franklin.

My dear Madam,

I wrote you yesterday. I have this morning received a letter from Lieutenant Rogers, declining to accept the command of the contemplated Expedition.* His letter, or rather a copy, I

* Lieut. de Haven, aet. 34, with passed Midshipman Griffin, aet. 24, as his second in command, eventually led the Expedition.

LIFE OF LADY FRANKLIN

enclose. I shall now fall back on my original idea, which I think the best after all.

I shall purchase two small schooners of about seventy tons and put them in order as soon as possible, and take the chance of procuring officers and men. I intend they shall sail about the 1st of May.

With much respect,
Your friend,
HENRY GRINNELL.

Henry Grinnell to Lady Franklin.

New York,
March 19th, 1850.

Dear Madam,

Your note of the 22nd February came duly to hand, as also the papers accompanying it. I have made some progress with the expedition, having purchased one vessel of ninety-one tons, and am now in treaty for another of about one hundred tons, which I shall probably purchase this day or to-morrow. The one purchased is in the ship carpenter's hands, going through the process of strengthening, etc. I hope yet to see these vessels take their departure from Sandy Hook for Lancaster Sound. Lieutenant de Haven is now here assisting me. I see no insurmountable difficulty in the way, except procuring men, and here there is a difficulty. The officers who are to command this Expedition are all from the Navy, and they say it is indispensable that the discipline in the Expedition should be military, otherwise there will be but little chance of any fortunate result. To get rid of this obstruction, I shall probably have to apply to our Government, and obtain the passage of an Act giving the Secretary of the Navy power to furnish men from the Navy. I have already sounded the President and his Cabinet, and they send me word that everything they can legally do they are disposed to do. I shall go on with the vessels and leave nothing undone that I have the power of doing, so that if the Expedition

200

HENRY GRINNELL, ESQ.
From a Photograph by Alex. Bassano

LIFE OF LADY FRANKLIN

does not go, I cannot censure myself.   My expectation is that I
shall be able to remove all difficulties.

I refer you to Mr. Burrows' letter for further particulars.

With much respect,

I am your friend,

HENRY GRINNELL.

P.S.—A numerously signed petition to Congress to allow thirty
men from the U.S. Navy to man Mr. Grinnell's vessels was sent
in on March 30th.

Captain Phillips superintended the equipping of the ninety-
ton schooner, *Prince Albert*, which was commanded by Captain
Forsyth.   He returned before the end of 1850, and the *Prince
Albert* was at once sent out again by Lady Franklin in command
of Mr. Kennedy in 1851.   He unfortunately went to the N.W.,
instead of, as Lady Franklin insisted, to the S.W. of the Gulf of
Boothia ; exploring Wellington Channel, instead of the shore of
King William Island, but he discovered the fact of the existence
of a channel between Boothia and North Somerset and named it
after Lieutenant Bellot of the French Navy, who, as well as Sir
John Franklin's old companion in 1819, the seaman John Hepburn,
were with him on board.

Lady Franklin to Henry Grinnell.

33 Spring Gardens,

19th April, 1850.

My dear Sir,

Every letter I receive from you and Mr. Burrows convinces
me more and more what an arduous work you have taken in hand,
so arduous and prompted by so lofty a spirit of generous philanthropy that in your own touching and energetic language it seems
to you that the successful crowning of your enterprize will make
you " feel as though your work was done on this earth."   May
it please God to reward this self-sacrificing and noble devotion

LIFE OF LADY FRANKLIN

and though this one work alone is enough *whatever be its issue,* to make your life illustrious, may you live to do good in many ways for long years to come in the favour of God and honoured and beloved by men. I do so entirely sympathize and agree with you in your view of the necessity of getting naval authority over your crew that I assure you I should be better satisfied at your *abandoning* the enterprize than at your undertaking it under fearful disadvantages; I should feel with you that it would be a heavy burden of responsibility to bear if such a hazardous Expedition were launched without every possible safeguard. If your earnest endeavour to obtain this object should unfortunately fail, do not distress yourself on my account; you have done all that *man could do.* My debt of gratitude will be the same as ever.

There are two points of search so totally unprovided for at present that we are striving at home by private means if we can add one small vessel to the universal Expedition for the especial search of one of these. I think I mentioned them before, viz., Smith's Sound in one direction and Regent's Inlet with its W. Passage in another; I enclose a plan of the latter. Our Government has done so much that I cannot attempt to strive to obtain more from them, nor can I much expect that the public in general should take any other view of the question than that with six ships despatched under Admiralty orders about to be afloat, everything ought to be accomplished.

*   *   *   *   *

I beg my kind regards to Lieutenant de Haven and Mr. Griffin. I shall write a line to my kind friend Mr. Burrows.

JANE FRANKLIN.

Henry Grinnell to Lady Franklin.

New York,
30th April, 1850.

My dear Madam,

I wrote you this morning, since which I have received a letter from the President, of which the following is a copy :—

LIFE OF LADY FRANKLIN

Washington,
April 29th, 1850.

Henry Grinnell, Esq.,
New York.

Dear Sir,

Your favour of the 25th inst. has been duly received. You have doubtless had the gratification to observe that the Bill authorizing the Executive to furnish officers and seamen to the vessels which you have in so liberal a spirit fitted out to join in search of John Franklin has already passed the House of Representatives. It will doubtless pass the Senate at an early day and I have only to add that I shall be happy to give the assistance of the proper departments under the law in the most efficient manner, so as to contribute as far as possible to the success of the Expedition. I cannot doubt that it will redound to the great credit of its projector and the country.

I remain, with high regards,
Yours very sincerely,
Z. TAYLOR.

Lieutenant de Haven to Henry Grinnell.
U.S. Brig Advance
off St. John's, Newfoundland.
June 7th, 1850.

My dear Sir,

My progress this year has been much slower than I anticipated, in consequence of heavy winds and heavy weather,—in a gale on the 29th we parted from our consort* ; this, however, was not a subject of regret to me, as her sluggish movements retarded our progress considerably, and I thought that both vessels would make better progress separated. The sailing qualities of this vessel are admirable. We have had several opportunities of trying her speed with coasters and fishermen, and beat them all with ease. She will no doubt improve, too, as she becomes lighter. Yesterday we made the Southern Cape

---

* The *Rescue*.

LIFE OF LADY FRANKLIN

of Newfoundland and at the same time fell in with several ice-
bergs. We have continued to meet them since and now have at
least twenty in sight around us.

The officers and men are all in good health and spirits, and with
myself are sanguine as to the success of the enterprise which you
had the mind to conceive and the ability to institute. There
is a vessel now near us, by which I hope to be able to forward
to you these few lines, probably the last that you will receive from
us until the fall. I write to the Secretary also. With many kind
regards for your family.

I am, Sir,

Truly and gratefully yours,

EDWIN J. DE HAVEN.

Mr. Henry Grinnell was as voluminous a writer as Lady Franklin
herself, and in the year 1850 he was in constant communication
with Lady Franklin. He gave his son an introduction to her,
and her invariable kindness and warmhearted reception of all
who took a practical interest in what, during the fifties, was the
absorbing object of her life, caused Robert Grinnell to write to
his father, " Her manners are so kind and agreeable that before
we parted I really loved her."

Mr. Henry Grinnell to Lady Franklin.   New York.
7th October, 1851.

My dear Lady Franklin,

I intended to have written to you by this steamer a full account
of the proceedings of the *Advance* and *Rescue,* or rather my reflection of them, but I must defer it for the present. The *Rescue*
came in this morning and I have been all day with the officers;
they as well as the officers of the *Advance* have not yet come down
to serious thoughts, being much excited by their return home and
meeting with their friends. I am happy to say that every man
that went out in the Expedition has returned home in good
health ; this to me is a great satisfaction, but I feel sad, sad, that
the great object of the Expedition has not been accomplished.
Your husband and your countrymen have not been rescued and

LIFE OF LADY FRANKLIN

restored to their home and country. I find no fault with the
officers and men of the American Expedition ; they have done
all that could be expected of them ; there is not one of them that
would not go on a similar Expedition if their services were required.

You ask me a very grave question, what will my Government
do, provided your Government do not send out another Expedition ? I cannot answer this at present. My Government simply
carry out the will and voice of the people. What that is time
must disclose, but, my dear Lady, so far as I am able to judge,
the prevailing opinion is in this country that all hope is extin-
guished ; there are some, the officers of the American Expedition,
myself and some few others, still think there is a lingering hope.

By the American steamer for South Hamilton I sent you a
list from the papers announcing the arrival of the *Advance*. I
now enclose some duplicates.

Most sincerely I am,

With great respect,

Your friend,

HENRY GRINNELL.

In a letter, dated New York, 18th November, 1851, Mr. Grinnell
says that he has offered his ships again to the Government, and
has received from the Naval Secretary the following answer :—

Navy Department,

10th November, 1851,

Sir,

Your letter of the 8th instant on the subject of another expedition for the search for Sir John Franklin and his party, and
lending to the Department for that service the two brigs *Advance*
and *Rescue* has been received and respectfully considered. The
Department will very willingly lend its aid in fitting out another
expedition to the Arctic regions in search of Sir John Franklin
and his companions, should Congress authorize it. *It does tender
you thanks for your generous offer.*

I am, very respectfully,

Your obedient servant,

W. A. GRAHAM.

205

LIFE OF LADY FRANKLIN

A copy of the New York paper, *The Albion*, of November the 8th, 1851, gives a very full account of a banquet given by British residents of New York, on November 4th, in honour of Mr. Grinnell and of the American officers recently returned from the North Polar Seas. The English consul at the port was in the chair ; and on either side of him, Griffin, who had commanded the *Rescue*, and Cornelius Grinnell, representing his father, who was not present.

Lieutenant de Haven of the *Advance* was also unable to be there. After a well merited eulogy of Mr. Grinnell by the chairman, his son replied.

The best speeches were made by Griffin, and by Dr. Kane the intrepid Arctic explorer, whose book was at the time anxiously expected, and by a New York merchant, Mr. R. Irvin.

The whole tone of the meeting was one of regret that they had not found and brought back Franklin and his men, and confidence that they would still be able to do so. This note comes out very clearly in the toasts which the three speakers above mentioned proposed at the end of their speeches. Passed Midshipman Griffin's was " Health, happiness, and success to Captain Kennedy of the *Prince Albert*, his officers and men." Dr. Kane who said in the course of his speech " God bless old Sir John Ross ; there is but one British officer I would more gladly meet than he, and that is the one we were all in search of, Sir John Franklin (cheers). I speak as if he were still alive, and I do so because in all our explorations and in those of others, I have seen nothing to convince me to the contrary (cheers), and I earnestly hope the search is not ended, and that the rescue of Sir John Franklin is yet reserved to his nation and the world. In conclusion allow me to give you this sentiment—' The Country of Sir John Franklin. Honoured in all the records of his adventurous life, and still more honoured in the record of her attempts to rescue him.' "

The toast was hailed with loud acclamations.

Silver medals were then presented to each of the officers, and two days later to all the crews ; later in the evening other enthusiastic speeches were made. Mr. Irvin concluded a fine speech thus :—" Sir, they must not be abandoned. Even if they have perished we want to know where and how they sunk under their sufferings. We want to track their pathway through the cheerless waste, and to know and mark to all time, the spot where their humble spirits bowed to the Will of God, and they laid them down to their last sleep. We want to recover the memorials they left behind them, the records of their trials and sufferings, their last tokens of affection to friends and kindred ; perhaps some touching memento from their gallant chief to his noble and devoted wife, whose name will go down to posterity almost as illustrious as his own. In the confidence that they will not be abandoned, Sir, allow me to give you as a toast, ' the next Expedition in search of Sir John Franklin and his comrades—may it be honoured to bring them back in safety to their Country.' "

Young Mr. Grinnell said that for the last two years Sir John Franklin had occupied all his father's thoughts ; and that he felt that his work was not yet finished. He ended by giving, at the request of his father, the following toast : " The rescue of Sir John Franklin and his companions ; may it never be abandoned until his fate shall have been positively ascertained."

Lady Franklin to Mr. Henry Grinnell.

Bedford Place,
November 21st, 1851.

My dear Mr. Grinnell,

Yesterday and the day before there came a shower of your New York papers, all genial and refreshing, full of the banquet and the medals, of the praises of one who does not love to be praised, and of the well-deserved honours paid to the brave men who have so worthily accomplished his and the nation's bidding. You may be sure that we have been very much gratified with all this. I am proud and delighted that my countrymen in New York have thus nobly expressed their own feelings and that of the nation to which they belong. There is not an Englishman at home who does not feel that his own heartfelt sentiments were spoken on that festive occasion, and it was so kind and generous of them all, and of the American officers in particular, to express that noble confidence and hope in the future. Without doubt the cypress as well as the laurel ought to have hung on the festive walls, but in the strength of that we look for renewed exertion and long enduring effort. The sentiments of our own country-men and allies in America will be reflected here and give new stimulus to our people, amongst whom, however, there is not wanting, and especially amongst those who best understand the subject, a very high degree of revived interest and hope. Many of the best Arctic Authorities (if Authority has anything to do in the matter) think our prospects more hopeful now than they appeared two or three years ago, doubtless on account of the search being narrowed and the course taken by the missing ships ascertained. I believe I may state that Sir Edward Parry and Sir J. Richardson are of this opinion. What charming speech makers are Dr. Kane and Mr. Griffin, and how kindly the latter spoke of my poor little *Prince Albert*, now left all alone with the " red cross of St. George at her poop " in those icy solitudes. I am glad he formed so good an opinion of the crew. What a pity Captain de Haven was obliged to be absent, and shall I say the same of you, or rather shall I not sympathize with that truly English feeling, rare perhaps even among Englishmen, but very rare indeed in people of any other race, that shrinks from applause and suffers not the left hand to know what the right hand doeth. Your son worthily filled your place, and what a noble toast you put into his mouth! I am grateful for it and for all your generous intentions respecting your own two little ships and for moving Congress to take up the cause afresh. . .

And now with a heart overflowing with gratitude and affec-tion, may I not say, to you for all you have done for me, and all you are trying to do,

Believe me, dear Mr. Grinnell, sincerely yours,

JANE FRANKLIN.

Sophy is much pleased by your kind remembrance and the privilege you gave her of writing to you. I wish there was a

LIFE OF LADY FRANKLIN

spare Arctic medal and that I could get possession of it, but I fear this is out of the question. Is it not ?

Lady Franklin to Mr. Grinnell.   21 Bedford Place,
                                                        November 28th, 1851.

My dear Mr. Grinnell,

I am about to send to the American Embassy two volumes of Sir J. Richardson's just published work, of which I will beg your kind acceptance. Should they be thought, however, too large and heavy for the Embassy bag, I must defer them until early in January, when Mr. Alfred Wallie, an American gentleman who has lately brought me a letter from Dr. Bartlett of New York, has offered to take back with him anything I may have to send.

Dr. Bartlett tells me I am to have a silver medal as a specimen of the honor paid to your well-deserving officers and men. I wish it had arrived; I long so much to look at and show it, and I am very anxious also to have a full and particular description (a drawing would be still better) of the gold medal which has been presented to you, my best and kindest of friends. They have acted just after my own heart, my good countrymen in New York.

Yesterday I was indulged with the reading of Commander de Haven's very interesting letter to our Admiralty written off Proven. This was a very kind and considerate act, which I much appreciated.

It falls to my excellent friend, Mr. Barrow, in the absence of Captain Hamilton, to acknowledge this mark of respect and attention, and he is pleased with his commission. He will probably tell Captain de Haven how much valued it would be if he would send an abstract of his Arctic labours to the Admiralty at as early a period as possible in order that they may be printed with our own Arctic Papers at the opening of Parliament by order of the House.

I am obliged to conclude rather abruptly, my head being very painful.   Believe me with sincerest regard,

Ever yours,
(Signed) JANE FRANKLIN.

LIFE OF LADY FRANKLIN

My dear Sir,

My Aunt is too unwell to add more, but wishes me to mention that in the report of the Geographical Society, the speech of M. Osborn is very imperfectly given, but that it was received with much enthusiasm and entirely dispersed the gloomy feelings which had been elicited by the dreary picture presented by Captain Ommaney. The officers of your late Expedition will remember Lieutenant Osborn when in command of the *Pioneer*.

I am, dear Sir,

S.C.

Lady Franklin to Dr. Kane.

December 19th, 1851.

My dear Mr. Kane.

Your letter has given me great comfort and satisfaction; I hardly know how to thank you for it sufficiently. We are longing for the appearance of your book ; it will, I am sure, be one of the most graphic, most touching, and most eloquent histories of Arctic adventure, if I may judge by the few specimens I have seen of your able pen, and what I have heard of it and your ardent and generous heart.

You cannot indeed do me greater service than by counteracting the despondency and very irrational impression which seems to have been produced by the return of all the expeditions, and which in this country have been aggravated by the fortuitous assertions of Sir John Ross and Captains Austin and Ommaney that my husband and his companions must, after one winter spent at Beechey Islands, have turned their backs upon their work, and in returning home perished in Baffin's Bay ; a "fool libel" indeed, as Lieutenant Osborn calls it, on those brave men, and in direct opposition to the declared intentions of my husband, who, in a letter to Colonel Sabine from Whale Fish Island, tells him that if after a second winter the health of his crews permit, he would have some new plans, thus contemplating even in the third year the starting afresh at it even on a new Expedition."

* * * * * * *

210

LIFE OF LADY FRANKLIN

The Secretary of the United States Navy to Lady Franklin.

Navy Department of the United States,
Washington.

January 12th, 1853.

" My dear Madam,

I thank you very heartily for your letter of the 3rd of December, and for the very kind terms in which you speak of my young friend Dr. Kane. It has afforded me a very lively gratification to have it in my power to second his generous zeal on your behalf, by giving him permission to join the new expedition, which, through the aid of Mr. Grinnell and Mr. Peabody, and others in your own country, is about once more to tempt the perils of Arctic navigation in search of your gallant and unfortunate husband. I am very sensible of the important service which the skill and experience as well as the high scientific accomplishments of Dr. Kane may enable him to render in this interesting adventure, and, therefore, did not hesitate to give to him every facility which my position in the control of the American Navy had placed at my disposal. I shall comply with his wish, in giving him a few valuable subordinates who may be found necessary to his immediate service, and I have already commended his enterprize to the favourable notice of Congress, to bespeak for him such consideration hereafter as may enable him to turn his labours to the best account. I am happy also to assure you that what I have done in this matter touches the heart of our country and opens it to the most earnest sympathy in your cause. The participation of Mr. Grinnell in this noble act of philanthropy, which has been inspired by your anxiety and suffering, is regarded here as you regard it in England, and already finds its reward in universal commendation.

I am much obliged to you for the chart published by your Admiralty. I, with my countrymen, trace with great interest the progress of the adventurous voyagers whose track is there delineated, and we shall await with new crews and eager expectation the tidings which shall bring us the further research of our friends who are now preparing to cast themselves upon the same rough seas and dangerous pathways of the North. That you may see how the Government responds to your hopes and wishes I take the liberty to send you, with this, the newest report of this Department, which is now submitted to the attention of Congress. I am sure it will gratify you to know that all I have said in it, in regard to yourself and the Expedition to which I have attached Dr. Kane, is received by the members of our National Legislature with the kindest approbation and with the unqualified commendation of the President, who unites with me in the most sincere good wishes to yourself and earnest prayer for the success of your Expedition,

I beg you to believe, my dear Madam,

that I am most truly and faithfully,

Your obedient servant,

J. P. KENNEDY.

It has been very justly observed by Dr. Guillemard in his article in *Blackwood* on " Franklin and the Arctic," that " Franklin added to our sum of knowledge as much after his death as before it ; for it was the ceaseless endeavour to discover him that made our knowledge of the Arctic what it is."

1847-1854

It may not be out of place here to give a short resumé of the work done in sending out search expeditions between the years 1848 and 1854.

The *Erebus* and *Terror* having been victualled for three years, which Sir John said might possibly be made to do for four, it was clear when in 1847 no news had reached England from them and the three years would be up early in 1848, that something must be done at once by way of relief. So in the summer of 1847 the Government arranged with the Hudson's Bay Co. to despatch large supplies of provisions to all their most northern stations and to warn all the Indians to be on the lookout to assist any of the crews they might fall in with.

212

LIFE OF LADY FRANKLIN

Large rewards were offered to the masters of all the whaling ships for any news of the ships or their progress, and for any reliable information regarding the fate of the missing Expedition a reward of £2,000 was offered by Lady Franklin.

In 1848 nothing having yet been heard of the ships the Government sent out the *Enterprise*, 471 tons, and the *Investigator*, 420 burthen, under Captain Sir James Ross with Captain Edward Bird second in command. Also a second expedition was sent under Sir John Richardson and Mr. John Rae to examine the northern coast of America, whilst a third expedition consisting of the *Heron* and *Plover*, under Captain Kennett and Commander Moore, was sent to Bering Strait. Sir James Ross sailed from England on June 12th, just a year and a day after Sir John Franklin died and sixteen days after the final abandoning of the *Erebus* and *Terror* and the start on April 26th, 1848, for their last journey under Captains Crozier and Fitzjames for Back's Fish River. The officers and men then numbering 105 souls, there having been apparently 33 deaths during the past three years.

Sir James Ross was beset by the ice to the north of the spot where the *Erebus* and *Terror* had been so long imprisoned. He missed the *North Star*, which had been sent out with provisions for his use, and returned to England in the autumn of 1849. Sir John Richardson also returned about the same time without success, and now the Government offered £20,000, to which Lady Franklin added £3,000, to any exploring parties who had been able to render efficient assistance to Sir John Franklin, his ships or their crews. The Government lost no time in re-equipping and re-commissioning Sir James Ross's ships and sending them out in command of Captain Collinson and Commander M'Clure, and these vessels left England in January, 1850, and in May a squadron consisting of the *Resolute* and *Assistance* with the steam tenders *Intrepid* and *Pioneer*—the first full-powered steamers employed in the ice, and with such good results that steam whalers became the order of the day in future,—sailed under command of Captains Horatio Austin and Erasmus Ommaney. But Lady Franklin would leave no stone unturned, and hence the correspondence

LIFE OF LADY FRANKLIN

we have given above with Captain Penny, who with Captain Stewart sailed in a couple of whaling brigs named the *Lady Franklin* and the *Sophia* under Government orders to Jones' Sound and Wellington Channel in April, 1850.

Captain Ommaney discovered the spot on Beechey Island at the southern end of Wellington Channel, where Franklin had passed his first winter after a most successful exploration of that channel as far north as lat. 77 and all round Cornwallis Island; and subsequently Captain Penny found on Beechey Island the graves of three of the seamen who had died there.

Meantime, Lady Franklin at her own expense equipped and sent out the 90-ton schooner, *Prince Albert*, under Captain Forsyth, and Sir John Ross in his 74th year took out a small schooner and a little 12-ton yacht, so that there were fifteen vessels all engaged in the search for Sir John's Expedition in the autumn of 1850. All these ships returned in 1851 except the *Enterprise* and *Investigator*. These vessels spent four winters in the ice. Coming from the west by the Straits of Magellan, they parted company in the Pacific and never met again, but Captain M'Clure has the honour of having discovered one, if not two, north-west passages, and to him and his crew in the *Investigator* the Government awarded the sum of £10,000 for the discovery. This was in 1854, and, of course, it was not known until the *Fox* (Captain M'Clintock) returned in 1859, that Sir John Franklin had made the discovery of a North-West Passage a good deal to the south of M'Clure's as early as 1847. The *Prince Albert* had returned in 1850, and was at once re-equipped by Lady Franklin and sent out in 1851 under command of Captain Kennedy. It is interesting to know that the veteran John Hepburn, who was with Sir John in his adventurous land journey in 1819, was one of the crew of the *Prince Albert* in this, its second expedition. Another was the French naval officer, Lieutenant Bellot, after whom the strait is named separating Boothia Felix from North Somerset, which Captain Kennedy discovered to be an island.

Lady Franklin, not satisfied with what was accomplished now in the autumn of 1852, fitted out as her third personal contribu-

LIFE OF LADY FRANKLIN

tion to the cause, the little screw steamer *Isabel*, under Commander Inglefield, who returned within three months. But the Government had not been inactive, and in April, 1852, had sent out the recently returned ships *Assistance, Resolute, Intrepid and Pioneer*, with the *North Star* (Captain Pullen) attached as a depot ship. Sir Edward Beechey was in command of the squadron, with Captains Kellett, M'Clintock and Sherard Osborn under him. It is curious that all these expeditions were directed to Wellington Channel and the north, whereas Franklin, who had explored that channel before his first winter, had been instructed to direct his investigations to the south-west and not the north-west, and indeed it was in the south-west portion of the map of the Arctic regions that he had discovered the North-West Passage.

All these four ships were unnecessarily abandoned in Melville Sound, by Sir Ed. Beechey in May, 1854, and the officers and crews were brought back to England in the *North Star, Talbot* and *Phoenix*, but the *Resolute*, which had rescued the crew of M'Clure's vessel the *Investigator* in 1852, subsequently, as the ice broke up, drifted out by Barrow Strait, through Lancaster Sound and Baffin's Bay to Davis' Strait, a distance of nearly 1,000 miles, where she was picked up in September, 1855, by the American whaler, *George Henry* (Captain J. M. Buddington), and finding her watertight, he decided, with a skeleton crew such as could be spared from the whaling barque, to take her into the American port of New London, which he reached on Christmas Eve, 1855. Her Majesty waived all claim to her and handed her over to Captain Buddington. The Americans bought her for 40,000 dollars, repaired and refitted her and sent her back to England as a gift from the American people to Queen Victoria, December 1856.

The abandonment of this whole squadron put a stop to all further Government search expeditions; and things were no better in America. The ship *Advance*, equipped and sent out from America by Henry Grinnell in 1850, was again equipped in 1853 by Messrs. Grinnell and George Peabody, and Dr. Elisha Kane was put in command. He wintered in lat. 78. 38, but after

215

LIFE OF LADY FRANKLIN

two years in the ice, he had to abandon her and made his way with all his men to the W. Coast of Greenland and got back to New York in October, 1855. But whilst Kane was still held fast in the ice,—the Hudson Bay Co. had in 1853 engaged Dr. Rae to complete a survey on the west coast of Boothia Felix. He, in 1854, met some Esquimaux in Pelly Bay, from whom he got some information about the *Erebus* and *Terror*, and also obtained various articles which had evidently belonged to officers on those ships, and returned to England, and although he had not made out for certain what had been the actual fate of the Expedition, the Government made sure that they were lost, and voted Dr. Rae the sum of £10,000 as a reward for his discovery. This was in 1854, and a further expedition undertaken by the Hudson Bay Co., in 1855, under the leadership of Mr. Anderson, added little to what Dr. Rae had discovered.

Lady Franklin was now the only person left to continue the efforts which were so apparently hopeless, to find out what had been the fate of the missing ships ; though the hope of her seeing her husband again must have long been given up. She had herself sent out three vessels, and still another was to be equipped by her before she could cease her splendid and tireless activities.

Lieutenant Hartstene to Lady Franklin.
Recd. 31st October, 1855.

> U.S. Barque *Release*
> Lievely, Isle of Disco.
> September 18th, 1855.

My dear Madam,

In accepting the tablet to be erected to the memory of your gallant and universally lamented husband, I felt myself in charge of a sacred trust, and had indulged the hope of fulfilling it in a manner agreeable to your own and my wishes, but the severity of the last two seasons had so effectually blocked Lancaster Sound with heavy-packed ice as to have prevented my getting beyond Cape Bullen, although strenuous efforts were made with our

steamer on both shores to force a passage. It is a source of deep
regret that though we have closely examined both shores of Baffin's
Bay, Smith Sound as far as the ice would permit to Pelham Point,
and Lancaster Sound as far as Cape Bullen on the north and Stanley Point on the south, and have been successful in finding Dr.
Kane and his associates, no traces whatever were discovered of
the long-absent *Erebus* and *Terror*. As we are *en route* for the
U. States, I have thought it advisable to leave the tablet in charge
of Mr. Olrick, the Royal Inspector at this place, believing that it
will be more convenient to be removed thence when an opportunity
shall offer.

With respects and sympathy,
I am, dear Madam,
Very respectfully,
Your obedient servant,
H. J. HARTSTENE,
Lt. Commanding
U.S. Arctic Expedition.

Mr. Grinnell to Lady Franklin.

New York. 19th February, 1856.

My dear Lady,

I have to acknowledge the receipt of your and Miss Sophie's
letter of the 25th of January, accompanied with the report of Dr.
Kane to the Admiralty, as also the very interesting paper read
before the Paris Geographical Society, giving to your husband
and his party the first discovery of the North-West Passage.
This paper expresses my view entirely. . . . . I will take care,
so far as lies in my power, that your husband's party shall have the
credit which I am of the opinion it is justly entitled to in this
country, and I may say there is no question on the subject with
those who understand it. I learn from Mr. Perkins, of the firm of
Perkins and Smith, of New London, that Mr. Crampton, your Minister, has given up all claim to the *Resolute*. This does not satisfy me.
I want our government to pay the salvage and send that ship to
England and give her up to whom she belongs—probably 30 to

LIFE OF LADY FRANKLIN

50,000 dollars would only be required to carry out this object.
It appears to me it is nothing more than ordinary comity between
two nations that such an act should be consummated. There
is not much power invested in our officials, and the slow progress
of obtaining an act of Congress, by which alone it could be done,
is a tedious one to bring about. Mr. Perkins has gone on to
Washington this day in relation to this matter.

Dr. Kane came over from Philadelphia yesterday afternoon
and has been with me this night to a late hour ; he leaves to-morrow morning. The more I see of the Doctor the more I appreciate
him for his talents. I know him intimately. Dr. Hawks says
he is a genius. So think I.

. . . . . The Doctor is now fully engaged with his book, which
will probably be out in the course of a month or six weeks. He
informed me that you should have one of the first copies. I
have no doubt it will be a work that will do credit to him and to the
country.

. . . . . Now as to the political affairs between this country
and yours, rest assured there never can be any war between them.
As I have before stated to you, the *people* of the *two countries*
would never consent to anything of the kind, let Lord Palmerston
and President Pierce act as they may.

At all times, my kind regards to Miss Sophia,
I am with great respect,
Your friendly,
HENRY GRINNELL.

New York. 19th July, 1856.

My dear Lady,

I have yours and Miss Sophia's letters up to the 4th inst.
What seems most important in them to you I will first reply to.
Dr. Kane came to New York day before yesterday and returned
yesterday. He passed an hour or more with me at my house. I
never saw him look so bad ; he is but a skeleton or the shadow of
one ; he has worked too hard. He says he must be off, and now
thinks of leaving in about ten days for Havre, from there to

LIFE OF LADY FRANKLIN

Switzerland; pass a month among the glaciers, quietly, recruit his health and then go to England. I think this is a good plan and one which he will probably adopt. He is every other day attacked with the remittent fever, better known here as a fever and ague. I do not fear for the Doctor's life if he will only carry out his plan or some other equally good. As soon as he comes to a positive determination I will let you know.

With continued respect,
I am, yours truly,
HENRY GRINNELL.

P.S.—*I enclose an extract from my Mother's letter.*"

Dr. Kane is here, but truly miserable. I *never saw him* look so ill. He goes to-morrow to the water cure, and says he has written Neal (Cornelius) that he shall meet him in Switzerland in a *few weeks*. Father is anxious he should comply with Lady Franklin's wishes, but at present he looks as though he would never be able to take another voyage. He has rheumatism, chills and fever, and remains of scurvy.

Dr. Kane to Lady Franklin.

Giraud House,
Philadelphia.
July 24th, 1856.

My dear Lady Franklin,

I have just seen your letter to Mr. Grinnell and write at once to reassure you. It was my intention to have sought repose and health by a few weeks' sojourn in Switzerland, but I will come to England to confer with you, and return for a longer visit after I have attempted to relieve your cares. Probably my friend, Grinnell, will accompany (me) across the Channel and return with me to London at a season better suited for sight-seeing.

For myself, my sole object is to see you and fully say to you much that under our present relations cannot be written. You may keep me according to your pleasure, as my first and only thought will be your interests and those of the cause which you represent.

My book, 900 pages of *ad captandum* sacrifice, has left my hands. It will, at least, establish for me the character of a hard worker, and, with friends like yourself, shew where are my sympathies. Give my best regards to Miss Cracroft and expect a notice of my departure. I shall not leave for at least two weeks.

Mr. Grinnell has perhaps told you that, in common with many of my recent party, the American summer bears hardly upon me. I have no *fault* of health but a complete inability to withstand hot weather and indoor life.

Faithfully always,
Yr. friend and servant,
E. K. KANE.

Mr. Grinnell to Lady Franklin.
Recd. 24th October, 1856.

New York, 3rd September, 1856.

My dear Lady,

I have just received yours of the 18th ult. Dr. Kane was present at the time ; after reading it I gave it to him to read. He has written you a hurried note, which you will find herewith, by which you will notice he answers your question in relation to his letter to you in the affirmative. I went with the Doctor to-day and took passage for himself and servant (Morton, who was with him during the first and second Arctic voyage) in the steamer *Baltic* to leave on the 11th inst. Dr. Betton and family of Philadelphia, with whom the Doctor is intimately acquainted, have taken passage in the same vessel. The Doctor improves slowly in health. I trust it will be entirely restored by his visit to England.

The *Resolute* is being put in complete order at the Navy yard ; new topmasts, top-gallant masts, some new yards, rigging, etc. a complete new suit of sails. She will be fully in order by the 20th and will no doubt take her departure before the 1st of November. It is the intention of this Government to hand her over to yours in an unostentatious quiet manner. I think this is proper.

This country is politically convulsed throughout, and will

continue so until after the 4th of November ; if Freemont is elected President I really fear that something much worse will follow, all occasioned simply on the question whether slavery shall be allowed in territories which the North or South or the General Government have anything to do with. Buchanan stands the best chance, Hillmore next. I am nominated as one of the Hillmore Electors of this State.

My kind regards to Miss Sophia,
I am,
Truly yours,
HENRY GRINNELL.

Lady Franklin, London.

Dr. Kane to Lady Franklin.

Dated 29th August.
Received 20th September, 1856.

My dear Lady Franklin.

Mr. Grinnell has doubtless told you that I have been delayed in Washington, working for the resolution with regard to the purchase and return of the *Resolute*. I write to announce its passage.

This vessel, fitted with a propeller of sufficient power, would in many respects be suited for an expedition and, if intended by the Admiralty for that purpose, would certainly save you much expense and anxiety. Take such action on this suggestion as you may see fit, and expect from me the fullest co-operation. I may yet have time to confer with you by letter before my departure, as I am unwilling to leave for England before recruiting my health. The delay of a few weeks will not affect your interests and I feel that I would do wrong to enter upon fresh labours before being prepared for them.

With my sincere regards to Miss Cracroft,
I am, my dear Madam,
Very faithfully,
Your friend,
E. K. KANE.

Lady Franklin, London.   Philada., August 28th, 1856.

LIFE OF LADY FRANKLIN

Lady Franklin to Mr. Grinnell.

Llanrwst, Denbighshire.
September 18th, 1856.

My dear Mr. Grinnell,

I received your most welcome letter yesterday at Carnarvon, and hasten on our way back to Liverpool to thank you for it and to congratulate you on the successful result of your efforts respecting the *Resolute*. It is a noble achievement on your part, and I hope will be properly appreciated by our Government. There is something of romance in it which captivates my imagination as well as touches my heart. If your magnificent conception and generous feelings did not do this, I should be very dull and very hard indeed, but you must not expect the Admiralty to feel any of the poetry of the incident, still less to be very demonstrative in the matter. Still, I hope they will do their duty, as there are many English hearts who will feel on the occasion all that you or even I can desire. I feel sure that Dr. Kane is much gratified by your success. The Board are all now, I believe, *gadding* about or holiday-making like the rest of the world. By and by—*i.e. to say* in about six weeks from this time,—will I think be the right moment for pressing them for distinct declaration of their intentions, and if these are not such as can reasonably satisfy me, then I shall make bold to ask them for the loan of this noble gift of the *Resolute* with which to accomplish our private expedition. I think there can be little doubt that in one way or the other, in a national or a private expedition, the ship will go into the Arctic seas again. I am particularly pleased with the terms in which the *Times* states she will be presented to the British Government, viz., " in token of the deep interest felt by the United States in the service on which the ship was engaged at the time she was abandoned." I hope the official intimation of the gift will embody some such significant sentiment. I would like to see Dr. Kane arrive, fully restored to health, in command of her, but I do not know whether such a thing could be as his command, so I will try and limit my wishes to the entire recovery of his precious health, about

LIFE OF LADY FRANKLIN

which I am deeply anxious, not for my own sake alone, but for that of his country, his parents, and all who love and honor him.

Received 1st November, 1856

H. Grinnell to Lady Franklin.

New York, 17th October, 1856.

My dear Lady,

Your letter of the 26th ult. I received on board the *Baltic*, seeing Dr. Kane off, about fifteen minutes before she cast off. After reading only a few lines I gave it to the Doctor to read. He scanned it over, but had not time to understand it completely, and before this reaches you you will probably have seen Dr. Kane. He in person can reply to it much better that I can in writing.

. . . . . . I was on board the *Resolute* yesterday; she is now completed and so reported to the Navy Department, nothing more to be done than the appointment of officers and men and placing stores on board. Everything that was found on board on her arrival at the Navy Yard that was in a state of preservation, has been put in as good order as could be, packed in boxes and casks and put on board again. All the stores are returned as well as spare rigging, etc., etc. She is now really a fine looking vessel ; so far as hull, sails, spars, etc., she is in a condition to go on a three or five years cruise in the Arctic regions. The expenses at the Navy Yard will probably be about 15,000 dollars. Her first cost to Government was 40,000. Captain Hartstene will have the command. You may look for her at Portsmouth the last of November.*

In a letter written on November 11th, he says :

" Well, our great political controversy is over and this country is safe for years to come. Mr. Buchanan is elected President for four years from the 4th of March next. Mr. Hillmore was my first love, but I am well satisfied with the result. In visiting the *Resolute* to-day I took with me Mr. Delaine, connected with *The*

* NOTE.—She really sailed on November 13th,

Times. We passed two or three hours together, with others. He takes his departure to-morrow in the steamer. I hope his visit to this country will prove productive of good."

Dr. Kane to Lady Franklin.

> Adelphi Hotel, Liverpool.
> 22nd October.

My dear Lady Franklin.

I have arrived quite an invalid, and am now at the Adelphi, Liverpool. It is only my anxiety to see and confer with you which prevented my immediate departure for some Continental hot baths, and I shall make your residence in London the seat of my first call.

I leave, should nothing change my movements, on Friday, for London, expecting to stay at Morley's.

Pardon the extreme fatigue which shews itself in this letter and believe me, dear Lady Franklin,

> Faithfully your friend,
> E. K. KANE.

Lady Franklin,
    Pall Mall.

Lady Franklin to Dr. Kane.

> Wrangle Vicarage,
>   near Boston,
>   Lincolnshire.
>   25th Oct., 1856.

My dear Dr. Kane,

How much I grieve that the so long desired moment of your arrival finds me distant alike from London and Liverpool upon some family business which will not admit of my taking the first train to meet you. Mr. Robert Grinnell will tell you that we long hoped to be the very first to welcome you at Liverpool, where, or in the neighbourhood within easy recall, our summer has mainly been passed,—but this was not to be, and so far from regretting that you did not arrive sooner in your then state of health, my fear now is lest you should have committed any imprudence in coming so soon. I can permit myself to say this because you well know how delighted I am at the prospect of seeing you and at the conviction that you are at last safe among us, and my greatest anxiety now is that you should not do or think anything to worry you, but give a whole month at least, after consulting one of our best physicians, to the process of cure. It is only a very few days ago that, being at Ben Rhydding and Ilkley Wells in the neighbourhood of Harrogate, we were saying to one another that if we could only know that you were on the eve of arriving we would linger there and persuade you instantly to join us and keep you in that healthy atmosphere, drinking and bathing in (if it were the right thing for you to do) those mineral waters. But in some way or other, and in the most favorable place, we must get you well before we enter upon that business which is so near to our hearts, tho' I find it difficult to thrust it from me in writing to you to whom I owe so much.

I am sure you will be entirely candid with me, and tell me whether from the state of your health or from any other cause, you would find it difficult or inadvisable to meet me at Cambridge on my way into Essex, where, at the house of my sister, Mrs. Majendie of Hedingham Castle, we should have the opportunity for that quiet intercourse which is required, and could discuss other arrangements. I must unfortunately go to Hedingham within a short period, as a deed is lying there awaiting my signature, and I must not omit to tell you that my sister and her husband have long contemplated the pleasure of receiving you there and have made me promise to bring you. Cambridge lies directly in our way from Lincolnshire to Hedingham, and we could spend a day or two there if you liked (as it is a very interesting place) before we proceeded to Hedingham, but in this and in all things you must let me feel that it is your comfort and gratification which will guide my movements.

I received the telegraphic announcement of your arrival along with your kind letter of the 3rd from New York last night, on arriving here from the extreme north of the county, too late

LIFE OF LADY FRANKLIN

to reply to it, and at once I have put off all my visits to my husband's family to hasten to meet you; too happy to do so. I cannot hear from you before Sunday morning, when I shall be at *Lincoln*—to which Post Office will you address your reply? I hope you have already seen Mr. Barrow and Colonel and Mrs. Sabine, who are amongst the few people returned to London.
Sophy begs kind regards.

Most sincerely yours,

JANE FRANKLIN."

Miss Cracroft to Mr. Grinnell.

November 14th 1856.

My dear Mr. Grinnell,

You will, no doubt, hear by the present mail from your son Cornelius, who to our infinite relief has arrived from Paris. He will tell you doubtless that he has been shocked by the appearance of Dr. Kane, whose state he thought *we* received too despondingly, and therefore did not attach to my aunt's strong representations the importance he now finds they should have had. His arrival has accomplished (as we felt it would) the speediest possible removal of poor Dr. Kane to a warmer climate, and he sails for the W. Indies on the 17th. He has been most strongly urged to prefer Madeira, but he has, after much vacillation, decided upon the W. Indies, which has the perhaps overwhelming advantage of being nearest to the United States. I cannot describe to you how unhappy and absorbed my aunt has been by Dr. Kane's illness— and I cannot say anything which will more strongly prove this than that it is considered to jeopardise all our hopes of future search because she cannot turn her mind to the necessary representations to our Government which depend upon her alone. It is most deplorable and unfortunate, but we can only hope that when her mind is in some degree relieved by the fact that Dr. Kane is on his way to such a place as *may* restore him, she will turn to other consideration of vital importance, to the resumption of the search. Without pressure from her, in fact, the Government will not resume it. Her representations will be timed so as to connect themselves with the arrival of the *Resolute*, and

226

LIFE OF LADY FRANKLIN

we have had many enquiries as to whether there had been, or would be, any expression of hope on the part of America that this splendid gift would be applied to the search in which she was originally engaged. Had your Government intimated such an expectation, the object would have been secured, but Dr. Kane fears that they have not done so, and failing this, persons well able to judge have suggested that if some expression of this hope and expectation were put forth in the American newspapers, it would have great weight in England. The *Times* correspondent duly chronicles the facts about the *Resolute*, and if he could add such an observation as I have suggested, it would certainly prove advantageous ; but if he does not, the observations of your own papers upon the point would be copied into the English ones.

My aunt is writing to Mrs. Kane by this mail, and afterwards we go to Camberwell to see Dr. Kane with your son, Cornelius, who tells me that there will be some relations of Mr. Wood in the vessel with Dr. Kane. This, with the fact that he has relations in Cuba to whom he will go, has quieted my aunt's mind upon a point which really has caused me the deepest anxiety on her account, ever since she suggested that she ought to accompany him and see him comfortably settled in his new abode—a step which not only would have irrevocably sealed the fate of the future search, but would have seriously affected her health, by the anxiety of such a position and by the effect of the W. India climate, which is absolutely dangerous to her constitution.

You will like to hear that at the first meeting since the summer of the Geographical Society on Monday last, an unanimous resolution expressed to Dr. Kane the sympathy of the Society and their admiration of his heroism and endurance.

. . . . . . We fear he will be disappointed at the sale of his book in England, but the fact is that people believe it to be full of horrors, and the most unfortunate impression has been produced among those unacquainted with the details of Arctic work, that these are necessarily incidental to a private expedition.

My aunt sends you kindest regards.

S.C.

227

LIFE OF LADY FRANKLIN

Mr. Weld's review, in the *Athenaeum*, though differently intended, has really deterred people from reading it, from the character he gives of the sufferings.

Miss Cracroft to Mr. Grinnell.

November 21st, 1856.

My dear Mr. Grinnell,

As we cannot be quite sure in the absence of your son, Cornelius, from London, that he had written to you by this mail of the departure of Dr. Kane, we send you a few lines to tell you that he embarked for Cuba in the *Orinoco* mail steamer, on Monday last, the 17th. Your son went down with him and saw him on board, and reports that he performed the journey with much more ease and comfort than could have been expected. He has the very best cabin in the ship and will be surrounded by friends anxious to do all in their power for him.

Even more satisfactory than all this has been the result of his having consulted another physician, considered now the most eminent in London. It was this Dr. Watson whom my aunt most earnestly desired he should see from the very first, but he had already spoken to Sir H. Holland, and it was in vain that she pleaded and urged that if he wanted an excuse he might tell Dr. Watson, whom she knows, that he had consulted him to please her.

However, at last he did go, and we have the comfort of knowing that, ill as he is, Dr. W. expresses his hope that the removal to a better climate and repose will restore to him his past health and vigour. So he writes to my aunt, in a letter expressing his high admiration of Dr. Kane, and the favour done him by permitting him to be of any service to one so distinguished. It is an additional comfort, too, that Dr. Watson has inspired Dr. Kane with a full confidence in his great skill and judgment.

S.C.

228

LIFE OF LADY FRANKLIN

C. Grinnell to Lady Franklin.

Star Hotel, Southampton.
December 15th, 1856.

My dear Lady Franklin,

It is well that I came here instead of Portsmouth, as the Queen is to visit the *Resolute* at 10 o'clock to-morrow morning, and the Consul McCroskey has engaged a steamer to take us on board at 8 o'clock. After the Queen's visit I will be able to tell you of Hartstene's movements.

In haste,
Faithfully yours,
C. GRINNELL.

Mr. Grinnell to Lady Franklin.

DEATH OF DR. KANE.

New York,
24th February, 1857.

My dear Lady,

Last evening I intended to devote to writing you and others, but while doing so I received a telegraphic dispatch, dated the 23rd, at New Orleans, as follows :—

" We learn by a private dispatch, that Dr. Kane died at Havana on the 16th inst. The sad intelligence was brought by the *Cahawba*, which arrived at New Orleans yesterday.

" The greatest sympathy," says the dispatch, " was shown by the authorities of the Island, who attended his funeral in a body."

And so the world bids farewell to one of her manliest and noblest sons. It is a consolation, that though a young man, he died in the fulness of his fame. He had not lived in vain, and his memory will be lasting.

This event is not unexpected to me, but now that I know it to be a positive fact, it has such an effect on my mind that I cannot answer your and Miss Sophia's letters by this steamer— but will endeavour to by the next. No doubt the Doctor's remains will be brought to Philadelphia. Cornelius and myself will go there to attend the funeral.

The Geographical Society will meet on the evening of the 26th, when the only business transacted will be in relation to Dr. Kane. I have no doubt it will be an interesting and affecting meeting.

My love to Miss Sophia, and am with great respect,

Your friend,

HENRY GRINNELL.

Lady Franklin,
London.

Miss Cracroft to Mr. Grinnell.

March 13th, 1857.

My dear Sir,

My aunt sends you two letters which will we know have weight with you, and if you can act upon the suggestion they contain, there is no doubt that the Admiralty would at once place the *Resolute* in my aunt's hands for the search. From what we hear, it is not the feeling of the Board as a whole that we have reason to be afraid of, as they would probably not be displeased to have a fair reason for resigning a vessel they do not intend to make use of in the search, and which is therefore valueless to them. All that is wanted is to have a representation of your wish that the ship should be made over to my aunt, signed by a few friends and sympathisers (there need not be many in addition to yourselves) and the thing would be done, we are sure.

Independently of the advantage to my aunt of possessing this fine ship with the costly equipment put into her by you, we feel sure that the fact of its being made over to her for the search which she is compelled to make at her own cost will excite the greatest sympathy and add to the friendly feeling between our countries to which the restoration of the *Resolute* contributed so largely.

LIFE OF LADY FRANKLIN

Miss Cracroft to Mr. Grinnell.   Pall Mall,
                                        August 13th, 1857.
My dear Sir,

        .   .   .   .   .   .

The *Resolute* affair still hangs on, to our very great vexation
and inconvenience, for here we are still in London, detained by it
week after week.   Sir Charles Wood has been formally spoken
to on the subject of giving her up, by several members of the House
of Commons, and he did not give any refusal to their request.
And the same gentlemen with others, members of an influential
deputation to Lord Palmerston, laid the question before him also.
Lord Palmerston shewed (as he has always done) his desire that
the *Resolute* should be yielded for the purpose of an expedition,
and promised to speak to Sir C. Wood about it.   No one has
any hope whatever that *the Government* will send her out, but if
they will give her up, we must try whether public subscriptions
will be sufficient for the provisioning and payment of wages.

We must have already mentioned that your memorial was
called for in the House of Commons, and, with others to the same
effect, has been ordered to be presented and printed.   Apparently,
however, they have not yet been issued, and we hear the pressure
of late upon the printers has been very great.

                                                S.C.

The *Fox* sailed at the beginning of July, but in August, as this
letter shows, there was still some idea of obtaining the *Resolute*,
and provisioning her and sending her out as a tender or depot
ship for the *Fox*.

                        1859
Mr. Henry Grinnell to Lady Franklin.

                                        New York,
                                    12th October, 1859.
My dear Lady,

The information, which reached us on the 8th instant, of the
return to England of Captain M'Clintock, and of the consummation of his object, has caused intense interest and excite-

ment in this country, perhaps quite as much so as in old England ; it is the general subject of conversation, the political affairs of Europe and this country are insignificant in comparison. I can truly say I thank the Great Disposer of events for the result attained by *your expedition* under the command of that most able and excellent officer, M'Clintock. He has acquired a just fame for himself, which the pages of history will never allow to be obliterated.

For yourself, it is better I should say nothing, for I have not the command of words to define the estimate I entertain of your character. I am not alone in this ; the whole community are with me. I am from all quarters congratulated on the event, as though I had a part in bringing it about—it is you, however, that is intended, through me.

I suppose now there can be no question as to your husband's Expedition being the first to ascertain the water communication with the Atlantic and Pacific, north of the American Continent, or otherwise the North-West Passage.

Again with my kind regards to you and Miss Sophia, believe me to remain truly

Your friend,
HENRY GRINNELL.

Lady Franklin in New Zealand

Supplement to page 89

NOTICE

MY book, which contained many interesting letters written by Sir John and Lady Franklin during the six and a half years when he was Governor of Tasmania, was far too long for any publisher to undertake to bring it out, and I had to cut it down to one third of its size. This necessitated the leaving out of a great deal ; and amongst other things the letters describing Lady Franklin's visit to New Zealand were most unfortunately, and quite contrary to my intention, omitted.

I have had these pages now printed and inserted in the end of the volume, and all copies which after this date are sent out to New Zealand will be furnished with them.

W. F. RAWNSLEY.

August 1st, 1923.

IN NEW ZEALAND

From Sir John Franklin to Mrs. Simpkinson.

" Government House,
"23rd February, 1841.

" Jane embarked, leaving this letter to be finished by me, and I undertook to inform you of her having accepted at my recommendation the very kind offer of the captain of the *Favourite* to

take her to New Zealand. The *Favourite* is a sloop of war having
excellent accommodations and a gentlemanly set of officers,
and the season for such a trip is particularly good. I therefore
considered such an opportunity of Jane's seeing New Zealand
should not be lost, . . . and I hope to welcome her home again
by the Queen's birthday, May 24th. Miss Williamson and Mr.
Bagot, my A.D.C., are her companions. The captain's cabin
has been placed entirely at Jane's disposal. Herself, Miss W.
and the maid are to occupy it at night, and I believe arrangements have been made by the officers to invite the captain and
his party to dine with them daily, so that the cabin may be left
for the use of the ladies.

" New Zealand is an object of peculiar interest at all times
and especially now when colonization and emigration are going
so rapidly forward, and the question as to the adjustment of
the titles to the land is on the tapis.

" I heartily wish that I could have accompanied the party.
I went a little way down in the ship, and enjoyed the gratification of seeing the management of a ship-of-war under sail, which
to me is always a great treat."

NOTE—They left Hobarton on the 20th February and arrived
in ten days at Port Nicholson.

Lady Franklin's next letter to her husband is of thirty-five
quarto pages, dated :

" Auckland,
" Government House,
" 21st April, 1841.

" My dearest Love,
" You may have received Port Nicholson papers, and if so,
will have read the address which was presented to me and to
which I returned a verbal answer. I have not seen this paper,
and am therefore ignorant of what they made me say, except
so far as Captain Hobson, from whom I learnt the fact itself,

has communicated to me my sayings. He merely told me, however, that he thought it a very neat speech, and a very proper one, like a good wife who preferred her husband's praises to her own. Hearing that an address was being prepared to present to me, I said I hoped it was not so. But time passed on, and I heard no more of it, and had quite persuaded myself that the threatened shower had passed over, the more so as I had begged Mr. Bagot, who was frightened to death at the idea of it, to make known my feelings, when on the last day while at dinner, and within an hour of our embarkation (in H.M.S. *Favourite*), a rap came at the dining-room door with a request to know when the deputation could be received. Colonel Wakefield was about saying that it was so late they could not be received at all, which, appearing to me rather a rude message, I corrected it in form, though not in substance, by saying I was not prepared for the announcement, and was under the necessity of going on board immediately.

" There was then a proposal to send it after me, a proposal I could not endure, and which on a former occasion I had resisted at Port Phillip, when it was proposed there to send the address after me to Government House at Sydney, but I suggested that if they would give me the address into my own hands or convey it on board, I could in two words thank them *viva voce*, for the honour they intended me, and for the kind sentiments which I felt sure I should find in it, and which I should read as soon as we had embarked.

" With this contrivance I was getting into the boat, and we were making off when Colonel Wakefield, who had taken leave of me, hurried back to say the deputation would come off instantly in another boat to the ship to present the address. It was very rough weather and the captain was very impatient, our own boat bobbed about so much that we had some difficulty in getting on board, and the deck was a scene of noise and bustle under orders to make sail. I went down into the cabin, which was a heap of trunks, boxes and bedding, in the utmost confusion, rolling about, and ourselves holding on. In this position and expecting every instant to be under weigh, it was announced to me that the deputation had arrived, and I was asked where I would receive them. I determined in the cabin, tho' there was no room as yet for them to stand, preferring this to the deck, where the scene would have been a matter of amusement for all the officers. Two gentlemen whom I did not know, and whose names I am yet ignorant of, presented me with the parchment, or, rather, requested first to be allowed to read it to me. I thought I was to have been spared this ; however it could not be helped, so all of us holding on by the table as well as we could, we listened to your praises, and then I made, I assure you, a very pretty and ready reply, for I watched sharply what they said to me, and according to prescriptive rule slightly alluded to all, or most of it. There was nobody I cared about who was listening, and Mr. Bagot looked as gracious and happy as a prince, seeing, as he did, that I spoke for myself, and that it was not he who would have to speechify for me. . . . .

" I learnt from Colonel Wakefield that the 110,000 acres which have been confirmed to the N.Z. Company, at and around Port Nicholson, are all taken up and that their next purchaser. must take their land in another district, their right to which is still in abeyance. Colonel Wakefield told me that if I, or any-body belonging to me, wished to make any future purchase, the best way to do it would be to purchase in London of the New Zealand Company and then send out here to an agent to select, and that he would be happy at any time to be of any service.

" To return to Port Nicholson, and our voyage ; we arrived there in ten days, I went on board a little disordered inside, and my complaint increasing with the motion of the ship it turned into a species of slight dysentery, which reduced me extremely, so that the first two days after anchoring I was not well enough to land, and on the third, when I did land, I was not strong enough to walk from the beach to Colonel W's. house, tho' only a few hundred yards, but had to be carried. The complaint however had left me, and during the few days I was on shore I recovered, to the astonishment almost of Dr. Kilroy and everybody else. Colonel Wakefield has a very comfortable house. He gave me a sitting-room and two bedrooms for our exclusive use, besides the free use of the dining-room, and of another private sitting-room which had a fireplace, and within which he was content to lodge himself in a closet.

" He desired us to order whatever we pleased of his housekeeper, and for the first two days he went out himself to dine at the club in order to be out of our way. Another day, when he found I was better, he had some people to meet me at dinner.

" He told me he intended to visit V.D.L., and I expressed on the occasion all that gratitude and politeness required. We were very favourably impressed with the respectability of all the people we saw at Port Nicholson ; of its elegibility as the site for the Capital I do not feel very confident to speak, but I am inclined to think Captain Hobson has chosen the better place, on account of there being so much more available land for building and cultivation at Wellington, a few miles to the north.

" We stayed nearly a week at Port Nicholson, and sailed for Akaroa, where we found the Frenchman with ill-disguised alarm making ready for battle, and it was nothing, I think, but the fact of there being ladies on board which convinced him that our assurance of the continuance of peace was perfectly correct.

" We found Akaroa a most beautifully snug and picturesque harbour, but its banks are exceedingly mountainous, and seem little adapted for a settlement of any importance. There are about sixty French and German emigrants there—men, women and children, all of the class of labourers, simple-minded harmless individuals. There is also living there M. de Beligny, the agent of the Bordeaux Company, which sent them out, and who, I am told, is a very agreeable and gentlemanly person. Captain Lavand is, I think, quite prepared to learn that this Company's claims will not stand against those of any other rival candidates, and he is fully aware that if they do the proprietors or occupants are subjects of the Queen of Great Britain.

" I found Captain Lavand all that Captain Stanley had represented him to be, the most frank, honest-hearted Frenchman I ever met with. We liked Captain Cecile, but I prefer Captain Lavand a thousand times to him. He gave me a detailed account of the French settlement there, denied all action on the part of the French Government of forming a penal colony, or arrogating any sovereignty, and said that if France did such a foolish thing it would be a pleasant circumstance for England, since on the first outbreak of war, their colony would fall into our hands. I asked him if the news of war between the two countries were to arrive while we were there, what would he do ; and if he were to take the *Favourite* what would he do with *us*, ladies. He said he would take us back instantly to Hobart. ' I thought as much,' I replied, ' mais sans saccager la ville ?' I added. ' Ah madame,' he replied, as if shocked. I thought it as well to add, however, that a short time ago, he might have done this with impunity, but that now we had guns arrived and forts erecting. A shade came over his face, which I accounted for by his interpretation of this fact looking very much like war, and of war, tho' he did not say so, it was evident to all of us he was very much afraid, knowing very well that he would be sure to be taken somewhere or other before he got back to France.

" He told me what a pity is was we had not sent to him to take us about in his ship ; he would have done it with pleasure, and would be delighted now to take us back to Van Diemen's Land. I told him we might yet be glad of his services in the event of the *Favourite* not being able to take us, but as the Captain (Dunlop) was extremely anxious to return thither, we could not leave his ship, except in the case that he were ordered elsewhere, and in that case we would let him know and claim his services. In the most earnest and solemn manner he said he trusted—he put his faith in me—that I would tell him if there was likely to be war or not, and if not, he would come to us immediately at our summons, either to Waitemeta, Bay of Islands, or wherever we chose, and take us to Hobart.

" He and his officers evinced the most ardent and even impatient desire to visit Van Diemen's Land. They knew so well, they said, the noble hospitality you had exercised there towards their compatriots, and Captain Lavand sent me a number of the " Annales Maritimes et Coloniales " (an official Admiralty publication), in which is an article of M. Cecile on V.D.L. with the praises of its inhabitants, many of whom are mentioned by name. I will send it if I can lay my hand on it, and you can let Lady Pedder, and all whom it concerns, see it ; and pray let all the good Hobartians know that the French frigate *Aube* expects great things from them all.

" We lodged at Akaroa, in a newly built and unfinished store, a small portion of which was fitted up with flags by M. Lavand for our accommodation. The building was raised on piles about four feet from the ground, and a passage into the rooms was effected by some rude blocks of wood placed as steps before the door.

" On to this fact hangs my next unlucky tale. I was going out of one of these rooms (a sort of gallery) in the dark, and forgetting I believe that the floor I was upon was raised above the ground, on which the doorway (for there was no door) opened, I stepped out, missed the step, and came down on the ground, four feet below, striking in my way, I believe, the blocks I should have trodden on. I lay on the ground in great pain, almost afraid to move lest I should find I had broken my leg ; this was not the case, however, though I was half inclined to attempt making some signal to the ship for the Doctor ; however the next day he seemed to think little of it from my description, and said he would not advise me to do anything to it. During the four or five days I remained at Akaroa, I followed his advice, but continued to suffer much, and particularly in walking ; my walking being limited, however, to moving from the store to the boat and up and down the ship's side, for dinner, etc.

" On embarking from Akaroa my leg was worse and Dr. Kilroy said I must by no means put it to the ground, and that it would probably confine me a long while. There is nothing visible, but the doctor thinks I have probably lacerated the tendons or muscles of the leg, by the great stretch I gave them, and that it will be long in healing, though he seems to have no fear whatever of its coming right at last. It has been a most unfortunate accident to me, rendering me helpless as to walking and very troublesome to others.

" On landing at Auckland I had kept my crib a week in the cabin, and in it I received a visit from Captain Hobson, who, notwithstanding my helplessness, advised me not to miss the opportunity which was just about to present itself of witnessing a very large missionary meeting of Christian natives at Waikato, on the west side of the island, for which he was about setting off himself. He said the journey would be chiefly performed by boats, and the land part could be managed by bearers in the manner in which ladies usually travel in this country.

" I was the more induced to accept this proposal as I found (though not from him) that Mrs. Hobson had very insufficient accommodation for us, and was herself crowded into a small dwelling quite inadequate to the wants of her family, while the wooden Government House was putting up.

" It was agreed that Miss Williamson should remain with her, however, during our absence.

" This expedition was accomplished with great satisfaction by all the party . . . . . .

" The separation of New Zealand from New South Wales gives great satisfaction not to the Governor only, but to everybody, and congratulations and addresses are pouring in upon him.

. . . .

" We received your packet of letters from Port Nicholson on our arrival at Auckland, brought by some private hand. Mr. Halswell arrived himself soon after at Auckland and left a card for me . . . . .

IN NEW ZEALAND

"The Government officers here have more spirit than with us, and have been subscribing together for a newspaper to support the Government. A printing press has arrived from Sydney and an editor who has been similarly engaged before. . . . . . .

"I wish we had put more stock on board, or at least more sheep. We bought four more at Port Nicholson for £9, but at Akaroa and Auckland they were not to be had. People live here almost entirely on pork, but it is very delicate and more like veal than pork.

"I am extremely anxious to get back, and desirous of being home again. My thoughts are constantly fixed on what may be going on while I am away.

"I had almost forgotten to tell you about the first crown sale of land in New Zealand, the foundation of her capital city of Auckland. Great excitement prevailed on this occasion and though a small portion only of the town was sold, it realised high prices. It was put up to auction, contrary to the usual plan and contrary to what Captain Hobson supposed his instructions might be if they came in time ; but, fortunately, they did not, so instead of selling it at a fixed price he has sold it by auction, and by the prices realized has proved that his choice of a site is approved of, and that his mode of selling is the most profitable.

"I told Captain Hobson that although it was not true that I had purchased land at Port Nicholson, yet, that finding myself here at the foundation of his capital and at the first legalised sale, and having a real interest in New Zealand, which I should like to preserve, I should like to have a small bit of his new town, providing, by so doing, I kept out no on else, and could get from it such a rent as would give me fair interest, with the power of giving a small sum yearly to the mission. He seemed pleased, and referred me to the Surveyor General, who bid for three allotments for himself, and gave me the choice of either. The allotment we chose (I say we, Mr. Bagot and Miss Williamson being sharers with me) is at the lower end of Queen Street—the great street (to be) of shops near the water . . . .

LIFE OF LADY FRANKLIN

" At Waikato we saw above a thousand natives assembled to hear preaching and be catechised. Two hundred and twenty partook of the Communion on the Sunday, and about one hundred and twenty men, women and children were baptized. This was a curious and interesting sight. At the missionary meeting they held forth in very animated harangues, to propose or second resolutions. One of them was to deplore the Governor's absence, and to thank me for my presence, and scarcely a native addressed the Assembly without, as I am told, an allusion to me. I like much what I have seen of the missionaries, and am glad to learn that their land acquisitions are likely, in all, or most cases, to be confirmed to them. We are going to set off from hence to Waimate, the great missionary agricultural establishment, in order that we may be back in readiness for any opportunity of departure. . . . . .

" The missionaries' houses are the only inns in New Zealand. It the traveller did not find refuge there he might lie in the woods, and then the traveller goes home and writes a book, and says how rich and comfortable they are, full of this world's goods, very sly, very covetous, grudging what they do give, and giving nothing more than they can help. Who can wonder if they look sometimes with a little shyness at travellers, particularly at the Navy, who have been the hardest upon them.

" For my own part, I found the missionaries and the natives the most interesting things in New Zealand, though the scenery is often grand and beautiful, and the climate healthy and delightful.

" The climate, however, is wet. It is not in that respect so convenient as ours, nor do I think the sky quite so clear, but I should think it less variable, and on the whole more soft. The winds while we were there were often boisterous, but they were seldom cold. . . . . ."

For EU product safety concerns, contact us at Calle de José Abascal, 56–1°, 28003 Madrid, Spain or eugpsr@cambridge.org.